DATE DUE

			PRINTED IN U.S.A.

MAR 3 0 2015

Online Learning in Music

ONLINE LEARNING IN MUSIC

Foundations, Frameworks, and Practices

Judith Bowman

OXFORD
UNIVERSITY PRESS

OXFORD
UNIVERSITY PRESS

Oxford University Press is a department of the University of Oxford.
It furthers the University's objective of excellence in research, scholarship,
and education by publishing worldwide.

Oxford   New York
Auckland   Cape Town   Dar es Salaam   Hong Kong   Karachi
Kuala Lumpur   Madrid   Melbourne   Mexico City   Nairobi
New Delhi   Shanghai   Taipei   Toronto

With offices in
Argentina   Austria   Brazil   Chile   Czech Republic   France   Greece
Guatemala   Hungary   Italy   Japan   Poland   Portugal   Singapore
South Korea   Switzerland   Thailand   Turkey   Ukraine   Vietnam

Oxford is a registered trademark of Oxford University Press
in the UK and certain other countries.

Published in the United States of America by
Oxford University Press
198 Madison Avenue, New York, NY 10016

© Oxford University Press 2014

Library of Congress Cataloging-in-Publication Data
Bowman, Judith.
Online learning in music : foundations, frameworks, and practices / Judith Bowman.
pages cm
Includes bibliographical references and index.
ISBN 978-0-19-998817-4 (alk. paper)—ISBN 978-0-19-998818-1 (alk. paper)
1. Music—Instruction and study—Computer network resources.   I. Title.
MT1.B706O55 2014
780.71'1—dc23
2014001077

CONTENTS

PREFACE

This book aims to set forth a scholarship of online teaching and learning in music in higher education. It is not a how-to manual. Rather, it presents ways to think about online music instruction at the course level from design to development to effective practices. It provides a background that will help readers place online learning in music in the larger context of higher education. It addresses quality issues and concerns that have been voiced with regard to online learning in general, and it summarizes research to date that will give readers a sense of the status of online learning in music.

Most important, it outlines theoretical frameworks and provides specific examples of how learning experiences in various music subdisciplines function within those frameworks. To promote ongoing scholarship and informed practice in tune with the 21st century, it outlines an agenda to advance the research on online teaching and learning in music.

I would like to thank Norman Hirschy, my editor at Oxford University Press, whose enthusiasm, support, and guidance for this project were invaluable. I am grateful to Duquesne University for a Presidential Scholarship Award that aided me in the completion of this book. And I wish to thank Dean Edward Kocher at Duquesne University for his support of online learning efforts in the Mary Pappert School of Music.

INTRODUCTION

Online learning in music is a young field whose variety reflects both the multidisciplinary nature of the field and the multiple models of online learning. This multiplicity presents opportunities and challenges—opportunities to develop creative new approaches and challenges to stretch the boundaries of music instruction to harness the power of new technologies and pedagogical models in the service of the art and craft of online music instruction. Some academically oriented music courses such as music history, music education philosophy, and psychology of music may fit within existing models of online learning. Others make unique demands upon existing structures and call for models and approaches tailored specifically to their requirements (e.g., music theory and applied music studies). There is no single model for online learning in music; innovative instructors may develop multiple models on the basis of current theories and theoretical frameworks.

BOOK OVERVIEW

This book situates online music learning in higher education within the general context of online learning, and it shows how the richness and complexity of music disciplines both fit within and challenge the existing boundaries of the field. It presents scholarship in the developing field of online learning in music, makes research-based recommendations for practice, and proposes future research and development directions. It is organized in three parts that address background, theoretical frameworks, and practice.

Part I, Background and Development, provides context for online learning in music. Chapter 1 gives a brief historical overview of online learning. It documents the growth of online education and highlights the disappearing distinctions between traditional and online instruction. Chapter 2 deals with the quality and effectiveness of online learning, including common misperceptions and issues regarding academic integrity. It provides a summary of accreditation standards for online learning in general and online learning in music. Chapter 3 presents a broad overview of research on online learning and describes the small but growing body of research on online learning in music that includes philosophical studies, program and course evaluations, and studies of pedagogical strategies in various music subdisciplines.

Part II, Theoretical and Pedagogical Frameworks, focuses on design and development issues and presents theoretical frameworks that contribute various perspectives on online learning. Chapter 4 presents a conceptual framework for teaching with technology (TPACK). It extends the framework to online learning in music and aligns it with a sequential approach to course design for significant learning. Chapter 5 addresses interaction within a learning community as a criterion for quality online instruction and describes theoretical frameworks predicated upon the idea of an online learning community and collaborative learning.

Part III, Teaching and Learning in the Online Classroom, addresses pedagogical issues. Chapter 6 describes the design of fully online courses in terms of composing the course, choreographing learning experiences, and course delivery, with emphasis on creating an online learning community. Employing the same analogies of composition and choreography, chapter 7 describes the design of blended courses, with emphasis on integration of in-class and online work. Chapter 8 focuses on the art of online teaching, and it portrays the instructor who conducts the course as a director of learning. It explores troubleshooting techniques and problem prevention, and it addresses faculty development issues that include preparation of pre-service music educators for K–12 online instruction. Chapter 9 presents published effective practices and external rubrics for online instruction, not as prescriptions but as points from which online music instructors can move forward. It includes anecdotes from the field that illustrate various approaches to some challenges. Chapter 10 looks to the future of online learning in music based upon current trends and offers an agenda for future research and development.

This book is for college music faculty who wish to teach online or to redesign their face-to-face courses in a blended format, for music teacher educators who want to prepare pre-service or in-service music educators for K–12 online teaching, and for music professors or other professionals involved in faculty development for online music instruction.

Readers who are interested in developing entire online music programs will find useful references to courses and programs throughout the book, including brief outlines of existing online music programs in appendix B. They are directed particularly to chapter 3, which provides short overviews of studies that document the design, development, and implementation of an online graduate music education program, as well as a descriptive analysis of nine NASM-accredited programs. Those readers are encouraged to seek out those articles separately and to examine the national and NASM accreditation standards that are outlined in chapter 2.

Given the growth of online learning, the integration of current technologies into face-to-face classrooms at all levels from K–12 through higher education, the growing popularity of massively open online courses (MOOCs) and blended models such as the flipped classroom, and perhaps most important, the role of the Internet and digital technologies in everyday life, online learning is a critical area for all involved in music in higher education.

PART ONE

Background and Development

CHAPTER 1

The Protean Nature
of Online Education

As with every form of education, distance learning is a continuous journey of evolution
to enable even more effective learning and uncover instructional techniques to match
individual learning styles.

—John G. Flores, *Expanding the classroom: Mobile learning across America*

INTRODUCTION

Distance education has an extensive and well-documented history, existing in
various forms from the correspondence courses of the early 20th century, to
educational television of the 1950s, to interactive TV (ITV) of the 1990s, to
the Internet-based courses of the late 1990s through the present. That history
is summarized but not detailed here. For an overview of the development and
use of distance learning and collaboration in general education and their more
recent integration into music education, the reader is directed to a chapter by
Rees (2002) that includes a review of research on distance learning in music.

Analyses of distance education have provided various windows onto
the nature and evolution of distance learning. Dirr (1999) described four
generations of distance education: correspondence education, televised
instruction, online courses available on the Internet, and completely virtual programs of study. Taylor (2001) identified five generations of distance learning, each characterized by specific delivery technologies. The
first generation/correspondence model relied upon print technology for
delivery of learning materials, as well as for communication between student and instructor. The second generation/multimedia model utilized

printed study guides in addition to audio and videotaped materials, along with computer-managed or computer-assisted instruction and interactive videos. Both models accommodated asynchronous communication. The third generation/telelearning model employed audioconferencing, videoconferencing, and broadcast TV, which supported synchronous communication. The fourth generation/flexible-learning model is generally characterized by online delivery via the Internet. This model, which uses interactive multimedia, web resources, and both synchronous and asynchronous computer-mediated communication, is presently being adopted as more institutions offer distance/online courses and programs. Finally, an emerging fifth generation/intelligent, flexible-learning model would make use of the same technologies as the fourth generation/flexible-learning model, but it would additionally include automated courseware production features, as well as automated response systems based upon previously stored student and faculty interactions. Although some have criticized these kinds of characterization schemes as reductionist (Saba, 2011), they provide a useful analysis, as the available technologies of the past influenced the shape of distance education, and new technological tools impel continuing changes in distance and online education.

DEFINING DISTANCE AND ONLINE EDUCATION: WHAT'S IN A NAME?

While distance education originally served students geographically separated from educational institutions, "distributed learning" became a designation to indicate changes in the clientele for distance education as on-campus students began taking online courses, whether due to schedule conflicts, personal preference, or simply convenience. As Mayadas & Picciano (2007) observed:

> When online learning burst into the academic consciousness in the mid-90s, there was a rush by many of these institutions to downplay their locality, and to emphasize their role in meeting the needs of all kinds of geography-independent and global student populations. However, many of these same institutions eventually came to realize that many of their local and in some cases even their residential student populations were as interested in enrolling in online learning courses as were students living afar. (pp. 4–5)

Distributed learning has been described as "an instructional model that allows instructor, students, and content to be located in different, noncentralized locations so that instruction and learning occur independent of time and place" (Saltzberg & Polyson, 1995, p. 10). In the context of distance learning and collaboration in music, Rees (2002) observed that "[d]istance learning is now being subsumed under the classification of distributed learning" (p. 258). More recent terminology includes the use of "distributed learning" and "learning community" in reference to "orchestrated mixtures of face-to-face and virtual interactions among a cohort of learners led by one or more instructors, facilitators or coaches over an extended period of time" (Means, Toyama, Murphy, Bakia, & Jones, 2010, p. 4). Rees also noted "some evidence of employing the Internet as the primary vehicle for distance instruction" with "video streaming, desktop videoconferencing, web-based course management systems, chat rooms, threaded discussion groups, and on-line testing" among the resources being used for online instruction (2002, p. 259), suggesting that distance education was by that time evolving into online education.

Online education itself has multiple faces, and precise definitions have been somewhat elusive. Some terms are used interchangeably while others are used inconsistently, and various definitions are provided in the literature and reports of online education at all levels. A U.S. Department of Education-sponsored meta-analysis and review of online learning research defines online learning as "learning that takes place partially or entirely over the Internet" and "excludes purely print-based correspondence courses, broadcast television or radio, videoconferencing, videocassettes, and stand-alone educational software programs that do not have a significant Internet-based instructional component" (Means, et al., 2010, p. 9). A report on K–12 online learning policy and practice (Watson, Murin, Vashaw, Gemin, & Rapp, 2012) defines online learning as "teacher-led instruction that takes place over the Internet, with the teacher and student separated geographically" (p. 11). The same report defines blended learning as "[a] combination of online and face-to-face instruction in which the student learns at least in part at a supervised brick-and-mortar location away from home and at least in part through online delivery with some element of student control over time, place, path, and/or pace" (p. 11).

Annual surveys of online education in the United States (formerly called the Sloan Surveys of Online Learning) have attempted to provide some clarity by creating definitions of online education based upon the percentage of content delivered online. The designations and their definitions, which have remained essentially unchanged since the publication of the first report in 2003, are as follows: Online courses are those in which at least 80 percent of the content is delivered online. Face-to-face instruction includes both traditional and web-facilitated courses in which 0 to

29 percent of content is delivered online. Blended or hybrid instruction, which blends online and face-to-face delivery, is a course in which 30 to 80 percent of content is delivered online. In addition to these designations, the reports also provide a brief description of each type of course. An online course is one in which "most or all of the content is delivered online. Typically have no face-to-face meetings." A traditional course is one "with no online technology used—content is delivered in writing or orally." A web-facilitated course is one that "uses web-based technology to facilitate what is essentially a face-to-face course. Many use a learning management system (LMS) or web pages to post the syllabus and assignments." A blended/hybrid course "blends online and face-to-face delivery. Substantial proportion of the content is delivered online, typically uses online discussion, and typically has a reduced number of face-to-face meetings" (Allen & Seaman, 2013, p. 7). Further, online courses themselves may be asynchronous or synchronous, based upon the use of common meeting times, and are likely to include both modes. Asynchronous elements might include recorded lectures, threaded discussions, individual blogs, class wikis, and e-mail. Synchronous elements might include audio chats and desktop videoconferencing that complement and build upon work done in an asynchronous mode. They may be self-paced or they may follow a schedule corresponding to that of face-to-face courses.

The National Association of Schools of Music (NASM), designated by the U.S. Department of Education as "the agency responsible for the accreditation throughout the United States of free-standing institutions, and units offering music and music-related programs (both degree- and non-degree-granting), including those offered via distance education" (NASM, 2013, p. 1), has also developed definitions of distance learning and correspondence courses as a basis for standards for those types of learning. The definitions, which apply to programs delivered either fully or partially by distance or correspondence learning, are as follows:

a. Distance learning involves programs of study delivered entirely or partially away from regular face-to-face interactions between teachers and students in classrooms, tutorials, laboratories, and rehearsals associated with coursework, degrees, and programs on the campus. Normally, distance learning uses technologies to deliver instruction and support systems, and substantive interaction between instructor and student.

b. Correspondence education is provided through one or more courses by an institution under which the institution provides instructional materials, by mail or electronic transmission, including examinations on the materials, to students who are separated from the instructor.

Interaction between the instructor and the student is limited, is not regular and substantive, and is primarily initiated by the student. Correspondence courses typically are self-paced. (p. 78)

The U.S. Department of Education's definitions for correspondence courses and distance education were changed effective as of July 1, 2010, to clearly distinguish between correspondence courses and distance education. Because the department uses the new definitions when it performs audits, it is advisable to be aware of them, as there are consequences for the use of federal aid. According to the new definitions, a correspondence course is one for which the institution provides instructional materials electronically or by mail to students "separated from the instructor." The course is ordinarily self-paced and student/instructor interaction is "limited, is not regular and substantive, and is primarily initiated by the student." Distance education uses one or more listed technologies for instructional delivery to students "separated from the instructor" and, in contrast to correspondence courses, to support "regular and substantive interaction between the students and the instructor, either synchronously or asynchronously" (Electronic Code of Federal Regulations, §600.2). Primary distance education technologies include the Internet, one- and two-way transmissions through various communications devices, including open broadcast, broadband lines, or wireless devices, and audioconferencing. Details of these regulations may be found in appendix A.

GROWTH OF ONLINE EDUCATION

The growth of online education has been well documented since 2003 in the annual Sloan Surveys of Online Learning. The 2013 report (Allen & Seaman, 2013) reveals that during the fall 2011 term, over 6.7 million students, or 32 percent of all students in higher education, took at least one online course. These figures represent a 9.3 percent growth rate over the previous year, and although this is the lowest recorded increase, it still exceeds the growth rate of the overall higher education population (–0.1 percent). With regard to the future growth of online education, the report points out that, although the growth rate may be slowing, the absolute number of students taking online courses has continued to increase at rates consistent with previous years. The 2010 enrollment increase over the previous year was 563,258, and the 2011 enrollment increase was 572,512.

Although online education in music is not specifically addressed in these reports, it is also expanding, with online courses and entire online programs becoming more common, particularly in music education at the graduate level. However, as Webster (2007) noted, there is little research at this time on their effectiveness. Hebert (2007, 2008a) and Phillips (2008) explored some philosophical and pedagogical issues relevant to online doctoral and master's degrees in music education. Hebert (2007) predicted continued growth for online music education programs based on the growth of online learning in general and its advantages for in-service teachers, including convenience, inclusive discussions, and networking with colleagues. He also outlined some challenges, including skepticism about the quality and effectiveness of online learning, securing interdepartmental collaboration, and concerns about academic integrity and secure testing. Phillips acknowledged the success of online programs with knowledge-based content, but pointed out the challenges to development of musical skills and teaching skills at both doctoral and master's levels. On the other hand, Hebert (2008a) noted the suitability of more theoretical study for graduate-level music education, given research expectations particularly at the doctoral level, and detailed the increasing opportunities for online mentoring supported by technological advances.

Austin (2007) pointed out the progression of online learning in music education from online courses to fully online degree programs, and he listed several universities offering online master's degrees in music education. Among the factors attracting students were convenience in terms of time and location due to the asynchronous nature of the programs, customized and accelerated learning, and lower cost. Criticisms from various sources included questions about the quality of student learning, inadequate mentoring (in contrast to Hebert's assertion), and the integrity of online assignments. Groulx & Hernly (2010) studied the nine available NASM-accredited online graduate music education programs, each with at least 80 percent of their programs online. The authors, in line with the general research on online learning, emphasized that an online degree is neither better nor worse than an on-campus degree, but is simply an additional option for reaching an intended clientele. Examination of curriculum, program, and application and enrollment factors revealed that course requirements were typical of on-campus music education programs, while also reflecting the differing philosophies of the institutions offering them. Research courses were an element common to all the programs. Programs varied in the amount of required on-campus study, from none to several summer sessions. Nearly all the students in these programs were in-service teachers, the audience for whom the programs were designed. Generally, convenience and flexibility of scheduling were cited as benefits of any online graduate programs, with a perceived lack of human interaction and lack of curricular choice, specifically electives, constituting the drawbacks. Benefits for music educators included the ability to remain in one's current position while pursuing an advanced degree.

DISAPPEARING DISTINCTIONS

The concept of distance education has been interpreted both literally, as physical separation of teacher and students by place and time, and non-literally, in a conceptual sense. Moore (1993) described distance education as a pedagogical concept, rather than merely a geographic separation of students and teachers, and labeled the resulting psychological and communication space that would need to be bridged as "transactional distance." He noted as well that some transactional distance exists in any type of education, including the face-to-face kind. Additionally, examining the ways people learn in both face-to-face and online settings can lead to a reversal of the common perception of distance education. Face-to-face education can be perceived as distancing, while online learning can be perceived as connected, as conventional educational practices often begin at a conceptual level rather than an experiential level. Web-based technologies, on the other hand, provide connected learning, as they support direct experience that can be captured, shared over the Internet, and connected to concepts within the discipline (Batson, 2011). Further, within certain professional programs such as teacher education, online education eliminates the separation of the formal learning venue from its practical application: It allows teachers to carry out their studies within the context in which they will be used (Garton & Richards, 2007; Groulx & Hernly, 2010).

Although definitions of online education and its subsets have been formulated, and some distinctions have been made, the lines between categories delineated in the literature of online education and what is actually happening in both online and face-to-face classrooms are blurring. Consequently, delivery mode designations are becoming less definitive. Rees (2002) pointed out a trend toward use of the same technologies and pedagogies in on-campus and off-campus instruction in music: "As the technology and pedagogy blur distinctions between how students in these populations receive instruction, so will distance learning lose much of its identity as a discrete mode of instructional delivery" (p. 258). Garrison & Vaughan (2008) predicted the same fate for blended learning: "…the blended learning distinction will dissolve as a useful label. The reason is that all learning will be blended to some degree. Blended learning will just be the way learning occurs" (p. 155). More recently, Cavanagh (2012) has provided further corroboration of the blurring of boundaries between the traditional and nontraditional with regard to both students and delivery modes, observing that students are more concerned with getting the courses they need than with delivery modes and the categorical labels attached to them (p. 216). For students who require flexibility, online courses are simply another option for meeting curricular requirements. Taking Garrison & Vaughan's assertion about blended learning one step further, Cavanagh suggests that in a postmodality era, online learning is becoming simply "learning" (p. 215).

DIGITAL TOOLS FOR LEARNING AND FOR LIFE

As noted previously, each generation of distance education has utilized its contemporary technologies for instructional delivery, and although online education utilizes digital technologies, those technologies permeate contemporary culture. Digital tools are not limited to the education arena or solely to online instruction: They are used on a daily basis for both personal and educational purposes. Students expect to continue using them in the classroom, and instructors in traditional classrooms aim to increase their teaching effectiveness by integrating current technologies into their pedagogy. Further, the course categories described by the Sloan Consortium— traditional, web-enhanced, blended, and online—outline a path that highlights both the differences and the similarities among the four types. These designations also suggest a sequence of course development that instructors might follow as they gradually integrate technology into their pedagogy. They might begin by using selected digital technologies within a conventional face-to-face course. The next time the course is offered, they might choose to regularly replace one class meeting with some online work, which would match the Sloan definition of a blended course. Finally, they might redesign the course as an online offering that would include both synchronous and asynchronous components. Again, the lines begin to blur from one iteration to the next. It is not completely clear at what point a web-enhanced course would definitively become a blended course, and there is no separate designation for an online course that involves an initial in-person orientation meeting and includes on-campus or local students. The clearest distinction between the types may well be the primary locus of access, whether that is a traditional classroom or the Internet.

Within current online education, other technologies are used in addition to Internet-based tools. At the same time, face-to-face instruction is enhanced with the use of computers, the Internet, and other technologies: Online elements merge with face-to-face elements to produce either a web-enhanced or blended model. For example, online instruction might be combined with other educational technologies, including web-based applications and collaboration technologies, but these technologies may also be used in face-to-face instruction. Moreover, all learning in an online course does not necessarily occur in the online environment or by means of web-based resources; within an online course a substantial amount of content might be accessed using more traditional means. Online instructors may use traditional print textbooks in addition to instructor-developed content made available on the web. And as all necessary research and reference materials have not yet been digitized, brick-and-mortar libraries and their print resources are used by both online and on-campus students. Likewise, within traditional face-to-face courses, there is often in-class and out-of-class use of digital tools by both instructors and students. As instructors become more familiar and comfortable with contemporary digital tools, they are likely to use them in their face-to-face teaching practice without thinking of their course as being web-facilitated. Content for both online and face-to-face courses might be housed within a learning management system (LMS) for review and study in preparation for class meetings—the idea behind the flipped or inverted classroom. Both online and face-to-face instructors might make use of asynchronous discussion boards, albeit perhaps for different purposes. Their function in an online course might be as a primary means of communication and discussion of assigned topics, while in a face-to-face course, they would provide a way to extend classroom discussion. Online and face-to-face instructors might likewise use blogs for student journaling and wikis for collaborative research projects. These tools and others function well within multiple types of courses, and the same tools can be used in online and face-to-face environments. The major difference would be the nature of the educational environment itself: online or face-to-face.

IMPLEMENTATION PATTERNS AND RESULTS

Online education has followed an implementation pattern similar to previous technology integration efforts. Early implementations tend toward the familiar, resembling what people are already doing. In online education, this resulted in mirroring the face-to-face classroom online, a replication of current practice with the expectation that it would be a more efficient and effective way of achieving the same outcomes. This level of implementation is likely responsible for the finding that online instruction is at least as good as or slightly more effective than face-to-face instruction. Later implementations aim to use new technologies to achieve what was not possible before, introducing innovative new practices with potential to transform education. In online education, web 2.0 technologies are among the innovative tools with transformative potential, but available research has not yet provided evidence for such transformation.

Research on new approaches and on integration of new technologies into instruction has followed a consistent pattern, and the research on online education continues in this direction: A new technology is adopted and perhaps adapted for educational purposes. It is tested first for feasibility to determine whether it is possible to teach with this technology. Next, it is tested for effectiveness, which usually has involved a comparison with a traditional or conventional approach with the hope or expectation that the new approach or technology will be shown to be more effective or superior to the traditional one. This places the research within a defining framework that highlights the need for change in both research strategies and teaching models. Research to date generally supports the effectiveness of online education as compared with traditional face-to-face education, with results ranging from no significant difference to modest superiority in online learning outcomes. But in the case of online instruction as compared with traditional instruction, it is not a matter of either/or, or replacing one with the other. It is more a matter of both/and, in different contexts. First, online instruction and face-to-face instruction often serve different constituencies, with online offerings providing options where there may not have been any before. Second, with the blurring of distinctions between online and face-to-face instruction, "both/and" takes on new meaning as blended learning becomes more common in on-campus courses and residential students enroll in online courses. While institutions, organizations, and individuals are attempting to clarify definitions and refinements of online education, students are selecting the courses they need without concern for delivery mode. In this case, there is no pitting of one approach against another, but the coexistence of two approaches that creates flexibility and additional options. Garrison & Vaughan suggest that "…the time has come to reject the dualistic thinking that seems to demand choosing between conventional face-to-face and online learning, a dualism that is no longer tenable, theoretically or practically" (2008, pp. 4–5). Keeping in mind that current technologies have the capability to support high-quality learning experiences, it would be more productive and useful to investigate how best to use web-based technologies in support of high-quality learning outcomes rather than continue to pit instructional delivery modes against each other.

REFERENCES

Allen, I. E., & Seaman, J. (2013). *Changing course: Ten years of tracking online education in the United States*. Babson Survey Research Group and Quahog Research Group, LLC. Retrieved from http://sloanconsortium.org/publications/survey/index.asp

Austin, J. (2007). *Navigating a flat world: The promise and peril of online graduate music education programs*. Paper presented at the September 2007 Symposium on Music Teacher Education, Greensboro, NC.

Batson, T. (2011). The classroom is 'distance learning;' The web is connected learning. *Campus Technology* (May 18). Retrieved from http://campustechnology.com/articles/2011/05/18/the-classroom-is-distance-learning-while-the-web-is-connected-learning.aspx

Cavanagh, T. B. (2012). The postmodality era: How "online learning" is becoming "learning." In D. G. Oblinger (Ed.), *Game changers: Education and information technologies* [PDF e-book version] (pp. 215–227). Retrieved from http://net.educause.edu/ir/library/pdf/pub7203.pdf

Dirr, P. J. (1999). Distance and virtual learning in the United States. In G. M. Farrell (Ed.), *The development of virtual education: A global perspective* (pp. 23–48). Vancouver, CA: Commonwealth of Learning. Retrieved from http://www.col.org/resources/publications/Pages/detail.aspx?PID=277

Electronic code of federal regulations. Retrieved from http://ecfr.gpoaccess.gov/cgi/t/text/text-idx?c=ecfr&sid=0900b7322acc5a5a10c558b8fe15ad7b&rgn=div8&view=text&node=34:3.1.3.1.1.1.23.2&idno=34

Flores, J. G. (2011). *Expanding the classroom: Mobile learning across America*. Retrieved from http://www.usdla.org/assets/pdf_files/USDLAWhitePaper.English.FINAL.9.15.pdf

Garrison, D. R., & Vaughan, N. D. (2008). *Blended learning in higher education: Framework, principles, and guidelines*. San Francisco: Jossey-Bass.

Garton, S., & Richards, K. (2007). Is distance education for teacher education second best? *The Teacher Trainer 21*(3), 5–8. Retrieved from http://www.tttjournal.co.uk

Groulx, T. J., & Hernly, P. (2010). Online master's degrees in music education: The growing pains of a tool to reach a larger community. *Update, 28*(2), 60–70.

Hebert, D. G. (2007). Five challenges and solutions in online music teacher education. *Research and Issues in Music Education 5*(1). Retrieved from http://www.stthomas.edu/rimeonline/vol5/hebert.htm

Hebert, D. G. (2008a). Forms of graduate music education: A response to Kenneth Phillips. *Research and Issues in Music Education 6*(1). Retrieved from http://www.stthomas.edu/rimeonline/vol6/hebert.htm

Mayadas, A. F., & Picciano, A. G. (2007). Blended learning and localness: The means and the end. *Journal of Asynchronous Learning Networks, 11*(1), 3–7. Retrieved from http://files.eric.ed.gov/fulltext/EJ842682.pdf

Means, B., Toyama, Y., Murphy, R., Bakia, M., & Jones, K. (2010). *Evaluation of evidence-based practices in online learning: A meta-analysis and review of online learning studies*. Center for Technology in Learning, U.S. Department of Education. Retrieved from http://www2.ed.gov/rschstat/eval/tech/evidence-based-practices/finalreport.pdf

Moore, M. G. (1993). Theory of transactional distance. In D. Keegan (Ed.), *Theoretical principles of distance education* (pp. 22–38). New York: Routledge.

National Association of Schools of Music. (2013). *Handbook 2013–2014*. Retrieved from http://nasm.arts-accredit.org/index.jsp?page=Standards-Handbook

Phillips, K. H. (2008). Graduate music education. *Research and Issues in Music Education* 6(1). Retrieved from http://www.stthomas.edu/rimeonline/vol6/phillips1.htm

Rees, F. J. (2002). Distance learning and collaboration in music education. In R. Colwell & C. Richardson (Eds.), *The new handbook of research on music teaching and learning* (pp. 257–273). New York: Oxford University Press.

Saba, F. (2011). Distance education in the United States: Past, present, future. *Educational Technology* 51(6), 11–18.

Saltzberg, S., & Polyson, S. (1995). Distributed learning on the world wide web. *Syllabus* 9(1), 10.

Taylor, J. C. (2001). *The future of learning—learning for the future: Shaping the transition.* 20th International Council on Distance Education World Conference, Dusseldorf, DE [online]. Retrieved from http://www.fernuni-hagen.de/ICDE/D-2001/final/keynote_speeches/wednesday/taylor_keynote.pdf

Watson, J., Murin, A., Vashaw, L., Gemin, B., & Rapp, C. (2012). *Keeping pace with K–12 online learning: An annual review of policy and practice.* Evergreen, CO: Evergreen Education Group. Retrieved from http://kpk12.com/

Webster, P. R. (2007). Computer-based technology and music teaching and learning: 2000–2005. In L. Bresler (Ed.), *International Handbook of Research in Arts Education* (pp. 1311–1328). Dordrecht, NL: Springer.

CHAPTER 2

Quality Assurances

Quality online education will be realized only when traditional views of content and pedagogy are reconceptualized within new frameworks that include technology.

—Cheryl L. Ward & Susan N. Kushner Benson, *Developing new schemas for online teaching and learning: TPACK*

QUALITY AND EFFECTIVENESS

Quality in online learning is frequently equated with learning effectiveness as demonstrated by learning outcomes. National reports and reviews of research on online learning provide considerable data that support the effectiveness of online learning. The previously mentioned Department of Education meta-analysis and review of online learning research (Means, Toyama, Murphy, Bakia, & Jones, 2010) provides current research-based support for the effectiveness of online instruction: Learning outcomes for students in online courses were found to be "modestly" superior to those of students in traditional face-to-face courses (p. xiv). Nevertheless, questions regarding the quality of online education persist, often based on perceptions and comparisons with traditional or face-to-face education. However, because comparisons place traditional education in the forefront, they actually obstruct the most salient issue: the unique characteristics of the online environment. The focus on delivery medium masks the more significant issue of appropriate pedagogy—the way the medium and technologies are used in support of learning. At a fundamental level, the characteristics of a high-quality online course and a high-quality traditional course should be the same. Among those characteristics are relevant content, current scholarship and materials, sound pedagogical techniques and strategies, intellectually challenging activities and experiences appropriate to the level of the course, use of technology appropriate to the course, and interaction with a vibrant learning community.

Accreditation standards provide benchmarks for quality online education that are evaluated periodically on an institutional basis; however, these standards generally reference equivalence to on-campus courses and programs. External rubrics such as the *Quality Matters*™ rubric offer detailed criteria for design and evaluation of online courses. The seven principles for good practice in undergraduate education (Chickering & Gamson, 1987), and particularly their application to online learning (Graham, Cagiltay, Craner, Lim, & Duffy, 2001; Palloff & Pratt, 2003), outline characteristics of quality education and how that quality may be achieved in an online environment (see chapter 9). These principles also tend to support the idea that the essential elements of quality education do not depend upon the delivery medium.

Perceptions, misperceptions, and concerns

Comparisons between online and traditional face-to-face education are often made, with face-to-face instruction held up as the standard of quality. Rees (2002) observed that "[h]istorically, distance learning has been dismissed by the higher education community as a second-rate substitute for in-class teaching. Commonly held criticisms were concerns over quality of course content and delivery as well as lack of direct contact between teacher and student" (p. 259). Dede noted "a widespread misconception that, for everyone, face-to-face is the 'gold standard' in education" (Grush, 2006), and that "any form of online learning is second best to any form of face-to-face learning" (Downs, 2006). That perception persists to a certain extent; a recent national faculty survey (Seaman, 2009b) revealed that 80 percent of faculty without online development or teaching experience believe that online outcomes are "inferior" or "somewhat inferior" to those of face-to-face instruction (p. 6), while a majority of faculty with online experience believe its outcomes are as good as or better than those of face-to-face instruction. At some level, it appears that the face-to-face standard is the gold standard because it is the practice we know. A recent report on K–12 online learning (Watson, Murin, Vashaw, Gemin, & Rapp, 2012) presents a different view of the gold standard, suggesting a movement toward use of technology to transform education regardless of delivery mode, rather than a pitting of one delivery mode against another: "The gold standard of quality in any classroom is the teacher.... Digital learning does not represent an alternative to teachers; it presents a new opportunity for innovative teachers seeking new challenges—or seeking to work in a technology-rich environment that is similar to that of most other professions" (p. 63).

It is worth noting that it is possible to find high-quality learning and low-quality learning in both online and traditional face-to-face classroom settings. In a statement for *The Chronicle of Higher Education*, Carol Twigg, president and CEO of the National Center for Academic Transformation, admitted to being "somewhat mystified about the continuing concern about quality assurance in online learning, particularly when it is directed at accredited colleges and universities. The characteristics of a good face-to-face course are the same as those of a high-quality online-learning course" (Forum: Has the quality…, 2010). She identified student and faculty support, dependable infrastructure, and effective assessment as determinants of any high-quality learning experience, regardless of delivery mode. These elements are addressed in the standards of the various accrediting bodies. Therefore, rather than fixating on delivery mode, it would be more productive to examine internal elements of quality instruction and learning, and on a more global level, to evaluate all educational settings on the same basis. Additionally, in many cases, the same faculty who teach online courses also teach in the face-to-face classroom, so it would seem that if the face-to-face program and courses are of high quality, then the online courses should also be of high quality. The more pressing issues are pedagogical ones, such as what techniques and strategies make the best use of the technological tools available to teach a specific content in a particular context, and whether the online courses were designed or redesigned to maximize the potential of current interactive, collaborative, and creative technologies. Further, the continued blurring of distinctions among distance, online, blended, and face-to-face learning environments suggests that any quality assurances would need to be applied to all educational settings, rather than just to the online environment.

Annual surveys of online education in the United States have typically polled campus leaders, primarily chief academic officers and academic technology administrators, who speak for both themselves and their faculty members. Administrators generally report that while they expect continued and growing demand for online courses, they have concerns about quality. They consider online outcomes inferior to those of face-to-face instruction, and they report that their faculty also question the value of online learning. Direct faculty representation has typically been missing from these reports; however, a recent survey brings the faculty perspective into the picture. *Conflicted: Faculty and Online Education, 2012* (Allen, Seaman, Lederman, & Jaschik, 2012a) presents the views of over 4,500 faculty, 25 percent of whom are teaching online courses. The findings reflect the title of the report: conflicted. Faculty who teach both online and blended courses express the most positive views about online learning. Two-thirds of those surveyed consider online outcomes at least somewhat inferior to face-to-face outcomes. The other third considers the outcomes comparable, and even faculty who are teaching online courses express concern about the quality of online outcomes. Details of those concerns are not provided; faculty were merely asked whether online education can be as effective as face-to-face instruction in helping students learn. These results do corroborate the administrators' views that their faculty members question the value of online learning. The findings of this study are generally in agreement with previous surveys: Faculty who have developed or taught online courses view online learning more positively than those who have not, and those who have not had online experience express negative views about online outcomes. Nevertheless, regardless of their views, a majority of faculty have recommended online courses to students (Allen, et al., 2012a). However, this recommendation may not be as paradoxical as it seems, because in some cases, an online course may be the only option available. As is the case with most surveys of this type, music is not specifically represented, though it may be included in the categories of humanities and arts.

Academic integrity and student verification

Other issues frequently voiced in discussions of online learning include finding effective ways to verify student identity, promote academic integrity, and prevent cheating. There is a perception that online education is inferior because it is easier to cheat online. It is possible to use an online proctoring option or other means to discourage or eliminate cheating, but it may be more effective to use a variety of assignment types and tools that make this kind of proctoring unnecessary.

Academic integrity is at the heart of regulations enacted as part of the reauthorization of the Higher Education Opportunity Act (HEOA) that address the issue of authenticating the identity of distance learning students. The current legislation requires that institutions offering distance learning courses or programs have processes in place to verify that the student who registers for such courses or programs is the same student who participates in, completes the course or program, and receives academic credit (H.R. 4137, §496). The requirement is stated in terms of the responsibility of accrediting agencies or associations:

ii. the agency or association requires an institution that offers distance education or correspondence education to have processes through which the institution establishes that the student who registers in a distance education or correspondence education course or program is the same student who participates in and completes the program and receives the academic credit; (§496)

Security mechanisms for compliance include a secure login and password, proctored exams, and other technologies and practices that provide an effective means of verifying student identification. Use of a learning management system ordinarily ensures compliance with this regulation, as most are password-protected. Additionally, HEOA requires that any authentication procedures must protect student privacy and that students must be informed at registration of any additional charges for these procedures.

In 2008, the Western Interstate Commission for Higher Education's WICHE Cooperative for Educational Technologies (WCET) surveyed 170 directors of distance/online programs about their policies and practices regarding academic integrity. A response rate of about 32 percent (55 responses) revealed that a little more than half of the institutions did not have an academic integrity policy specific to online courses and programs. Respondents reported having various types of policies, including a remote proctoring policy, and use of the same policy for online and on-campus classes. Of design practices for online courses, the most frequently cited were use of assignments that require written work like papers and online discussions, use of multiple assessment strategies such as low-stakes quizzes, group work, and capstone projects, informing students about avoiding plagiarism, and use of timed tests. With regard to student identity verification, about two-thirds of respondents reported wide use of physical proctoring for exams; requiring a student ID and login password was also mentioned. At the time of the survey, most respondents were not using challenge questions, webcam monitoring, or biometrics to verify student identity.

GUIDELINES AND STANDARDS FOR ONLINE EDUCATION

Guidelines and standards have been developed that address most of these issues and concerns. The Sloan Consortium has compiled research on elements considered to constitute quality in online education; the regional accrediting commissions have developed interregional guidelines for distance or online courses and programs; and the National Association of Schools of Music (NASM) has developed standards for distance learning programs in music. A summary of those guidelines and standards follows.

Pillars of quality online education

In the 1990s, the Alfred P. Sloan Foundation's Sloan Consortium established five pillars for quality online education. Frank Mayadas (Miller, 1997) of the Alfred P. Sloan Foundation first presented the five pillars as "assessment factors" that would demonstrate institutional quality. In order to support online learning in both distance and on-campus learning environments, each of the factors would need to show positive outcomes and progress. Mayadas recommended an attitude of continual improvement regardless of outcome, whether positive or less favorable, with efforts to improve what was working, as well as to find better outcomes for less successful approaches. In subsequent publications of the Sloan Consortium, these assessment factors or principles were called "pillars." The pillars, which include learning effectiveness, student satisfaction, faculty satisfaction, cost-effectiveness, and access, were intended to serve as "a framework for measuring and improving an online program within any institution" (Lorenzo & Moore, 2002, p. 3). The cost-effectiveness pillar was later amended to "scale" (Moore, 2005). One goal of the 2002 report, a synthesis of research on effective practices, was to confirm that online teaching and learning works in multiple disciplines and multiple types of institutions. The authors provide a commonly understood definition of quality and place it within a broader context, pointing out that

> [q]uality in online education is often thought to mean "learning effectiveness," and that is certainly one element, and it is one of the pillars. However, learning effectiveness has greater meaning when it is combined within a framework that encompasses all five pillars. (p. 3)

Learning effectiveness

Research on learning effectiveness, the focus of the first pillar, was found to support the idea that online learning can be as good as and sometimes better than traditional face-to-face learning (p. 4). This section of the report emphasizes that interaction—with content, the instructor, and other students—is key to effective online learning, just as it is key to effective instruction in a traditional setting. Active learning assignments, in which students are required to think about and respond to course content, are advocated as a path to effective education. Further, the report stresses the importance of building communities of inquiry that promote higher-order thinking, as well as collaboration of students with other students and instructors, with small group discussions playing a key role in the process.

Supporting pillars

The remaining pillars—student satisfaction, faculty satisfaction, cost-effectiveness, and access—support learning effectiveness in context and exert an influence on it, with student and faculty satisfaction most closely related to instructional issues. The second pillar, student satisfaction, is associated with high-quality learning outcomes; this information is often obtained through student surveys that reveal whether students are satisfied with what they learned. Student satisfaction is also impacted by academic and administrative support services. Retention and graduation figures for online students are cited as among the best indicators of student satisfaction. The third pillar, faculty satisfaction, involves the increased interaction with students, as well as the flexibility for both faculty and students that is afforded by the digital environment. It is associated with various types of administrative and academic support that allow faculty to focus on instructional aspects such as course development, delivery, and interaction with students.

Interregional guidelines for evaluating online courses and programs

Guidelines for distance education/online learning, developed by the Council of Regional Accrediting Commissions to assist in the planning process, as well as to serve as an assessment framework, may provide a more fully developed representation of quality in distance or online education (Middle States Commission on Higher Education, 2011). The guidelines consist of nine hallmarks of quality for distance education, each with analysis/evidence criteria that relate specifically to the online environment and that apply the same standard of academic rigor to both online and face-to-face courses. The analysis/evidence criteria provide specific examples that indicate the extent to which an institution meets the various hallmarks.

Hallmarks for quality distance education

Some hallmarks, notably hallmark 1 ("Online learning is appropriate to the institution's mission and purposes"), address institutional mission and support issues while others are more directly concerned with curriculum, assessment, and academic integrity. Evidence for hallmarks 2 and 3 is relevant to institutional support: it addresses quality issues on a large scale. Evidence for hallmark 2 ("The institution's plans for developing, sustaining, and, if appropriate, expanding online offerings, are integrated into its regular planning and evaluation processes") stipulates that plans for expansion of online learning show that the institution can assure that "an appropriate level of quality" is maintained (p. 7). One example for hallmark 3 ("Online learning is incorporated into the institution's systems of governance and academic oversight") states that the institution "insures the rigor of the offerings and the quality of the instruction" (p. 8). Hallmarks 7 and 8 address issues at the institutional level. Evidence for hallmark 7 ("The institution provides effective student and academic services to support students enrolled in online learning offerings") concerns issues of web-based information about the online learning environment, orientation programs, technical support, access to library and other learning resources, and student proficiency with electronic learning resources. Evidence for hallmark 8 ("The institution provides sufficient resources to support and, if appropriate, expand its online learning offerings") includes institution-level budgets for online learning and technology plans that support online learning.

Hallmarks 4, 5, 6, and 9 are most closely related to instructional issues and are useful in the design and development of online courses and programs. Individual examples are summarized here.

Hallmark 4 directly concerns curriculum: "Curricula for the institution's online learning offerings are coherent, cohesive, and comparable in academic rigor to programs offered in traditional instructional formats." Nine examples of evidence address multiple facets of curriculum design, including overarching issues of online practice in the various disciplines, comparable rigor between face-to-face and online courses, and support for instructional interaction. Specifically, they state that knowledge of online practice appropriate to the discipline should be evident in curricular goals and course objectives, that on-campus courses and programs should serve as benchmarks for online offerings, and that learner/learner and learner/instructor interaction should be integral to course design and delivery. Other examples in this category include stipulations that curriculum design and a course management system support active faculty contributions, that scheduling helps students succeed and leads to timely degree completion, and that enrollment policies support appropriate faculty work with students. All are directly concerned with instructional quality and can be useful in the planning process (p. 9).

Hallmark 5 examines quality through the lens of evaluation: "The institution evaluates the effectiveness of its online offerings, including the extent to which the online learning goals are achieved, and uses the results of its evaluations to enhance the attainment of the goals." Eight examples of evidence are given, including overarching assessment issues and comparable evaluation processes for both face-to-face and online courses. Among the examples are larger-scale assessment issues including regular course evaluations and regular evaluations of academic and support services, with results in both cases used for course improvements. In line with the hallmark 4 call for on-campus courses and programs as benchmarks, this hallmark stipulates that online assessments should follow the processes used in on-campus courses or programs or, alternatively, just reflect good assessment practice (p. 10).

Hallmark 6 addresses the quality issue from the standpoint of faculty preparedness for online teaching: "Faculty responsible for delivering online learning curricula and evaluating the students' success in achieving the online learning goals are appropriately qualified and effectively supported." Six examples of evidence are given, with a general emphasis on proficiency with online teaching tools and good online pedagogical practices. The first examples highlight faculty selection and training by the institution. Criteria for faculty training programs include periodic offerings, use of proven good practices, and assurance of competency with institutional software. A separate example stipulates faculty proficiency with the institution's course management system, along with effective support in its use. Included in this category is student satisfaction with the instructional quality provided by online faculty (p. 11).

Finally, hallmark 9 emphasizes the responsibility of the institution with regard to general issues of quality and academic integrity in online courses and programs: "The institution assures the integrity of its online learning offerings." The four examples may be beyond the control of individual instructors, but they are nevertheless important considerations in the planning process. The first example addresses the frequently raised question of student identity; it stipulates effective procedures to certify that the student registered in an online course or program is the same one who participates in, completes, and receives academic credit for the course or program. It is noted specifically that this is a federal requirement with which all institutions must demonstrate compliance. The remaining examples detail academic integrity policies, specific reference to online learning within those policies, discussion of the policies with students, and incorporation of academic integrity issues in online faculty training (p. 14).

Best practices for promoting academic integrity

The issue of academic integrity is addressed in a list of best practices compiled by the Western Interstate Commission for Higher Education's WICHE Cooperative for Educational Technologies (WCET, 2009), a publication recommended in connection with hallmark 9 in the guidelines of the regional accrediting organizations. The list includes practices in the areas of curriculum, instruction, assessment, and evaluation, as well as institutional and support practices. Strategies listed under curriculum and instruction include stating and discussing the academic integrity policy, engaging students with the policy in various ways, such as asking students to reflect on the policy on the class discussion board, providing a lesson on avoiding plagiarism, fostering a community of integrity by assigning work in which appropriate collaboration is required, and asking questions that follow up on statements made in student papers. Assessment and evaluation strategies include providing rubrics for every assignment, ensuring faculty familiarity with learning management system tools that may reduce cheating, such as use of test banks with more questions than needed for a particular test and randomization of test questions, requiring annotated bibliographies and preliminary drafts for written work, and use of cumulative assignments. Also given are practices for reading and evaluating student work, such as comparing student writing on the discussion board with writing in papers and noting student writing that reads like an encyclopedia.

Standards for distance education in music

The NASM addresses distance learning programs, which for its purposes are any programs in which more than 40 percent of requirements are completed through distance learning. These are defined in the NASM handbook as "programs of study delivered entirely or partially away from regular face-to-face interactions between teachers and students in classrooms, tutorials, laboratories, and rehearsals associated with coursework, degrees, and programs on the campus" (NASM, 2013, p. 78). The handbook further states that in distance learning, technologies are used for delivery of instruction and support systems, as well as for "substantive" instructor/student interactions (p. 78). Broadly speaking, distance learning programs are required to meet all standards relevant to the type of program and its content, including operational and curricular standards. The standards applicable to distance learning programs address purposes and resources; delivery systems, verification, and evaluation; technical prerequisites; program consistency and equivalency; and communication with students.

Purposes and resources

The purposes and resources standard deals with issues of institutional support, such as adequate delivery systems to support distance learning goals, financial and technical support, and growth in resources and support systems sufficient to accommodate enrollment growth.

Delivery systems, verification, and evaluation

This standard provides for compliance with federal regulations regarding student verification: It requires processes to confirm that the student who registers for a distance course or program is the same student who participates in, completes, and receives academic credit for the course or program. Further, it requires processes to ensure student privacy and to inform students of any additional charges for verification procedures. It also mandates delivery systems that match the purposes of each distance program and establishment of evaluation points throughout the course or program.

Technical prerequisites

This standard requires the institution to publish requirements for technical competence and technical equipment for each distance course or program and to have a means for assessing how students meet these requirements prior to admission.

Program consistency and equivalency

The program consistency and equivalency standard requires the institution to demonstrate functional equivalency in cases in which the same course or program is offered both on campus and through distance learning. Also required are procedures to ensure consistent application of academic policies and procedures.

This standard requires clear and readily available course information, as well as instructions for communicating with instructors and other students.

Taken together, these guidelines and standards provide some clarity and direction regarding quality in online education in general and in online education in music.

REFERENCES

Allen, I. E., Seaman, J., Lederman, D., & Jaschik, S. (2012a). *Conflicted: Faculty and online education, 2012. Inside Higher Ed*, Babson Survey Research Group and Quahog Research Group, LLC. Retrieved from http://babson.qualtrics.com/SE/?SID=SV_bJHd6VpmahG2NGB

Chickering, A. W., & Gamson, Z. F. (1987). Seven principles for good practice in undergraduate education. *AAHE Bulletin, 39*(7), 3–7.

Downs, A. (2006). Online professional development for teachers: An interview with Chris Dede. *Harvard Education Letter 22*(4), 1–2. Retrieved from http://www.hepg.org/hel/article/308

Forum: Has the quality of online learning kept up with its growth? (2010). In Online learning 2010: Taking measure of online education *Chronicle of Higher Education* (November 3). Retrieved from http://chronicle.com/article/Online-Learning-The-2010/129636/

Graham, C., Cagiltay, K., Lim, B., Craner, J., & Duffy, T. M. (2001). Seven principles of effective teaching: A practical lens for evaluating online courses. *The Technology Source* (March/April). Retrieved from http://technologysource.org/article/seven_principles_of_effective_teaching/

Grush, M. (2006). Changing the gold standard for instruction. *Campus Technology* (May 21). Retrieved from http://campustechnology.com/Articles/2006/05/Changing-the-Gold-Standard-for-Instruction.aspx?Page=1

H.R. 4137, 110th Congress. (2007). *Higher Education Opportunity Act*. Retrieved from http://www.govtrack.us/congress/bills/110/hr4137

Lorenzo, G., & Moore, J. C. (2002). *The Sloan Consortium report to the nation: Five pillars of quality online education*. Retrieved from http://sloanconsortium.org/publications/freedownloads

Means, B., Toyama, Y., Murphy, R., Bakia, M., & Jones, K. (2010). *Evaluation of evidence-based practices in online learning: A meta-analysis and review of online learning studies*. Center for Technology in Learning, U.S. Department of Education. Retrieved from http://www2.ed.gov/rschstat/eval/tech/evidence-based-practices/finalreport.pdf

Middle States Commission on Higher Education. (2011). *Distance learning programs: Interregional guidelines for the evaluation of distance education (online learning)*. Retrieved from http://web.njcu.edu/programs/vision2015/Uploads/msche_guidelines-for-the-evaluation-of-distance-education.pdf

Miller, G. (1997). Asynchronous learning networks and distance education: An interview with Frank Mayadas of the Alfred P. Sloan Foundation. Reprinted from *American Journal of Distance Education, 11*(3), 71–75. Retrieved from http://sloanconsortium.org/mayadas_interview_97

Moore, J. C. (2005). *The Sloan Consortium quality framework and the five pillars*. Retrieved from http://sloanconsortium.org/publications/freedownloads

National Association of Schools of Music. (2013). *Handbook 2013–2014*. Retrieved from http://nasm.arts-accredit.org/index.jsp?page=Standards-Handbook

Online learning 2010: Taking measure of online education. (2010). *Chronicle of Higher Education* (November 3). Retrieved from http://chronicle.com/article/Online-Learning-The-2010/129636/

Palloff, R. M., & Pratt, K. (2003). *The virtual student: A profile and guide to working with online learners*. San Francisco: Jossey-Bass.

Rees, F. J. (2002). Distance learning and collaboration in music education. In R. Colwell & C. Richardson (Eds.), *The new handbook of research on music teaching and learning* (pp. 257–273). New York: Oxford University Press.

Seaman, J. (2009b). *Online learning as a strategic asset volume II: The paradox of faculty voices: Views and experiences with online learning*. Babson Survey Research Group. Retrieved from http://sloanconsortium.org/publications/survey/APLU_Reports

Ward, C. L., & Benson, S. N. K. (2010). Developing new schemas for online teaching and learning: TPACK. *MERLOT Journal of Online Learning and Teaching, 6*(2), 482–490.

Watson, J., Murin, A., Vashaw, L., Gemin, B., & Rapp, C. (2012). *Keeping pace with K–12 online learning: An annual review of policy and practice*. Evergreen, CO: Evergreen Education Group. Retrieved from http://kpk12.com/

WCET. (2009). *Best practice strategies to promote academic integrity in online education: Version 2.0*. Retrieved from http://wcet.wiche.edu/wcet/docs/cigs/studentauthentication/BestPractices.pdf

CHAPTER 3

Online Learning, Online Learning in Music

What the Research Reveals

HISTORICAL RESEARCH CYCLES

Research to date generally supports the effectiveness of online education as compared with traditional face-to-face education. A pattern of historical research cycles in music technology was mentioned previously, in which a new technology or approach is first tested for feasibility to determine its appropriateness for educational purposes, and then tested for effectiveness by comparison to a traditional approach, with the expectation that the new approach or technology will be at least as effective as or superior to the traditional one. This pattern appears to apply as well to the larger arena of online education with its associated technologies. Identifying such research tendencies or cycles is important because it places the research within a defining framework and illuminates the changes that need to occur, in both research and teaching strategies.

RESEARCH ON ONLINE LEARNING

There is a substantial body of research literature on distance learning and online learning in general. The annual Sloan reports and the recent Babson report (Allen & Seaman, 2013) attest to the growth and general effectiveness of online learning. The reports contain detailed information on the nature and extent of online education, and they provide a window onto its current status. Topics include the strategic position of online learning, the numbers of students learning online, online learning outcomes compared to those of face-to-face instruction, faculty acceptance of online education, faculty training for online teaching, and the future growth of online enrollment. Data for these reports were obtained from surveys of chief academic officers at more than 2,500 colleges and universities in the United States, and little change was noted from 2003 through 2012. On the issue of comparable outcomes, the reports consistently found that most respondents (more than 75 percent in 2012) perceived online learning outcomes to be "as good as or better" than those of face-to-face instruction. A "sizable minority" continues to consider online learning inferior to face-to-face instruction (p. 24). Regarding faculty acceptance of online education, less than a third of responding academic officers believe their faculty acknowledge the "value and legitimacy" of online learning. Less than full faculty acceptance of online instruction was noted even at institutions with comprehensive online programs (p. 27).

There are several meta-analyses of the general research literature on distance and online learning that are informative regarding their relative effectiveness (Bernard, Abrami, Lou, Borokhovski, Wade, & Wozney, 2004; Bernard, Abrami, Borokhovski, Wade, Tamim, Surkes, & Bethel, 2009; Means, Toyama, Murphy, Bakia, & Jones, 2010). Bernard, et al. (2004) found evidence that distance education and traditional classroom instruction were comparable, but felt the results were inconclusive due to weaknesses in the research, such as lack of random assignment, use of non-equivalent materials, lack of detail on characteristics of comparison conditions, and others. They did, however, find an advantage for asynchronous over synchronous distance education, as well as advantages for distance education when computer-mediated communication was used. Bernard, et al. (2009) conducted a more finely focused meta-analysis of experimental research literature in distance education that compared the effects on achievement outcomes of three types of interaction treatments (i.e., treatments designed to encourage student/student interaction, student/teacher interaction, or student/content interaction as defined by Moore [1993]). Combinations of interaction treatments were also investigated to identify differences in effects on achievement. They found that designing interaction treatments into distance education courses increased cognitive engagement and had positive effects on student learning, particularly in asynchronous courses.

In line with the recursive nature of historical research cycles in music technology, the U.S. Department of Education report (Means, et al., 2010) acknowledged the need to revisit the question of the relative effectiveness of online and face-to-face instruction because of the availability of contemporary online learning applications, including a broad range of web resources and collaboration technologies. Studies in this meta-analysis were conducted in 2004 or later, primarily in higher education, and subject matter included medicine or health care, computer science, teacher education, mathematics, languages, science, social science, and business. Music and the arts seem not to have been represented directly. The report addressed four questions: How the effectiveness of online learning compares with that of face-to-face instruction; whether supplementing face-to-face instruction with online instruction enhances learning; what specific practices might be associated with more effective online learning; and what conditions influence the effectiveness of online learning?

The literature reviewed in this U.S. Department of Education report was limited to studies of web-based instruction that involved controlled designs, with all effects based on objective measures of student learning; student or teacher perceptions and attitudes were not considered. Overall, purely online approaches were found to be as effective as conventional instruction, while blended approaches emerged as more effective than conventional classroom instruction. A review of studies that contrasted various online learning practices suggested that learning in purely online conditions and learning in blended conditions are ordinarily comparable, and that learning does not seem to be enhanced either by including more media such as video or by giving online quizzes. In the case of groups of students learning together online, guiding questions were found to influence their interaction style but not the amount they learned. The report stated that it was not the delivery medium, but rather differences in curriculum materials, pedagogical aspects, and learning time that produced the learning advantages. Along the lines of previous observations regarding weaknesses in the research (Bernard, et al., 2004), the report noted that professors or other instructors using their own courses conducted most of the research on online learning practices, and that the technologies, content, and activities selected tended to be ad hoc rather than theory-based. It pointed out that the field of online learning generally lacks a coherent body of research based on systematic testing of theory-based approaches. On this basis, the authors concluded that the findings of the meta-analysis

... should not be construed as demonstrating that online is superior as a medium. Rather it is the combination of elements in treatment conditions, which are likely to include additional learning time and materials as well as additional opportunities for collaboration, that has proven effective. The meta-analysis findings do not support simply putting an existing course online, but they do support redesigning instruction to incorporate additional learning opportunities online. (Means, et al., 2010, p. 51)

RESEARCH ON ONLINE LEARNING IN MUSIC

Although there is a considerable body of research on distance learning and online learning in general, comparatively little exists with regard to online learning in music. Online education in music is subject to the same issues as online education generally, but it presents additional challenges due to the nature of the various music subdisciplines (e.g., music education, music history, music theory, and music therapy), the appropriate representation of concepts, and the use of suitable pedagogies in those subdisciplines.

Rees (2002) reviewed the development of distance learning and collaboration in music and music education up to 2001. He found "some evidence of employing the Internet as the primary vehicle for distance instruction" with "video streaming, desktop videoconferencing, web-based course management systems, chat rooms, threaded discussion groups, and on-line testing" among the resources being used for online instruction (p. 259). Rees additionally noted that a good deal of the research consisted of anecdotal comparison studies of the effectiveness of on-campus versus off-campus instruction, with little research on effective teaching practices and the ways in which students learn at a distance (p. 269).

Webster (2007), referring to recent research in music technology, pointed out that since the research on computer-based technology and music teaching and learning has shown technological approaches to be at least as effective as traditional ones, music educators are less interested in continuing this line of research (i.e., pitting technological approaches against traditional ones). He suggested that the more interesting line of inquiry would be the complex interactions involved in learning music as an art. With specific reference to distance education, he also noted that while online courses and even complete online degree programs were becoming more common, there was little to no research on their effectiveness. Walls (2008) similarly recommended qualitative study of features of online learning that contribute to individual student learning and satisfaction on the basis that much research comparing online with face-to-face instruction has revealed no significant difference in effectiveness.

More recently, other authors have pointed out the small number of research studies of online learning in music. Keast (2010) observed that although music educators are moving toward online learning, research in this area is not as widely published as it is in other disciplines, and he characterized the status of research on online music education as "almost nonexistent" (p. 55). Dye (2007), focusing more narrowly on applied music instruction in an online setting, found systematic research in this area to be "minimal and incidental" (p. 19). Dammers (2009) noted that there was little research on synchronous applied instruction, in part because of the relative newness of desktop videoconferencing technology. Groulx & Hernly (2010) found a growing body of research literature on online graduate degrees, but few published studies referring specifically to online music education programs. Webster (2007, 2011b) noted that serious research on distance learning in music education is just beginning, but it shows potential for interesting results. He pointed out studies involving online mentoring, videoconferencing with high-quality sound, use of social media, and online communities of practice as notable examples of the kind of work being done.

LITERATURE OF ONLINE LEARNING IN MUSIC: 2000–2013

The following sections provide descriptions of research on various aspects of online learning in music carried out between 2000 and 2013. The categories include philosophical or theoretical studies, course/program design and evaluation studies, and reports of research in particular music subdisciplines, including applied music, music theory, composition, music appreciation, music therapy, and music education. In order to highlight changes of focus and progress in advancing methodologies, the studies appear chronologically within categories.

Philosophical or theoretical studies

Several researchers have studied the use of constructivist techniques as a philosophical basis for online instruction at graduate, undergraduate, and secondary school levels. Results suggested the effectiveness of constructivist approaches in the online environment.

Bauer & Daugherty (2001) reported on a project using a constructivist approach in an online graduate history and philosophy of music education course taught at two geographically distant universities. Various collaborative activities were used, including an online discussion forum for exploration of current topics in music education, web searches for sites related to the history and philosophy of music education, and development of a history and philosophy of music education website. An end-of-semester student questionnaire revealed overall positive reactions to the collaboration and interest in use of the web as part of the learning process, but also a lack of interest in a completely online course. At this time, they concluded that the most effective use of the Internet might be as a supplement to traditional instruction, and noted the potentially transformative effect of web technologies within a constructivist pedagogy.

As a way to help professors prepare students for a final unit exam on the sociology of music within an online sociology course, Brewster (2005) developed a constructivist-based portal, Constructivist-Inspired Summary Portal (CISP), which allowed students to choose various interactive methods of reviewing key concepts. No significant difference in final exam averages was noted between students who used the portal and those who were instructed to prepare as they had for other units. However, those who used the portal reported a moderate to high perception that it helped them study for the final exam.

Keast (2010) used constructivist principles as the basis for an online research activity involving American tune books within a face-to-face graduate-level music education course. The goal was to determine how students would use the online materials to construct content knowledge. Students' class presentations were scored higher than the assignment required, so results were deemed moderately successful. The results also suggest the feasibility and effectiveness of constructivist learning within online graduate music education courses, as has been found in other disciplines.

Bennett (2010) studied perceptions of students, teachers, and administrators regarding a secondary-level online music appreciation course, Experiencing Music 2200. This research was an exploratory case study and was conducted from a constructivist perspective. The pilot online delivery presented an opportunity for high school students in rural areas to study music with a specialist music instructor without respect to geographical location or class size, and it provided insights into a constructivist approach to online pedagogy. Based on the results, a second course was developed for online delivery, and a second online music teacher was secured.

Course/program design and evaluation

Course/program design and evaluation studies account for the largest number of studies in any category, which seems reasonable given both the status of online learning in music as a young field and the growing number of online courses and programs. Many of these are feasibility studies or case studies of particular courses or programs; however, the results may be useful to others engaged in the process of course and program design. Although the first study in this category predates the 2000–2013 time-frame, the author's point that a music specialist must be involved in the design process is an important one, with implications on several levels, including program effectiveness.

Schoueman (1999), noting the need for distance education for post-graduate music education students, used instructional design and distance learning principles in the design and evaluation of a graduate music education program. A particular challenge was effective facilitation of practical skills like singing, playing instruments, listening, and movement in the absence of direct physical contact. She concluded that a music education specialist should either lead the design effort or collaborate with an instructional designer to ensure program effectiveness.

Lee (2003) described the design and construction of a nine-unit introductory music therapy course for delivery through the Blackboard learning management system. Each unit consisted of a study guide and supplementary materials. Media in support of the course included e-mail, discussion forums, a virtual classroom, and supplementary multimedia materials. Students were assessed by means of online quizzes, an in-class midterm exam, journals, discussion forum posts, and a book review. Implications for future development of distance education in music therapy were drawn from issues encountered in the course.

Carney (2010) developed a blended learning environment that used web-based instruction to teach music theory to upper primary students in the private piano studio. Drawing from the fields of music education, educational technology, educational psychology, and interaction design, the approach was developed as a formative model and targeted toward instructional designers and music educators. The approach was intended to provide an optimum combination of face-to-face instruction, student, teacher, and parent collaboration, and interaction with a web-based program.

Two studies focused on finding solutions to more technical design challenges in online music instruction, each addressing technologies current at the time the research was reported. Chuang (2000) synthesized and improved upon web-based instruction guidance systems to develop detailed and useful guidelines for the design and development of web-based learning environments. The new guidelines were implemented, tested, and revised in the context of pre-college-level music fundamentals. The system was intended to serve as a framework for future research and theoretical development and as a guide for practitioners. Franklin (2008) studied sound and music-based interactivity in *Second Life®*, identified design challenges, and recommended appropriate design solutions. She developed a theoretical design model, a musicscape organized around timbre and accompanied by a database of acoustic instrument sounds. On this basis, she developed a college-level course for foundational work in musicscape design.

Three studies detailed the process of redesigning existing courses at the undergraduate and secondary school levels. These are particularly informative, as they present scenarios and raise issues that would apply to many instructors who intend to teach one of their existing courses online. Those instructors might find useful strategies here for adapting their face-to-face approaches to the online environment.

Ross (2001) conducted a feasibility study that involved the process of redesigning a traditional survey of popular music for online offering. Faculty unfamiliar with online learning raised various issues, including questions about technological capabilities of online learning such as synchronous meetings, concerns about assessment and cheating, and rethinking the concept of time in online learning. A comparative course description was developed as a model for future course redesign efforts. The course description and objectives remained the same, while various adjustments were made to the duration of the course, contact time, and type and weighting of assessments.

Scarnati & Garcia (2007) described the process of redesigning a junior-level music history course for online delivery. The large-enrollment jazz history and styles course was originally offered via interactive instructional television (IITV) in a traditional lecture-based format using a chronological survey approach that did not provide for interactivity and engagement with content. The authors changed the format to a reverse chronological one, employed a learner-centered pedagogy, and integrated online media resources, including videogames for teaching musical concepts, to promote engagement with content, knowledge construction, and interaction via discussion groups and collaborative group projects. The redesigned course was offered through the WebCT Vista learning management system. A student survey revealed mixed reactions to the reverse chronological format, predominantly positive responses to the multimedia components, and mostly positive responses to the videogames. Over half the students in the online course received A or B grades, but no grades from the previous IITV course were available for purposes of comparison. The authors concluded that the survey results support the effectiveness of the redesigned course.

Nakashima (2009) employed critical theory and a case study approach to document the redesign of a face-to-face secondary-level music appreciation course for online delivery. Interviews with course developers, field notes, and relevant government documents resulted in development of timelines, discussion of the redesign process, identification of challenges and opportunities along with current and future implications, and the posing of important questions regarding curriculum development for online environments.

A series of studies (Walls, Wolfe, Good, Powell, & Schaffer, 2004; Walls, Miranda, Schaffer, Gilbreath, & Good, 2005; Walls, 2008) describing successive stages in the design, development, implementation, and evaluation of an online graduate-level music education program provide valuable information and insights for anyone involved in similar program design endeavors. Program-level findings in this group of studies are informative regarding overarching issues. Results of specific instructional strategies provide a window onto how students learn online and the relative effectiveness of specific approaches.

Walls, et al. (2004) described the process of designing and implementing a blended distance learning master's program in music education. Reasons for creating the program included convenience for in-service teachers, who find it increasingly difficult to attend both academic year and summer courses, as well as drawbacks of short-term summer courses relative to the quality of the learning experience. They addressed issues of interaction, including learner/content, learner/instructor, learner/learner, learner/interface interaction, and the concept of perceived transactional distance. Varied kinds of interaction were found to support learning effectiveness, student satisfaction, and faculty satisfaction, three of the "pillars of quality online instruction" (Lorenzo & Moore, 2002). Preliminary evaluations suggest that graduate music education students, like distance students in other disciplines, value interaction and small transactional distance. Challenges included balancing the demands of interaction with faculty course loads and students' professional responsibilities, dealing with issues involving synchronous video, communicating specific interaction requirements and encouraging student participation, and determining optimal class size for various kinds of courses and the resulting cost-effectiveness issues.

Walls, et al. (2005) described the development, implementation, and evaluation of a distance learning master's program in music education. The development process included study of existing programs, obtaining campus approval and support for the program, and securing NASM, National Council for Accreditation of Teacher Education (NCATE), and regional accreditations. Instructional design models suitable for adult student needs and flexible delivery to both on-campus and distant students were also studied. Individual course implementations are described in some detail, each with unique configurations of technology, interaction, and other modifications appropriate to course content, student learning styles, and faculty teaching styles. Evaluation, described as an evolving process, included faculty and staff discussions, university teaching effectiveness surveys, questionnaires for entering and graduating students, and interviews with graduates of the program. Overall response to the program was positive.

Walls (2008) examined the impact of a graduate distance learning music teacher education program on the professional development of in-service music teachers, focusing on whether program goals were reached and how program delivery promoted achievement of the goals. Telephone interviews of graduates of the program and surveys of current and graduating students revealed a high level of satisfaction with the program, as well as positive changes in teaching philosophy, teaching practice, and personal growth. Program characteristics associated with the results included interaction with peers and with faculty, real-world application, academic quality, and integration of technology.

A similar study (Kos & Goodrich, 2012) examined music educators' perceptions of how their philosophies and teaching practices changed due to their participation in an online graduate degree program in music education. An additional interest was whether online coursework met their professional development needs. Analysis of semi-structured interviews with nine recent graduates of an online graduate music education program revealed several themes including relevance, empowerment, diversity, flexibility, and support systems. Some findings seem to pertain primarily to the nature of graduate study, while others suggest benefits specific to the online learning environment. Changes in teaching philosophy were attributed primarily to course content. Online discussion boards provided informal interaction with peers and allowed students to share pedagogical ideas that led in some cases to rethinking teaching practices. Coursework generally seemed to meet students' professional development needs; however, some felt they would have benefited from courses that were not offered online (conducting, Orff). The researchers concluded that a rigorous online graduate education can influence students' philosophies and classroom practices; however, they noted that some students may not be well suited to online learning and that some courses might be better suited to face-to-face settings.

One author focused specifically on assessment of an online music education course, designing various assessment tools that were integrated throughout the course. Smith (2010) described some tools, techniques, and assessments used to replicate the face-to-face classroom experience within a fully online music appreciation course delivered through the *Desire2Learn* learning environment in a community college setting. The assessment tools included embedded musical examples used during proctored exams, as well as in weekly lectures and other parts of the course. Assessments also included machine-graded self-evaluation quizzes, graded group discussions via a discussion board, and a research paper submitted electronically for grading and instructor comments. Smith noted that the primary focus of assessment was on development of critical listening skills, that the instructor determined assessment standards, and that assessment was achieved using tools of online technology.

Two studies focused on the status of online graduate degree programs in music education; one of the studies contained a detailed analysis of fully online graduate music education degree programs in the United States. These studies provide useful information on program design, point out perceived benefits and drawbacks of online programs, and illustrate the varied curricular models that may be employed to deliver online degree programs in music. Both were mentioned in chapter 1 in connection with the growth of online education in music.

Austin (2007) described the expansion of online learning in music education from courses to fully online degree programs and provided a list of several universities that offered online master's degrees in music education. Among factors attracting students were convenience in terms of time and location due to the asynchronous nature of the programs, customized and accelerated learning, and lower cost. Criticisms included questions about the quality of student learning, inadequate mentoring, and integrity of online assignments.

Groulx & Hernly (2010) conducted a descriptive analysis of nine programs that constituted the available NASM-accredited graduate music education programs in which at least 80 percent of the program is offered online. One element of the theoretical grounding of the study was a belief in online degrees as an additional option, rather than a judgment regarding the superiority or inferiority of a particular delivery medium. They examined curriculum, program, application, and enrollment factors within the nine programs. Course requirements were found to be typical of music education programs, but they also apparently reflected the differing philosophies of the programs studied, with research courses as an element common to all the programs. The amount of on-campus study required for degree completion varied, from none to several summer sessions. Convenience and flexible scheduling were cited as benefits of online graduate programs. A perceived lack of human interaction and lack of curricular choice, especially in elective course options, were pointed out as drawbacks. A particular benefit for these in-service music educators was the ability to remain in their current teaching positions while pursuing an advanced degree.

Research in specific music subdisciplines

The following studies are grouped according to subdiscipline in order to highlight the magnitude of work to date in each of the categories: applied music, music theory, music appreciation, music therapy, and music education. Studies of applied music and music education dominate in terms of numbers, although those numbers are small. There are fewer studies in each of the remaining categories.

Applied music

The research on applied music includes studies involving instruction of middle school and high school students, as well as college-level students. Instructional strategies reflect technological developments that facilitate improved instructor/student interaction. Although earlier studies in this category involve development and testing of materials for study, later ones tend to focus on use of videoconferencing environments for applied study.

Green (2003) compared the effectiveness of traditional and computer-assisted instruction on general music achievement and guitar performance skills (tonal, rhythm, harmonic, and melodic performance skills) of eighth grade students with higher or lower audiation abilities. All students used instructional content from the *Interactive Guitar* software. Results after five weeks showed that the type of instruction had no effect on either general music achievement or guitar performance skills, and that regardless of type of instruction, students with higher musical aptitude achieved higher levels of performance skills.

Yoshioka (2003) developed ancillary materials to provide online learning support for a published method for young, beginning piano students. Integration of ideas from Gordon's *Music Learning Theory* and Gagne's *Conditions of Learning* formed the basis of the web-based tutorial, which the author claimed could function as a virtual instructor and provide students with opportunities for asynchronous learning.

Ryder (2004) developed and tested an Internet-based unit of study on vocal science for high school-level choral music students, and studied its effects on both student knowledge of vocal anatomy, function, and health, and student attitudes toward the study of vocal science and online learning. Data were gathered through pre- and post-tests and surveys. All students showed significant gains in knowledge as a result of instruction. The surveys revealed that, in general, students were comfortable with Internet use for schoolwork, and they considered study of vocal science important.

Dye (2007) investigated desktop videoconferencing via iChat as an environment for applied music lessons for middle school band students. Results of 25 recorded lessons showed that most participant behaviors, such as instructors' diagnosing and directing of activities, and maintaining positive rapport and communication, were comparable to those in traditional applied lessons. However, a tendency toward less modeling of musical behaviors by instructors and more music-specific questioning among all participants was noted. All participants considered distance learning elements like reliable technology, suitable training, and instructional design important. On the basis of the results and with the capability of immediate feedback, the researcher found desktop videoconferencing to be a promising environment for applied lessons.

Dammers (2009) explored the feasibility of using personal computers and readily available videoconferencing technology for online applied music lessons between a college professor and an eighth grade trumpet student. He noted that there was little research on synchronous performance instruction, in part because of the relative newness of desktop videoconferencing technology. The advantages were the availability of lessons over a long distance, convenience, and ease of sharing recordings for duet playing. There were multiple challenges, including delay, interpersonal dynamics, visual limitations, the need to restrain movement due to the wearing of headphones, and issues related to volume control. Dammers concluded that this type of instruction, although feasible and functional, was not equivalent to face-to-face applied instruction because of the nature of music performance as a synchronous experience. However, he acknowledged that it could supplement music instruction. Possible applications included applied instruction in small towns and rural areas, clinics or master classes, and interviews with composers and performers.

Lockett (2010) studied perceptions of instrumental education students enrolled in a for-profit music academy regarding the effectiveness of online instrumental instruction as compared with face-to-face instrumental instruction. A survey revealed no significant difference in effectiveness scores between online and face-to-face learning and between Skype and iChat delivery. Student interviews suggested that in face-to-face instruction, students expected more instructor interaction and hands-on instruction, while technology, communication software, and learning through the instructor were the salient issues in online instruction.

Seddon & Biasutti (2010) studied learning strategies used by young adult students learning to play an improvised 12-bar blues on a keyboard in an asynchronous online environment over a period of six weeks. The three volunteer participants used a text, illustrations, and audio examples within a sequencing program. A distance facilitator was available through e-mail for support and advice. Each hour-long learning session was videotaped, and at the end of each session, participants sent MIDI files of their work to the facilitator for advice on how to proceed. Interviews with participants were conducted upon completion of the sessions. Video analysis revealed that learning activities consisted of instruction, copying, practicing, playing, and evaluating. The authors found the results to be supportive of concepts found in the literature regarding learning to play by ear.

Orman & Whitaker (2010) compared multiple aspects of face-to-face and online applied instrumental music lessons involving three middle school students—a saxophonist and two tubists. They analyzed extensive digital video and transcripts of all lessons for sequential instruction patterns, performance, focus of attention, eye contact, and other nonverbal behaviors. A comparison of face-to-face with online lessons revealed that teacher modeling and off-task behaviors occurred more frequently in face-to-face lessons, while student performance and eye contact increased in online lessons. They found few differences in focus of attention and issues related to venue, although there were concerns about audio and video quality.

In a particularistic case study involving online piano lessons at the college level, Kruse, Harlos, Callahan, & Herring (2013) studied the benefits and challenges to student and teacher of online piano instruction and the feasibility of offering this kind of instruction. The student, a fulltime middle school music teacher, studied secondary piano with a university professor during one 16-week semester; conducting the lessons using Skype allowed her to avoid a long commute to campus. Data collected using ethnographic techniques included eight 50-minute lesson observations, two interviews, and eight biweekly e-journals from both the student and the teacher. As in other similar studies, the participants were pleased with the naturalness of the interaction, the lesson-to-lesson continuity, and the flexibility regarding location. The student improved her piano skills and was able to apply them in her teaching. Obstacles included technological and financial issues: latency and the need to use the most current equipment. Both student and teacher agreed that online music teaching and learning could be successful, and by attending studio classes online, the student reversed her former discomfort with such classes. Among the implications cited were the need to consider music education professors' philosophical issues regarding online lessons and several issues about implementation: music education faculty's technological understanding, costs of equipment and its maintenance, and management of teaching and learning styles for best results in technology-mediated lessons.

Pike & Shoemaker (2013) compared acquisition of sight-reading skills by beginning piano students in a face-to-face environment with those in an online videoconferencing environment. Over a period of eight weeks, students in two different U.S. cities received weekly 15-minute individual sight-reading lessons. Online students connected via Skype and used digital pianos, Internet MIDI software, and acoustic pianos. All students practiced sight-reading between lessons using the same materials. Sight-reading post-tests revealed that both groups improved their sight-reading skills, with no significant difference between them. However, online students showed greater independence and self-directed learning than those in the face-to-face group. They also sustained greater engagement throughout the lesson: When the teacher spoke, online students looked at the computer screen, whereas face-to-face students continued to look at the piano. Online limitations on interaction stimulated more scaffolding of concepts by the teacher, leading to more integration of concepts for online students. The researchers concluded that online sight-reading instruction is a feasible alternative to in-person instruction and could supplement formal lessons. For optimum results, they provided recommendations regarding high-quality equipment, high-speed Internet service, and a student environment conducive to learning.

Riley (2013) investigated teaching and learning general music/composition using videoconferencing. Three music education majors in the United States taught 10 seventh grade general music students in Japan. Using Skype, the pre-service music teachers taught two 45-minute beginning composition classes focused on melody writing. Students worked two at a computer using a keyboard and an online notation program (Noteflight). Between lessons, they worked on compositions and received feedback from the pre-service teachers. Data included lesson plans created by the pre-service teachers, lesson videotapes, student compositions, mentoring comments, and reflections from pre-service teachers and students. The project was deemed successful, as students met lesson plan objectives and composed well-constructed melodies, while pre-service teachers provided well-formulated mentoring comments. Pre-service teachers and students alike expressed positive reactions to videoconferenced instruction. Challenges included limited video range and audio issues that caused difficulty in hearing student comments, while benefits included the multiple perspectives available to students. Difficulty establishing teacher/student relationships and the added time needed for all elements of the lessons were cited as drawbacks. However, Riley felt that the benefits outweighed the drawbacks, technological advances lessened the difficulties, and videoconferencing is becoming increasingly feasible for music instruction in distant locations.

Music theory

The research in music theory includes studies of specific instructional strategies at graduate and undergraduate levels, as well as some work at pre-college levels. Two of the studies revealed positive outcomes from use of online communication and collaboration.

In a case study, Walker (2001) investigated the effects of computer-mediated communication on learning in a graduate-level music analysis course. Within a computer conferencing community, students discussed class issues and prepared for the next class; they additionally collaborated on a web-based journal to post their work. Data were collected by means of observations, survey questionnaires, and interviews with students and the professor. Results indicate that this participation can benefit graduate students' learning, that journal work can focus their learning during the semester and result in high-quality professional work, and that student collaboration can result in valuable peer contributions to student learning.

Sinclair (2004) studied the effect of online communication on written achievement of undergraduate non-music majors enrolled in five sections of a music fundamentals class, as well as student perceptions of the online learning environment. Students participated in five weekly synchronous or asynchronous online study sessions; achievement data were gathered by means of a test, and perceptions were assessed through a course evaluation. Results revealed that regardless of group, all students increased their musical achievement, but decreases in involvement and task orientation were noted from pre-test to post-test.

Chuang (2000) and Carney (2010), cited in the Course/Program Design and Evaluation section of this chapter, also conducted research in the area of music fundamentals. Chuang developed guidelines for web-based instruction and tested them in the context of music fundamentals. Carney developed an approach for teaching fundamentals in the private piano studio.

Research in the area of music appreciation consists of studies conducted in courses titled as such (music appreciation), as well as in a small number of variously named music courses (jazz history, popular music). Most of these courses are offered at the college level, with community colleges and two-year colleges prominently represented. The studies deal primarily with aspects of the online learning experience, but also report on student perceptions and satisfaction with the courses.

McCabe (2007), noting the limited amount of empirical research on pedagogy that would result in successful online learning environments, studied the effect on student cognition of collaborative instruction in an online undergraduate music appreciation course. Students volunteered for participation in the study. Data from online surveys and discussion board posts revealed that small group collaborative work involving substantial discussion and interaction might elicit use of higher-order thinking skills, that students preferred independent work over small group work, and that they enjoyed the interaction in large group discussions. Overall, students preferred a variety of instructional strategies throughout the course.

Wright (2007) compared student satisfaction with course design, student/peer interaction, and student/instructor interaction between online and face-to-face sections of music appreciation courses offered at four community colleges. Survey results revealed that over half the students had no regular interaction with peers and no communication with instructors outside of class. Students listed historical aspects of music and learning to read music as outcomes that contributed to their lifelong appreciation of music. About half the respondents said that they were required to attend concerts on their campuses, and a third said that online students were not required to attend live concerts. Overall, students reported being very satisfied with music appreciation courses.

Eakes (2009) compared music achievement, music self-concept, and course satisfaction among students enrolled in different sections of a 10-week summer music appreciation course taught from either a chronological or a sociological standpoint, in either a face-to-face or an online setting in a two-year college. All conditions resulted in significant gains in music achievement, with those in both sociological sections scoring significantly higher than those in the chronological classes. There were mixed results on aspects of concert critiques and course evaluations between face-to-face and online students, but positive outcomes based on music appreciation instruction were noted in both face-to-face and online formats. Eakes recommended further exploration of effective online instruction.

Hunter (2011) examined the nature of student experience (i.e., the nature of interaction and engagement in learning) in an online jazz history course at the community college level. Data from interviews, surveys, discussion posts, and journal entries revealed that students' existing media habits influenced their class behaviors and course navigation habits, and that students' reasons for enrolling in the course (convenience and flexibility) also influenced their actions and class behaviors. Hunter reported limited engagement of students with peers, a pretense of participation and community building, and a seeming lack of sincere interest in the course. Further research on the capability of online courses to provide meaningful learning experiences, including a democratic learning experience, peer interaction, and community building, was recommended.

Stefanov (2011) studied perceptions of high school students and their teachers regarding online music classes and also investigated similarities and differences between the perceptions of students and teachers. The influence of music course content and online delivery platform on perceptions was also investigated. Areas of interest included instructor support, technology, class structure, assessment, student interaction, relevance, student autonomy, opportunities for creativity, and course delivery mode. Questionnaire and interview data indicated that course structure and the role of the teacher are strong influences on student perceptions, and that perceived advantages of the online environment include self-paced learning and less peer pressure. Participants noted some demands specific to the online environment, including the need to do extra work and exert greater self-discipline, and to have the ability to work independently. Academic and technical support issues influenced participant perceptions, and differences in perceptions between teachers and students seemed to be due to inadequate communication.

Music therapy

One study involving music therapy was found, Lee's (2003) design of an introductory music therapy course to be delivered through the Blackboard learning management system. Nine units were created, each containing a study guide and supplementary materials. Media support for the units included e-mail, discussion forums, a virtual classroom, and supplementary multimedia materials. Student assessments included online quizzes, an in-class midterm exam, journals, discussion forum posts, and a book review. Based on issues that arose during the course, the researcher drew implications for future development of distance education in music therapy. This study is also described in the Course/Program Design and Evaluation section of this chapter.

Music education

In addition to the studies listed here that focus on examination of specific instructional strategies, much of the work in course and program design has also been done in the area of graduate music education.

Student attitude

Three studies investigated student attitudes toward web-enhanced learning and an experimental approach best characterized as blended learning. All are somewhat exploratory and could be considered feasibility studies. Despite findings of generally positive attitudes toward Internet resources and web-based instruction, each researcher also reported skepticism regarding online courses.

Bauer (2001) studied attitudes toward web-enhanced learning in a face-to-face music education methods course. Students, junior and senior music education majors, expressed generally positive attitudes about Internet resources and asynchronous elements of the course. Remarks about online learning as impersonal, the lack of comfort using newsgroups, and the lack of interest in taking an online course were somewhat related to previous computer and web-based learning experiences.

Barry (2003) integrated web-based components, including materials that replaced traditional classroom instruction, and supplementary materials into a graduate music education research course. Results suggested the feasibility of this kind of combined instruction in graduate music education research courses. Students in this exploratory action research study generally found the combined classroom/web-based instruction to be useful, effective, and motivating, with convenience and self-pacing cited as strengths of the web-based lessons and lack of interaction as a weakness. An exception to the generally positive attitudes was one student who did not have e-mail at home. Students also expressed skepticism regarding fully online courses.

In the context of graduate-level music education, Fung (2004) studied the need for flexible learning, which he defined as any learning approach removed from conventional face-to-face instruction. Questionnaires were completed by 24 former, current, and prospective students, and interviews were conducted with three administrators. Overall, respondents recognized the convenience of Internet resources but were not convinced of the effectiveness of these resources in graduate music education. In addition, there was little enthusiasm for flexible learning, due in large part to concerns about lack of social interaction with students and professors. Fung noted the possibility that only theoretical courses, not practical ones, might be effective in flexible learning formats, and he concluded that such formats might be used to reach students not ordinarily reached by his program.

Mentoring

Several studies were focused on mentoring, and involved graduate and undergraduate students in electronic communities of practice. One followed the progress of elementary- and secondary-level students and teachers engaged in compositional activities. Earlier studies in this group explored the feasibility of electronic mentoring. The more recent studies appear to assume the effectiveness of online mentoring; these studies focus more directly on the benefits of specific aspects of mentoring relationships.

Bush (2001) investigated the feasibility of electronic mentoring to enhance learning in graduate-level music education coursework in a meaningful way. It was expected that mentoring would promote dialogue between music education students and practicing music educators, as well as discussion of topics related to music education methods. Graduate students teamed with three or four practicing music educators with different backgrounds (general music, instrumental music, etc.) and in different geographical locations. Students discussed weekly assigned questions with mentors and then discussed mentors' responses and reactions in weekly class meetings. Formal and anecdotal data were gathered. Students corresponded weekly with the instructor using an electronic journal, often reflecting on conversations with mentors. At the end of the semester, students completed a survey regarding use of electronic correspondence for educational reasons, and mentors were contacted for feedback. Results were generally positive. Benefits included a richer learning environment because of the varied backgrounds and locations of the mentors, the ability to share lesson plans among mentors and those graduate students who were also teaching, and the value of connecting with practicing music educators.

Reese, Repp, Meltzer, & Burrack (2002) created a multimedia website to be used for professional development in music education technology through a self-guided, informal learning approach. Data were gathered through pre- and post-tests, surveys, and interviews with practicing music educators. Results were somewhat mixed, showing positive but non-significant knowledge and attitude gains for both participants who used the site while enrolled in a music technology course and those who used the site but were not enrolled in a music technology course. Results also suggested that effective integration of technology into instruction would require a combination of personal interaction, formal instruction, and the resources of professional development websites.

Slotwinski (2011) examined student/teacher engagement in an online community of practice and its impact on their student teaching experience. Data on the nine participants were collected by means of interviews, document support, and a critical incident technique. Results showed that all participants discussed the benefits and impact of a positive relationship with cooperating teachers. Days and times of posts to a wiki revealed the benefits of asynchronous communication, with most posts dealing with the giving or seeking of advice. Each participant, based on individual needs, had different reasons for using the site and different ways of using it.

Shin (2011) studied the aspects of a mentoring project that helped teachers and students sustain their engagement in composing and teaching composition at elementary and secondary school levels. Data were gathered through interviews, observations, and student compositions matched with mentor comments. The necessity of asynchronous communication between students and mentors who are professional artists resulted in written comments that could be used by both teachers as a pedagogical tool and students for further reflection on their compositions. Results suggest that the mutually supportive relationships among the mentoring groups help to sustain their participation over time.

Reese (2013) investigated use of virtual field experiences and virtual mentoring in an elementary general music methods course. She assigned two or three pre-service music teachers to each of eight elementary general music teachers. Students observed two live-streamed 30-minute elementary general music classes followed by 30-minute post-observation conferences with their mentor teachers. In addition, they submitted three 30-minute field teaching videos to their mentor teachers via a private YouTube link followed by a 30-minute conference using Skype. Other data included student reflection papers related to each of the observations and conferences. Benefits to students included a more efficient use of time; a more realistic view of the elementary general classroom, attributed to the absence of visitors in the classroom; and a realistic outlook on the profession. Challenges included a limited view of the classroom due to use of a webcam, limitations on audio and video quality, and Internet reliability, lack of direct contact with students, and scheduling difficulties. Reese reported that the observations and mentoring experiences promoted interaction with experienced teachers and promoted the students' professional self-images. She recommended introducing such experiences prior to formal student teaching and extending virtual experiences to other courses, such as choral and instrumental methods.

SUMMARY

At this time, there is a body of research, including meta-analyses, that supports the general effectiveness of online education. Many studies comparing the effectiveness of online and face-to-face learning have revealed no significant differences: Online education was perceived to be at least as effective as face-to-face instruction. However, if pedagogical techniques appropriate to each medium, online and face-to-face, were used, then it would simply make sense that the medium itself would be less salient, and that the modes of instruction would be found to be equivalent in terms of effectiveness. That is, if context is taken into account when determining appropriate content, pedagogical techniques, and instructional technologies, the effectiveness of the two modes of learning should prove to be relatively equivalent (Adams, 2007).

Additionally, there is a smaller amount of research on online education in music including philosophical work, course and program development efforts, and studies of specific instructional strategies within various music disciplines that generally supports the feasibility and effectiveness of online learning in music and some specific strategies in particular. Although it is premature to draw any firm conclusions based upon the small amount of research on online learning in music, it is possible to identify a few threads running through some discipline-specific studies. A few findings seem particularly promising and suggest potentially productive directions for future research. Constructivist approaches have been beneficial in the online environment (Bauer & Daugherty, 2001; Brewster, 2005; Keast, 2010). Collaborative activities, as well as use of web 2.0 tools like blogs/journals and wikis, have been effective in maintaining interaction and achieving learning outcomes (Walker, 2001; McCabe, 2007; Slotwinski, 2011). Desktop videoconferencing appears to be a viable environment for applied music study (Dye, 2007; Dammers, 2009; Lockett, 2010; Orman & Whitaker, 2010; Kruse, et al., 2013; Pike & Shoemaker, 2013; Riley, 2013). Electronic mentoring of pre-service and in-service music teachers produced positive outcomes (Bush, 2001; Reese, et al., 2002; Reese, 2013). Some of the more recent activity in this area involved an online community of practice (Slotwinski, 2011). Most of these findings are in alignment with the results of the research on online learning in general.

As noted previously, there is a foundation of research that indicates the effectiveness of online learning in general and online learning in music. Moving ahead, it would be more productive and advantageous to investigate how best to use web-based technologies in support of high-quality learning outcomes, rather than continue to pit one instructional delivery mode against another. Webster (2007) noted that the growing number of qualitative studies of technology-based music teaching has increased our understanding of how people learn with technology, but he also pointed out the need for more substantive research on strategies for teaching with technology. It would seem that now is the time to reconsider the broader musical, educational, and technological contexts in which online education in music is implemented; to conduct qualitative studies of how people learn in online environments; to investigate specific strategies for online learning in music; and to direct more attention toward development of appropriate instructional models and practical teaching approaches. This agenda would help us understand which aspects of online education really matter, and would result in greater progress toward realization of the transformative potential of online education in music.

REFERENCES

Adams, J. (2007). Then and now: Lessons from history concerning the merits and problems of distance education. *Studies in Media Information Literacy Education*, 7(1), 1–14.

Allen, I. E., & Seaman, J. (2013). *Changing course: Ten years of tracking online education in the United States*. Babson Survey Research Group and Quahog Research Group, LLC. Retrieved from http://sloanconsortium.org/publications/survey/index.asp

Austin, J. (2007). *Navigating a flat world: The promise and peril of online graduate music education programs*. Paper presented at the September 2007 Symposium on Music Teacher Education, Greensboro, NC.

Barry, N. (2003). Integrating web based learning and instruction into a graduate music education research course. *Journal of Technology in Music Learning*, 2(1), 2–8.

Bauer, W. I. (2001). Student attitudes toward web-enhanced learning in a music education methods class: A case study. *Journal of Technology in Music Learning*, 1(1), 20–30.

Bauer, W. I., & Daugherty, J. F. (2001). Using the Internet to enhance music teacher education. *Journal of Music Teacher Education*, 11(1), 27–32.

Bennett, K. (2010). A case study of perceptions of students, teachers, and administrators on distance learning and music education in Newfoundland and Labrador: A constructivist perspective (doctoral dissertation). Retrieved from ProQuest Dissertations and Theses database (UMI No. MR64792).

Bernard, R. M., Abrami, P. C., Borokhovski, E., Wade, C. A., Tamim, R. M., Surkes, M. A., & Bethel, E. C. (2009). A meta-analysis of three types of interaction treatments in distance education. *Review of Educational Research*, 79, 1243–1288.

Bernard, R., Abrami, P., Lou, Y., Borokhovski, E., Wade, A., & Wozney, L. (2004). How does distance education compare with classroom instruction? A meta-analysis of the empirical literature. *Review of Educational Research, 74*(3), 379–439.

Brewster, M. S. (2005). The effects of a constructivist-inspired web-based summary portal on examination performance in music for an online course (doctoral dissertation). Retrieved from ProQuest Dissertations and Theses database (UMI No. 3180074).

Bush, J. (2001). Introducing the practitioner's voice through electronic mentoring. *Journal of Technology in Music Education, 1*(1), 4–9.

Carney, R. D. (2010). Using web-based instruction to teach music theory in the piano studio: Defining, designing, and implementing an integrative approach (doctoral dissertation). Retrieved from ProQuest Dissertations and Theses database (UMI No. 3417740).

Chuang, W. (2000). Formative research on the refinement of web-based instructional design and development guidance systems for teaching music fundamentals at the pre-college level (doctoral dissertation). Retrieved from ProQuest Dissertations and Theses database (UMI No. 9993557).

Dammers, R. J. (2009). Utilizing internet-based videoconferencing for instrumental music lessons. *Update: Applications of Research in Music Education, 28*(1), 17–24.

Dye, K. G. (2007). Applied music in an online environment using desktop videoconferencing (doctoral dissertation). Retrieved from ProQuest Dissertations and Theses database (UMI No. 3259242).

Eakes, K. (2009). A comparison of a sociocultural and a chronological approach to music appreciation in face-to-face and online instructional formats (doctoral dissertation). Retrieved from ProQuest Dissertations and Theses database (UMI No. 3365532).

Franklin, J. L. (2008). Dimensions of sound in virtual online immersive environments: A theoretical exploration (doctoral dissertation). Retrieved from ProQuest Dissertations and Theses database (UMI No. 3340474).

Fung, V. (2004). Perception of the need for introducing flexible learning in graduate studies in music education: A case study. *College Music Symposium, 44*, 107–120.

Green, B. (2003). The comparative effects of computer-mediated interactive instruction and traditional instruction on music achievement in guitar performance (doctoral dissertation). Retrieved from ProQuest Dissertations and Theses database (UMI No. NQ86051).

Groulx, T. J., & Hernly, P. (2010). Online master's degrees in music education: The growing pains of a tool to reach a larger community. *Update, 28*(2), 60–70.

Hunter, R. W. (2011). Learning in an online jazz history class (doctoral dissertation). Retrieved from ProQuest Dissertations and Theses database (UMI No. 3482765).

Keast, D. A. (2010). Implementation of constructivist techniques into an online activity for graduate students. *Journal of Technology in Music Learning, 4*(2), 41–55.

Kos, R. P., Jr., & Goodrich, A. (2012). Music teachers' professional growth: Experiences of graduates from an online graduate degree program. *Visions of Research in Music Education, 22*. Retrieved from http://www.rider.edu/~vrme

Kruse, N. B., Harlos, S. C., Callahan, R. M., & Herring, M. (2013). Skype music lessons in the academy: Intersections of music education, applied music and technology. *Journal of Music, Technology & Education, 6*(1), 43–60.

Lee, C. S. (2003). Introduction to music therapy: An interactive web course via Blackboard 5.5 (doctoral dissertation). Retrieved from ProQuest Dissertations and Theses database (UMI No. 3098610).

Lockett, W. (2010). Student perceptions about the effectiveness and quality of online musical instrument instruction (doctoral dissertation). Retrieved from ProQuest Dissertations and Theses database (UMI No. 3419163).

Lorenzo, G., & Moore, J. C. (2002). *The Sloan Consortium report to the nation: Five pillars of quality online education.* Retrieved from http://sloanconsortium.org/publications/freedownloads

McCabe, M. (2007). Learning together online: An investigation of the effect of collaborative instruction on students' demonstrated levels of cognition and self-reported course satisfaction in an online music appreciation course (doctoral dissertation). Retrieved from ProQuest Dissertations and Theses database (UMI No. 3257313).

Means, B., Toyama, Y., Murphy, R., Bakia, M., & Jones, K. (2010). *Evaluation of evidence-based practices in online learning: A meta-analysis and review of online learning studies.* Center for Technology in Learning, U.S. Department of Education. Retrieved from http://www2.ed.gov/rschstat/eval/tech/evidence-based-practices/finalreport.pdf

Moore, M. G. (1993). Theory of transactional distance. In D. Keegan (Ed.), *Theoretical principles of distance education* (pp. 22–38). New York: Routledge.

Nakashima, J. (2009). "Experiencing music 2200" online: A critical case study of the curriculum transfer process (doctoral dissertation). Retrieved from ProQuest Dissertations and Theses database (UMI No. MR57449).

Orman, E. K., & Whitaker, J. A. (2010). Time usage during face-to-face and synchronous distance music lessons. *American Journal of Distance Education, 24*(2), 92–103.

Pike, P. D., & Shoemaker, K. (2013). The effect of distance learning on acquisition of piano sight-reading skills. *Journal of Music, Technology & Education, 6*(2), 147–162.

Rees, F. J. (2002). Distance learning and collaboration in music education. In R. Colwell & C. Richardson (Eds.), *The new handbook of research on music teaching and learning* (pp. 257–273). New York: Oxford University Press.

Reese, J. A. (2013). Online status: Virtual field experiences and mentoring during an elementary general music methods course. *Journal of Music Teacher Education.* Advance online publication. doi: 10.1177/1057083713506119

Reese, S., Repp, R., Meltzer, J., & Burrack, F. (2002). The design and evaluation of use of a multimedia web site for online professional development. *Journal of Technology in Music Learning, 1*(2), 24–37.

Riley, P. (2013). Video-conferenced classes: American pre-service music educators teach composition skills to students in Japan. *Journal of Technology in Music Learning, 5*(1), 51–69.

Ross, V. (2001). Offline to online curriculum: A case study of one music course. Retrieved from http://www.westga.edu/~distance/ojdla/winter44/ross44.html

Ryder, C. O. (2004). The use of internet-based teaching strategies in teaching vocal anatomy, function, and health to high school choral music students, and its effect on student attitudes and achievement (doctoral dissertation). Retrieved from ProQuest Dissertations and Theses database (UMI No.3136262).

Scarnati, B., & Garcia, P. (2007). The fusion of learning theory and technology in an online music history course. Retrieved from http://www.editlib.org/p/104338

Schoueman, S. (1999). Instructional design for distance music education (doctoral dissertation). Retrieved from ProQuest Dissertations and Theses database (UMI No. 0801137).

Seddon, F., & Biasutti, M. (2010). Strategies students adopted when learning to play an improvised blues in an e-learning environment. *Journal of Research in Music Education 58*(2), 147–167.

Shin, H. (2011). Enabling young composers through the Vermont MIDI project: Composition, verbalization and communication (doctoral dissertation). Retrieved from ProQuest Dissertations and Theses database (UMI No. 3479343).

Sinclair, D. R. (2004). The effect of synchronous and asynchronous online communication on student achievement and perception of a music fundamentals course for undergraduate non-music majors (doctoral dissertation). Retrieved from ProQuest Dissertations and Theses database (UMI No. 3132257).

Slotwinski, J. A. (2011). Online communication as a mode of professional development among student teachers in music education (doctoral dissertation). Retrieved from ProQuest Dissertations and Theses database (UMI No. 3448039).

Smith, B. N. (2010). The role of technology in assessment of online music education courses taught at the community college level. In T. S. Brophy (Ed.), *The practice of assessment in music education: Frameworks, models, and designs. Proceedings of the 2009 Florida symposium on assessment in music education* (pp. 435–439). Chicago: GIA Publications.

Stefanov, I. B. (2011). High school music student and teacher perceptions of online learning environments (doctoral dissertation). Retrieved from ProQuest Dissertations and Theses database (UMI No. 3445716).

Walker, D. (2001). Computer-aided collaboration in a graduate-level music analysis course: An exploration of legitimate peripheral participation (doctoral dissertation). Retrieved from ProQuest Dissertations and Theses database (UMI No. NQ58954).

Walls, K. C. (2008). Distance learning in graduate music teacher education: Promoting professional development and satisfaction of music teachers. *Journal of Music Teacher Education, 18*(1), 55–66.

Walls, K. C., Miranda, M., Schaffer, B., Gilbreath, J., & Good, R. (2005). *Program development and evaluation of a distance learning graduate degree program in music education: Perspectives from students and professors.* Paper presented at the September 2005 Symposium on Music Teacher Education, Greensboro, NC. Retrieved from http://www.auburn.edu/~wallski/Clinics/SMTE05.pdf

Walls, K. C., Wolfe, S., Good, R., Powell, W., & Schaffer, W. (2004). Education at a distance: Perspective from the podium. *Hawaii International Conference on Arts and Humanities Conference Proceedings*, 6334–6349. Retrieved from http://www.hichumanities.org/proceedings_hum.php

Webster, P. R. (2007). Computer-based technology and music teaching and learning: 2000–2005. In L. Bresler (Ed.), *International Handbook of Research in Arts Education* (pp. 1311–1328). Dordrecht, NL: Springer.

Webster, P. R. (2011b). Key research in music technology and music teaching and learning. *Journal of Music, Technology and Education 4*(2/3), 115–130.

Wright, M. R. (2007). Texas community college music appreciation courses, online and traditional (doctoral dissertation). Retrieved from ProQuest Dissertations and Theses database (UMI No. 3295380).

Yoshioka, Y. (2003). A web-based tutorial for the beginning piano student (doctoral dissertation). Retrieved from ProQuest Dissertations and Theses database (UMI No. 3115088).

PART TWO

Theoretical and Pedagogical Frameworks

CHAPTER 4

Course Design/Redesign

Having a framework goes beyond merely identifying problems with current approaches; it offers new ways of looking at and perceiving phenomena and offers information on which to base sound, pragmatic decision making.

—Punya Mishra & Matthew J. Koehler, *Technological pedagogical content knowledge: A framework for teacher knowledge*

CONCEPTUAL FRAMEWORK FOR ONLINE TEACHING AND LEARNING

Analysis of published research on online learning and educational technology has revealed that the technologies, content, and activities used in these studies tend to be ad hoc rather than theory-based, with researchers using their own courses and serving as both researcher and instructor (Means, et al., 2010, p. xviii). Further, educational technology research has consisted predominantly of case studies, examples of best practices, and implementations of new pedagogical tools (Mishra & Koehler, 2006, p. 1018). These studies are useful in building an understanding of the use of technology for online instruction, as they illustrate how individuals have addressed or solved specific issues of online learning in their own contexts. They can therefore be informative for those experiencing similar situations. However, a theoretical and conceptual perspective is needed to support the broader context and provide general direction for everyday pedagogical decisions. A more systematic and effective approach to course design for online learning requires a conceptual framework that provides theoretical grounding and a basis for deep exploration of the online learning environment. It requires attention to the technologies, pedagogical approaches, curriculum materials, and learning activities that maximize the potential of the digital environment and support learning in this context.

Technological, pedagogical, and content knowledge (TPACK)

The TPACK framework, or technological, pedagogical, and content knowledge, developed by Punya Mishra & Matthew J. Koehler (2006) has potential to function as a conceptual framework for online learning. This framework is an expansion of an earlier model, pedagogical content knowledge, developed by Lee Shulman (1986). It has been applied to online education (Archambault & Crippen, 2009; Koehler, et al., 2009; Scott, 2009; Ward & Benson, 2010) and further applied to music education (Bauer, 2010a). Here it is further extended to online education in music in the context of higher education.

Shulman's pedagogical content knowledge

Lee S. Shulman, past president of the Carnegie Foundation for the Advancement of Teaching and professor emeritus at the Stanford University School of Education, formulated the concept of "pedagogical content knowledge" to counter the artificial separation of content knowledge and pedagogical knowledge that was typical in teacher education programs of the time (1980s). His research into teacher examinations of 1875 revealed a primary emphasis on content knowledge, with little attention to pedagogy. While serving in the 1980s as adviser for a state-level system of teacher evaluation, he noted a reversal in emphasis to a focus on teaching procedures, with little or no attention to subject matter knowledge. He characterized this overemphasis on pedagogy to the exclusion of content as "a blind spot that now characterizes most research on teaching, and, as a consequence, most of our state-level programs of teacher evaluation and teacher certification" (1986, pp. 4–5).

To remedy this situation, Shulman and colleagues initiated a research program to study the development of secondary school teacher knowledge. They investigated the "transition from expert student to novice teacher" (1986, p. 5) by exploring how college students transform their content expertise so high school students can understand; how novice teachers use content expertise to create accessible explanations of dense textbook readings or dispel student confusion; how they develop explanations, analogies, and examples; how they draw upon their content expertise while in the process of teaching; and other issues. To clarify the thinking about teacher content knowledge, Shulman organized it into three categories: subject matter content knowledge, pedagogical content knowledge, and curricular knowledge.

He defined pedagogical content knowledge as "subject matter knowledge *for teaching*," or "the particular form of content knowledge that embodies the aspects of content most germane to its teachability" (1986, p. 9). Pedagogical content knowledge constitutes the ways to represent and formulate a subject so that others can understand it. It includes knowledge of the commonly taught topics in a subject area, the most effective ways of representing those topics, and the most powerful explanations, analogies, and examples. Because there is no single best representation, teachers need to have various kinds of representations at their disposal. Pedagogical content knowledge, in Shulman's view, includes a grasp of what makes learning particular topics difficult or easy for students of different ages and backgrounds, including awareness of students' preconceptions and misconceptions. It requires that teachers develop strategies to address these learning issues.

Mishra & Koehler's technological, pedagogical, and content knowledge (TPACK)

Mishra & Koehler built upon Shulman's pedagogical content knowledge by adding technology to the mix and developing the TPACK theory or framework (2006). They note that in the 1980s, when Shulman developed the concept of pedagogical content knowledge, the technologies used in classrooms, including chalkboards, overhead projectors, and wall charts, were so conventional that they were not even considered technologies. That changed dramatically with the availability of computers, the Internet, and associated applications along with their potential to change the nature of the classroom. The addition of the third element of the model, technological knowledge, updated Shulman's concept in terms of the pervasiveness of digital technologies and the need to integrate them into teaching and learning. The addition of technology expands the original concept of pedagogical content knowledge (PCK) to technological, pedagogical, and content knowledge or TPACK.

Mishra & Koehler point out that parallel circumstances existed with regard to Shulman's work on PCK and their own work on TPACK. Before Shulman developed the PCK model, content knowledge and pedagogical knowledge were considered separately from each other. Likewise, technology has been considered separately from content and pedagogy, and

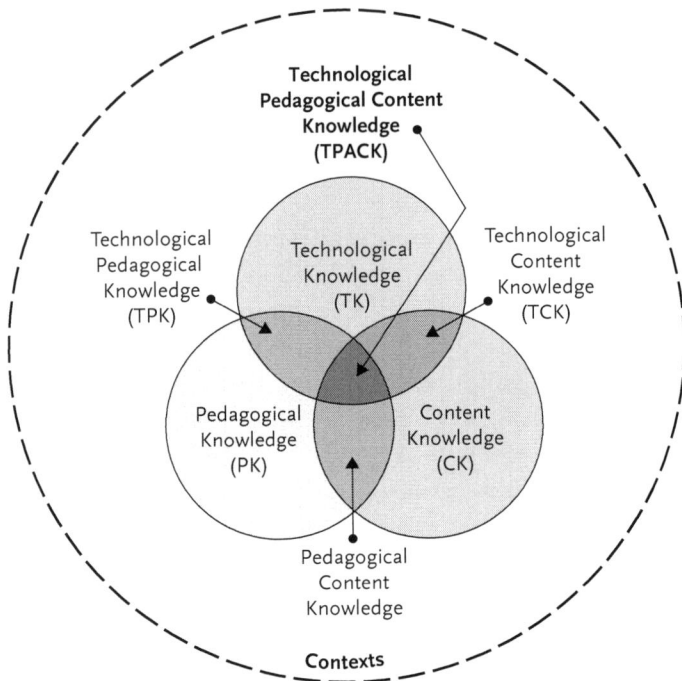

Figure 4.1 TPACK Conceptual Framework Model (Mishra & Koehler, 2006)
Source: http://tpack.org/
Reproduced by permission of the publisher, © 2012 by tpack.org

faculty development has often focused on development of skills with hardware and software, but without reference to subject matter or pedagogy. As Shulman's PCK connected content and pedagogy, Mishra & Koehler's TPACK brings together all three components (content, pedagogy, and technology) along with the relationships and interactions between and among them. The TPACK conceptual framework serves as both a theoretical and a practical way to explain the complex relationships and interactions among content, pedagogical, and technological knowledge within specific contexts (figure 4.1).

Mishra & Koehler explain that this framework

> ...emphasizes the connections, interactions, affordances, and constraints between and among content, pedagogy, and technology. In this model, knowledge about content (C), pedagogy (P), and technology (T) is central for developing good teaching. However, rather than treating these as separate bodies of knowledge, this model additionally emphasizes the complex interplay of these three bodies of knowledge. (2006, p. 1025)

As shown in figure 4.1, the components of the model can be considered separately (CK, PK, TK), as well as in combination with each other (PCK), with technology (TPK, TCK), and collectively (TPACK). As described by Mishra & Koehler, content knowledge (CK) is knowledge about the subject matter to be taught, including facts and concepts within a particular field, as well as ways to connect and organize ideas (e.g., organizing and sequencing topics in fundamentals of music theory at the college level). Pedagogical knowledge (PK) is general knowledge about the procedures and practices of teaching and learning, including knowledge of teaching techniques and characteristics of students. It includes understanding how students construct knowledge and acquire skills. Pedagogical content knowledge (PCK) resembles Shulman's idea. It includes knowledge of suitable approaches for teaching particular content and ways to organize content for improved teaching (e.g., specific techniques for teaching seventh chords to college freshmen in an introductory music theory course). Technological knowledge (TK) is knowledge and understanding of both standard and digital technologies. In the case of digital technologies, it includes skills with hardware and software, such as installing software programs and working with peripheral devices.

Technological content knowledge (TCK)

Technological content knowledge is knowledge about the relationships between technology and content, as well as how the use of technology can change the subject matter. Mishra & Koehler note: "Although technology constrains the kinds of representations possible, newer technologies often afford newer and more varied representations and greater flexibility in navigating across these representations" (p. 1028). Discovering and working with a new technology can reveal its potential to illuminate certain subject matter, so that beginning with technology and seeing how it may be used for instructional purposes may be preferable to the conventional approach of beginning with content, as has been the case in the past.

Technological pedagogical knowledge (TPK)

Technological pedagogical knowledge runs parallel to technological content knowledge: It is knowledge of the capabilities of different technologies as used in instructional settings and how their use might modify teaching. This category includes knowledge of the technological tools that might be used for a particular task, the ability to select the appropriate tool and ways to harness the tool's affordances, and knowledge of pedagogical techniques and the ability to apply those to technology use.

Technological, pedagogical, and content knowledge (TPACK)

Mishra & Koehler refer to technological, pedagogical, and content knowledge as "an emergent form of knowledge that goes beyond all three components" (p. 1028). It includes understanding how concepts can be represented using technology and knowledge of pedagogical strategies that employ technologies to teach content. It also includes knowing what makes certain concepts easy or difficult for students and how technology can help overcome such intellectual bottlenecks.

The TPACK framework

Generally speaking, TPACK is a framework for conceptualizing and integrating technology into instruction. With an understanding of content and the pedagogy appropriate to that content, teachers can make judgments about the affordances (benefits) and the constraints (limitations or challenges) of using particular technologies in their teaching. The interaction among these domains of knowledge (and especially the intersection of all three) supports the thoughtful, effective, and authentic integration of technology into classroom pedagogy. And because technology is constantly changing, TPACK also implies ongoing professional development, or a disposition toward adaptive expertise.

As a conceptual model, the TPACK framework provides a window onto the complex cognitive skills involved in teaching. This kind of knowledge involves an in-depth understanding of the relationships among content, pedagogy, and technology, and the particular contexts in which they function. Mishra & Koehler state that the TPACK approach "helps us identify important components of teacher knowledge that are relevant to the thoughtful integration of technology in education" (2006, p. 1044). They add that this framework provides "a language to talk about the connections that are present (or absent) in conceptualizations of educational technology" and that it "places this component, the relationship between content and technology, within a broader context of using technology for pedagogy" (p. 1044). In reference to application of the TPACK framework to instructional design, Mishra & Koehler point out that it promotes a critique of simplistic approaches toward development of teacher knowledge and helps to develop superior learning environments.

Additionally, it supports an integrated approach to faculty development in teaching with technology. This approach differs from the more common strategy of teaching technology skills separately from specific subject matter within a particular context, the approach often used in typical and standardized technology and music technology workshops. With regard to this type of training, Mishra & Koehler observe: "The leap of faith, however, is that by demonstrating their proficiency with current software and hardware, teachers will be able to successfully incorporate technology into their classrooms" (2006, p. 1031). Clearly, knowing how to use technology is not the same thing as knowing how to teach with technology. Rather, development of TPACK requires deep understanding of the complex interactions between and among the types of knowledge and practical experience in their applications.

Mishra & Koehler also argue for its usefulness in research and scholarship that investigates "the nature and development of teacher knowledge" (p. 1045). Elsewhere, they emphasize: "Teaching successfully with technology requires continually creating, maintaining, and re-establishing a dynamic equilibrium between each component" (Koehler & Mishra, 2008, p. 20). Finally, given the pace of technological change and the rate at which new technologies appear and older ones become obsolete, TPACK is not developed once and then used throughout a person's career. It is an ongoing effort that requires a flexible and adaptive understanding of teaching with technology.

Bauer (2012) corroborates these major claims for the model with respect to its application in music, noting

> ... it does appear that the general principles of TPACK have merit as a conceptual model for the integration of technology into music classes and rehearsals, as a potential framework for the design of professional development experiences for pre- and in-service music teachers, and as a theoretical construct for research. (p. 60)

Music TPACK

The general literature describes applications of the TPACK framework in various disciplinary areas, including literacy education, social studies, mathematics education, science education, teacher education, and arts education (AACTE Committee on Innovation and Technology, 2008). However, it is uncommon to find the framework applied to music education, although DePlatchett's (2008) description of TPACK in K–12 arts education included a brief discussion of music along with visual arts, dance, drama, and media production.

Bauer (2010a) extended Mishra & Koehler's framework to K–12 music instruction. Music TPACK involves integrating technology into the teaching and learning of music through the major ways in which people participate in music: by creating (composing or improvising), performing (singing or playing musical instruments), and responding (listening to, analyzing, and evaluating music). One example of the implementation of TPACK in K–12 music education is the use of an intelligent digital accompaniment application as a practice tool for students in a high school performing ensemble. This choice is based upon affordances provided by this technology, which include the opportunity to practice with an interactive accompaniment and receive immediate feedback on technical aspects of the performance. Bauer further expanded the music TPACK framework to include technological approaches to assessment of students' creations, performances, and understanding of music (2010b). In addition to the application of TPACK to music instruction, he addressed ways that in-service and pre-service music teachers might develop music TPACK, including specialized technology courses along with integration of technology into music education methods courses, active engagement with design activities in which they integrate technology into instruction, use of technology in field and peer teaching experiences, and modeling of technology use by college music instructors. He also emphasized that development of TPACK is a continuous process comparable to the ongoing learning and professional development required for any teacher. He has researched the development of in-service K–12 music teachers' TPACK, often in connection with music technology workshops (Bauer, 2010a, 2010b, 2012).

Bauer's work represents a thoughtful and thorough application of TPACK to K–12 music education along with recommendations for music teacher education and professional development opportunities for K–12 music educators. However, there is little evidence of parallel inquiry targeted toward higher education, where it is crucial that instructors develop their own TPACK in order to model it for their students. Implementation of music TPACK in higher education presents additional unique challenges, as it requires an extension and expansion of K–12 applications to accommodate the greater complexity and sophistication of college-level music study at undergraduate and graduate levels. Further, there are multiple contexts to be considered within higher education. Among them are undergraduate studies, graduate studies, the various music disciplines at each of these levels, traditional courses, online courses, and blended courses, all with specific technological and pedagogical requirements.

Creating, performing, and responding to music

As stated previously, music TPACK involves integrating technology into the teaching and learning of music through the major ways in which people participate in it (Bauer, 2010a). At the K–12 level, a musical goal or outcome in the category of creating music might be improvising a melody (content) over a digitally generated accompaniment (technology), first modeled by the teacher and then performed by the student (pedagogy). A performance goal might be development of effective practice habits through use of an intelligent accompaniment application and interaction with the immediate feedback generated by it. An outcome in the category of responding to music might be the use of a correct and accurate musical vocabulary to describe music listening experiences, compiled in a class wiki that is developed as a collaborative group project.

Responding to music: Higher education

Similar opportunities for creating and performing exist in higher education as well (e.g., with the use of intelligent accompaniment software during and outside of applied music lessons). However, the category of responding—listening to, analyzing, and evaluating music—is more common in other college-level music disciplines like music history and music theory, which constitute core studies in most music degree programs, as well as in foundations of music education, philosophy of music education, and music psychology. The activities associated with responding are also characteristic of music in general studies courses like music appreciation.

TPACK in the online learning context

There is wide agreement in higher education about the need for quality in online learning; however, there has been little inquiry regarding use of the TPACK framework to inform online instruction at that level (Ward & Benson, 2010, p. 484). Higher education instructors are more likely to have learned in traditional classrooms through instructor-centered approaches. It is probable that in their own educations, they experienced neither the integration of digital technologies into the classroom nor online instruction, so the transition to teaching online may not be intuitive. Additionally, there is a tendency for teachers new to instructional technology to use it initially to do more efficiently what they already do, then use it to do something they could not do before, and finally, use technology to transform content, pedagogy, and learning in a fundamental way. Given that pattern, it is not surprising that such instructors' first forays into online learning would tend toward the familiar, mirroring face-to-face courses and replicating current practices in the online environment. However, this approach of gravitating toward the familiar is rooted in traditional practice within the face-to-face environment, rather than in purposeful integration of content with technologies and pedagogies appropriate to the online environment. It is therefore unlikely to realize the potential of this environment or to achieve optimal outcomes, as it represents an attempt to apply the strategies of one environment to another in which at least some of those strategies are likely to be inappropriate or ineffective.

Rethinking content, pedagogy, and technology

Online courses need to be designed specifically for the online environment so they harness the potential of technologies and pedagogies that capitalize on the unique affordances and take into account the constraints of that context. Often, instructors who are transitioning to online learning will be teaching a course online that they have previously taught in a traditional face-to-face setting. The task in this case is adapting it to the online environment so that a course that was effective face-to-face will also work online. This transition requires rethinking of the subject matter, the pedagogy, and the technology: how to represent the content online, how the pedagogy will work online, and what technologies within the learning management system or outside of it will support the pedagogy and facilitate learning the content. Issues might include the uses of online media resources for content presentation, commercially available customizable online courses, asynchronous discussions and synchronous meetings, and others.

Music in the online context

As reported in the research literature, online music courses at the undergraduate level consist predominantly of academically oriented courses such as fundamentals of music theory, music appreciation, jazz, and popular music. At the graduate level, music education courses are most frequently reported, often as a component of an online graduate music education program. These types of courses may be included in the general category of responding to music, as outlined in Bauer's delineation of music TPACK, although they may also incorporate performing or creating to some degree.

Knowledge of music

Audio lectures or podcasts may be used to introduce or supplement textbook readings in any music course, as well as to provide an overview of a musical work incorporated in a listening assignment. Synchronous group discussions can be useful for initial exploratory discussions or brainstorming exercises in any music course. In a music history course, a synchronous meeting can be used to identify major issues for discussion of historical eras in music, such as the social milieu in which composers of a specific era worked, the philosophy of the time and its influence on composers and their works, and the technological development of the musical instruments for which they composed. Asynchronous discussions provide a venue for more extensive and thoughtful discourse on the topics identified in a synchronous brainstorming session. A class wiki provides an engaging way to create a cohesive portrait of a variety of topics—an overview of a musical era, a profile of a composer, an era-by-era exploration of ways composers have used humor in music, or a collaborative analysis of a musical composition.

Listening to music

Music listening tasks or assignments may be part of nearly any online music course, but are perhaps most characteristic of music history, music theory, and music appreciation courses, including jazz history and popular music courses. In these courses, online listening blogs make sense as the new listening journals. Ideally, they provide a record of increasing understanding of musical structure and style, as well as sophistication in the use of appropriate music terminology.

Music education/music research

Most students already use Internet resources for research whether they are enrolled in online or face-to-face courses. However, there are additional tools that can and should be added to students' repertoire of research technologies. Online bibliographic management programs facilitate the process of developing bibliographies and often accommodate collaboration. Blogs and wikis provide experiences with alternative writing styles that are particularly relevant to our digital age.

Developing TPACK

Most teachers are content experts, and in some ways, it is difficult to separate teachers' content knowledge from their pedagogical strategies, which may include use of standard technologies. However, new digital technologies may be less familiar to them and therefore have potential to "disrupt the status quo, requiring teachers to reconfigure not just their understanding of technology but of all three components" (Mishra & Koehler, 2006, p. 1030). The online environment with its associated technologies can be just such a disruptive force, obliging prospective online teachers to rethink their content, pedagogy, and technology.

Many professional development initiatives targeted toward online teaching consist of training in the use of a learning management system or workshops focused on specific technologies and techniques such as lecture capture, podcast creation, and others. These kinds of technology-centered workshops are easier to plan and execute than professional development efforts focused on more complex issues, such as determining appropriate technologies to support specific content areas and pedagogies to promote active engagement in the online environment. Although technology-centered training can be useful in providing instructors with ideas for effective ways to represent their subject matter and exert control over the mechanics of online instruction, technological training without reference to context and the interactions of content, pedagogy, and technology is unlikely to result in quality online teaching and learning. As Ward & Benson note, "Quality online education will be realized only when traditional views of content and pedagogy are reconceptualized within new frameworks that include technology" (2010, p. 487).

The TPACK framework applies the same deep reflection to technology customarily given to content and pedagogy choices. It has been used effectively in traditional classroom contexts; however, when the learning context is the online environment, the strategies used in a traditional setting must be altered or adapted to meet the needs of this inherently technological setting. The online context increases the complexity of the interactions among content, pedagogy, and technology. General issues to be addressed in making this transition include identifying the challenges of teaching specific music subdisciplines online in higher education, defining how TPACK informs preparation for online teaching, and determining what technologies are useful for music instruction in higher education. Some specific skills involved may be gleaned from surveys designed to determine the level of teachers' TPACK. However, because of the unique complexities of each individual instructional context, there is no single solution or plan that will apply to every course and every professor. Rather, professors must use the framework to develop individualized designs for their own situations.

In addition, two distinctive approaches to developing TPACK have been created, a design approach (Mishra & Koehler, 2006) and a learning activities approach (Harris & Hofer, 2009). Both approaches engage teachers in instructional planning tasks that require consideration of the interactions among subject matter, pedagogy, and technology. While they are not specifically designed for music instruction, and while they are primarily, although not exclusively, targeted toward K–12 settings, these approaches may also be useful in planning music instruction in higher education.

Learning technology by design

As noted previously with reference to the "leap of faith" (Mishra & Koehler, 2006, p. 1031), knowing how to use technology is not the same as knowing how to teach with technology. To bridge that gap, Mishra & Koehler created an approach to developing TPACK called "learning technology by design." This approach provides an authentic context in which teachers can develop the deep understanding required in order to teach effectively with technology, as development of TPACK is integrally connected with the development or redesign of courses: "Situations that call for reasoning about interactions (e.g., between technology, pedagogy, and content) are an inherent feature of the learning-technology-by-design approach" (2006, p. 1040). They created a one-semester course focused on online course design, with faculty and graduate student participants. Classes included whole-group discussions of principles and practices of online teaching, as well as small-group work on project design (2006, pp. 1038–1039). Creating an online learning community and related issues of the three-way interaction of students with content, the instructor, and other students were among the pedagogical issues explored. Technological issues were addressed as they arose with regard to instructional goals: Chat rooms and discussion boards were projected as technologies likely to support the interaction needed to build a learning community, a critical aspect of any online course regardless of subject matter (Koehler, Mishra, Hershey, & Peruski, 2004).

Learning activity types

Learning activity types (Harris & Hofer, 2009) and music learning activity types (Bauer, Harris, & Hofer, 2012b) extend instructors' existing experience and planning practice to include integration of technology. Use of this approach helps teachers develop their TPACK while they are engaged in instructional planning. By way of definition, Harris & Hofer offer this explanation of learning activity types:

> Each activity type captures what is most essential about the structure of a particular kind of learning action as it relates to *what students do* when engaged in that particular learning-related activity (e.g., "group discussion," "role play," "fieldtrip")....After teachers are familiar with a complete set of technology-enriched learning activity types in a particular curriculum area, they can effectively choose among, combine, and use them in standards-based learning situations, building their TPACK in practical ways while doing so. (Harris & Hofer, 2009, p. 3)

Harris & Hofer's learning activity types include knowledge building activity types (viewing a presentation, group discussion) and knowledge expression activity types (giving a presentation or performance). Though not specifically designed for online learning, these activity types could easily be adapted for use within an online course (e.g., viewing a presentation and participating in a group discussion). Viewing a presentation is a knowledge building activity type in which "[s]tudents gain information from teachers, guest speakers, and peers" through oral or multimedia presentation using synchronous or asynchronous means. Possible technologies for this activity type include "PowerPoint, Photostory, iMovie, Moviemaker, Inspiration, videoconferencing" (Harris & Hofer, 2009, p. 4). Online students might view a presentation of subject matter prepared by the instructor and delivered asynchronously by means of a PowerPoint presentation or a podcast. A guest presenter might address an online group synchronously using a desktop videoconferencing tool. Group discussion is another knowledge building activity type in which "...students engage in dialogue with their peers" using synchronous or asynchronous means. Technologies involved in this instance include "BlackBoard, discussion in Wikispaces, e-boards" (Harris & Hofer, 2009, p. 4). Online students can contribute to conversations with other course participants asynchronously or synchronously using communication tools built into learning management systems.

Building upon these learning activity types, Bauer, Harris, & Hofer developed a taxonomy of music learning activity types intended for beginning to intermediate students at the K–12 level (2012b). The taxonomy "reflects typical creating, performing, and responding activities and technologies for beginning to intermediate-level K–12 students" and "provides guidance for teachers to use when planning lessons that effectively integrate musical content, pedagogy, and technology" (2012b, p. 1). The National Standards for Music Education form the basis of these music learning activity types, and the relationship to each of the standards may be easily detected in their titles. The creating music category includes improvising and composing activity types, and the performing category includes singing, playing instruments, and reading and notating music activity types. The responding to music category includes listening and describing, analyzing music, and evaluating music activity types. The last two activity types in this category—relationships among music, the other arts, and non-arts-based disciplines; and relationships among music, history, and culture activity types—involve description and discussion of interdisciplinary connections. These activity types may lend themselves particularly well to online learning in higher education. For example, in the category of relationships among music, history, and culture, one activity is to "[d]escribe the various ways music is used in the world." In this activity, students "describe how music and people... interact in disparate musical environments" and "address how responding to music is an essential part of being human." Another activity in this category specifies that students "[d]escribe the historical, social, and cultural elements of a given musical composition," in which they "use digital and non-digital technologies to access information about a particular musical composition" (Bauer, Harris, & Hofer, 2012b, p. 13). The same technologies are listed for both activities, and they provide for both individual and collaborative work. Suggested technologies include audio/video sharing sites, presentation software, wikis, and discussion forums. The former activity might be adapted for use in an online course in ethnomusicology or psychology of music; the latter might be suitable for an online music history course.

The advantage of the learning activities approach is that the technology is considered as it will be used by the learner and is integrated into the learning experience. The focus on the students' learning experience clarifies how and why a particular technology is used. With some adjustments, this approach also has potential for online music instruction in higher education. General learning activity types and music learning activity types can be extended and adapted to online music instruction, as well as to the more specialized scholarly emphasis appropriate to the study of music at the college level.

Online course design

The TPACK model addresses the overall or big-picture issues of integration of technology into instruction: how subject matter, pedagogy, and technology dynamically interact with each other in the teaching and learning process within a particular educational context. The learning technology by design approach (Mishra & Koehler, 2006) engages instructors with course building or course revision using TPACK principles. The learning activities approach brings to this instructional planning process concrete learning activities that are aligned with learning outcomes (Harris & Hofer, 2009; Bauer, Harris, & Hofer, 2012b). By using these approaches, prospective online instructors may more easily develop the technological pedagogical content knowledge they need in order to teach effectively with technology and use that knowledge to design online music courses. In these ways, TPACK can inform preparation for online teaching and provide a framework for online course design.

DESIGN FOR SIGNIFICANT LEARNING

L. Dee Fink (2013) noted the need for change in college-level teaching in the areas of learning goals and teaching activities. He pointed out that many college teachers seem to emphasize lower-level cognitive skills such as knowledge and comprehension (Bloom, 1956), and that they have difficulty identifying teaching activities that go beyond lecture and discussion. To facilitate change in these areas, he proposed a new way to think about teaching in order to provide more effective, meaningful, and significant learning experiences for students: an approach to course design based on linking various types of significant learning with an integrated model of course design. His integrated course design (p. 69) provides a way to organize course elements into a coherent structure that incorporates learning goals derived from his taxonomy of significant learning (p. 35). Paralleling the idea of adaptive expertise in the TPACK model, he also stressed the need for continuous change in both the conceptualization and practice of teaching. Fink's system complements the two approaches to developing

TPACK. It accommodates and enriches the learning activity types, and incorporates ongoing development. While this model was not devised specifically for the online environment, it can be useful in the design of online courses.

Taxonomy of significant learning

Fink's taxonomy represents not just types of learning, but significant learning, learning that remains long after the course is over. It includes the categories of foundational knowledge, application, integration, human dimension, caring, and learning how to learn (pp. 34–37), each of which contains several subcategories of valuable learning. It is relational rather than hierarchical (p. 37): Each category of significant learning relates to, interacts with, and promotes other kinds of learning. A comparison of the taxonomy of significant learning with the well-known taxonomy of the cognitive domain (Bloom, 1956) reveals similarities, as well as important differences, notably Fink's addition of learning categories that go beyond cognitive types of learning.

Foundational knowledge

Foundational knowledge includes the basic information that students need to understand and remember—the conceptual structure and basic ideas of any discipline. This kind of knowledge is valuable to students because it provides the basis for all the other kinds of learning. Foundational knowledge in an undergraduate music history course might include major style periods and their characteristics, significant composers in each style period, and representative compositions.

Application

Application involves using knowledge in various ways. It includes developing specific skills and coordinating multiple tasks in order to manage complex projects. It also includes engaging in various kinds of thinking—critical, creative, and practical. The particular value here is that students learn how to make foundational knowledge useful. In an undergraduate music history course, application might include the ability to identify the style period of an unfamiliar composition through aural analysis.

Integration

Integration involves interdisciplinary learning and connections to everyday life—students making connections among ideas within a given course, across disciplines, and in their own life experiences. Making such connections produces greater intellectual vigor, which is a primary value of this kind of learning. Integration in an undergraduate music history course might involve explaining how the social-cultural milieu of a particular style period influenced the lives and artistic outputs of composers of that period.

Human dimension

This category includes students learning important things about themselves or others and discovering the personal and social implications of what they are learning. This may result in an enhanced self-image and greater awareness of one's possible role in life. The value of this kind of learning is that students become aware of the "human significance of what they are learning" (p. 36). Insight into cultural influences on composers of past eras may lead to increased sensitivity to issues confronting contemporary musicians.

Caring

When students enjoy what they are learning because they find it relevant or are fascinated by it, they care more about it and they may value it more. As a result, they will find the energy to learn more about it and integrate it into their lives. Increased awareness of challenges faced by present-day musicians might motivate students to attend concerts of contemporary music.

Learning how to learn

This category includes becoming a better student, learning how to do scholarship in a particular discipline, and becoming a self-directed learner. The value here is that students learn how to be lifelong learners. Motivated by in-class experience characterizing style periods, students would independently pursue an in-depth understanding of the music of one or more composers or eras.

Design for significant learning

Fink's model for integrated course design is organized into three phases: an initial phase that focuses on building a strong basis for the course; an intermediate phase that involves arranging the basic components within a course structure; and a final phase that entails refinement of the design. There are 12 steps in the integrated course design model:

Initial Phase: Build Strong Primary Components

   1. Situational Factors
   2. Learning Goals
   3. Feedback & Assessment
   4. Teaching & Learning Activities
   5. Integrate the Component Parts

Intermediate Phase: Assemble the Components into a Coherent Whole

   6. Course Structure
   7. Teaching Strategy
   8. Overall Set of Learning Activities

Final Phase: Finish Important Remaining Tasks

   9. Grading System
  10. Possible Problems
  11. Write Syllabus
  12. Evaluation of Course and Teaching (pp. 74–75)

In the initial phase, teachers consider features of the learning situation or "situational factors" (p. 75), formulate significant learning goals and assessment procedures, and develop teaching and learning activities. In the fifth and final step of this phase, they integrate learning goals with procedures for assessment and with learning activities so that all components are congruent. Features of the learning situation include its context (e.g., graduate/undergraduate, mode of delivery); the nature of the subject (e.g., theoretical, practical); learner characteristics (e.g., traditional/non-traditional age, current knowledge and experience, preferred learning style); teacher characteristics (e.g., teaching philosophy, subject matter expertise, teaching style); and any special pedagogical challenges presented by the course. These situational factors parallel the overall context component of the TPACK model. Teachers develop learning goals and assessments using the taxonomy of significant learning within a backward design process (Wiggins & McTighe, 2005). They identify a course goal, determine what performance will demonstrate student achievement of that goal, and then develop learning experiences and activities that help students reach the goal. The learning/music learning activity types (Harris & Hofer, 2009; Bauer, Harris, & Hofer, 2012b) can be useful at this stage, as they provide direction for development of learning experiences in the areas of creating, performing, and responding to music. Finally, teachers ensure congruence among goals, assessments, and learning activities. For example, in an undergraduate music education course, a goal may be for students to be able to integrate improvisation into the elementary general music class. The assessment would be based on a lesson plan and demonstration. Learning activities would involve experiences with improvisatory activities appropriate to elementary-level students.

In the intermediate phase, teachers create a thematic structure for the course in which they organize the concepts to be learned and develop an instructional strategy by combining and sequencing the learning activities they identified in the initial phase. This step echoes a key idea regarding use of learning activity types within the TPACK framework: When teachers are familiar with a relevant set of learning activity types, they can choose and combine them in an effective teaching strategy. In the last step of this intermediate phase, they integrate the thematic structure and instructional strategies into a complete plan of learning activities that includes in-class and out-of-class work and spans the timeframe of the entire course. In an online course, this would include online and offline learning activities.

In the final phase, teachers complete and refine the course design, devise a grading system, anticipate problems with the course design, write the syllabus, and plan how to evaluate both the course and their teaching. For an online course, they would also anticipate problems or challenges with technology and other related issues.

Active learning in online and distance learning

The integrated course design model consists of three elements: information and ideas, experiences (doing and observing), and reflecting. Each of these elements can be achieved through direct or indirect means, with preference given to direct experiences. Students can gain information and ideas directly by using primary sources and indirectly by using secondary sources like textbooks and lectures. They may access these sources in class, outside of class, and online, with online sources including a course website, the Internet, video lectures, and print materials. Receiving information and ideas, a more passive form of learning, is important but limiting: It needs to be complemented by more active engagement. "Doing" experiences include direct experiences, as well as indirect ones, such as simulations and role-plays. "Observing" experiences can include both direct, in-person observations and indirect ones accessed through films or oral histories. Online students can be instructed to "directly experience" or attend an event; they can also engage in indirect experiences online. Reflecting entails making meaning based on what students are learning and how they are learning. They can reflect as individuals through the use of journals or in dialogue with others as part of an online learning community. Online learners can engage in reflection directly, through use of class discussions and term papers, and they may reflect on the learning process itself through the use of blogs and e-portfolios that may be shared with others online (pp. 119–123).

In Fink's assessment, the primary strength of the online setting is access to information and ideas. A secondary strength is reflection achieved through journals, discussion boards, chat rooms, and e-mail, as some people feel freer to contribute online than in a face-to-face setting. The "weakest link," as he sees it, is limited opportunities for significant doing and observing experiences; however, he allows that as teachers find ways to provide effective experiences of these types, "good online learning will clearly be comparable with learning in good classroom courses" (p. 136). Fink applies this assessment to blended courses as well, noting that students in blended courses often acquire information or content online and engage in experiential learning activities during face-to-face class meetings. This assessment of strengths and limitations parallels the affordances and constraints aspect of the TPACK model.

Holistic learning model: Information and ideas, experiences, reflecting

The three components of active learning combine and interact to form a holistic learning model that provides a more complete and significant learning experience. Fink emphasizes that learning experiences should be representative of the three categories of information and ideas, experiences, and reflecting, with preference given to direct experiences when possible. He further advocates "*rich learning experiences* that enable students to achieve multiple kinds of significant learning all at the same time" (p. 123). Again, the learning/music learning activity types can be useful in planning these kinds of learning experiences that include activities in the categories of information and ideas, experiences, and reflecting.

In summary, course design considerations are addressed in a global fashion by the TPACK framework, brought into concrete focus with learning activity types, and organized within a course structure that emphasizes significant learning experiences. TPACK is a conceptual framework for integrating technology, pedagogy, and content within a specific context. Learning technology by design is an approach for putting TPACK into action by engaging teachers as curriculum designers. Music learning activity types provide a concrete basis for active learning experiences in music, and these music learning activity types can be adapted to online music

Table 4.1 ALIGNMENT BETWEEN TPACK AND DESIGN FOR SIGNIFICANT LEARNING

TPACK	Design for Significant Learning
Context	Initial design phase: Situational factors • Specific context, general context, nature of the subject, learner characteristics, teacher characteristics, special pedagogical challenge
Content Knowledge • Subject matter (facts & concepts, connecting & organizing ideas)	Initial design phase: Learning goals, feedback & assessment • Taxonomy of Significant Learning (foundational knowledge, application, integration, human dimension, caring, learning how to learn) Intermediate design phase: Course structure • Major topics in sequential order
Pedagogical Knowledge • Ways to organize & teach content Learning activity types Music learning activity types	Initial design phase: Teaching & learning activities, integration of component parts • Emphasis on active learning Intermediate design phase: Teaching strategy, overall set of learning activities • Combinations of learning activities • Instructional strategy for the course Final design phase: Remaining tasks • Grading system, possible problems, write syllabus, evaluation of course and teaching
Technological Knowledge • Understanding & skill with standard & digital technologies	Not addressed as a major component of the model
Adaptive Expertise	Need for continual change

learning in higher education. Fink's design for significant learning is a detailed course design model that can be used for design of online courses. The music learning activity types can be integrated into this model within the design phases that involve learning activities. Table 4.1 illustrates the alignment and integration of the TPACK framework, music learning activity types, and the design for significant learning model.

REFERENCES

AACTE Committee on Innovation and Technology (Ed.). (2008). *Handbook of technological pedagogical content knowledge (TPCK) for educators.* New York: Routledge.

Bauer, W. I. (2010a). Technological pedagogical and content knowledge for music teachers. In D. Gibson & B. Dodge (Eds.), *Proceedings of Society for Information Technology & Teacher Education International Conference 2010* (pp. 3977–3980). Chesapeake, VA: AACE.

Bauer, W. I. (2010b). Technological pedagogical and content knowledge, music, and assessment. In T. S. Brophy (Ed.), *The practice of assessment in music education: Frameworks, models, and designs* (pp. 425–434). Chicago: GIA Publications.

Bauer, W. I. (2012). The acquisition of musical technological pedagogical and content knowledge. *Journal of Music Teacher Education, 22*(2), 51–64.

Bauer, W. I., Harris, J., & Hofer, M. (2012b). *Music learning activity types.* Retrieved from College of William and Mary, School of Education, Learning Activity Types Wiki: http://activitytypes.wmwikis.net/file/view/MusicLearningATs-June2012.pdf

Bloom, B. S. (Ed.) (1956). *Taxonomy of educational objectives. The classification of educational goals. Handbook I: Cognitive domain.* New York: McKay.

DePlatchett, N. (2008). Placing the magic in the classroom: TPCK in arts education. In AACTE Committee on Innovation and Technology (Ed.), *Handbook of technological pedagogical content knowledge (TPCK) for educators* (pp. 167–192). New York: Routledge.

Fink, L. D. (2013). *Creating significant learning experiences: An integrated approach to designing college courses* (rev. ed.). San Francisco: Jossey-Bass.

Harris, J., & Hofer, M. (2009). Grounded tech integration: An effective approach based on content, pedagogy, and teacher training. *Learning & Leading with Technology, 37*(2), 22–25.

Harris, J., & Hofer, M. (2009). Instructional planning activity types as vehicles for curriculum-based TPACK development. In C. D. Maddux (Ed.), *Research highlights in technology and teacher education 2009* (pp. 99–108). Chesapeake, VA: Society for Information Technology in Teacher Education (SITE). Retrieved from http://activitytypes.wmwikis.net/file/view/HarrisHofer-TPACKActivityTypes.pdf

Koehler, M., & Mishra, P. (2008). Introducing TPCK. In AACTE Committee on Innovation and Technology (Ed.), *Handbook of technological pedagogical content knowledge (TPCK) for educators* (pp. 3–29). New York: Routledge.

Koehler, M., Mishra, P., Hershey, K., & Peruski, L. (2004). With a little help from your students: A new model for faculty development and online course design. *Journal of Technology and Teacher Education, 12*(1), 25–55.

Mishra, P., & Koehler, M. J. (2006). Technological pedagogical content knowledge: A framework for teacher knowledge. *Teachers College Record, 108*(6), 1017–1054.

Scott, L. C. (2009). Through the wicked spot: A case study of professors' experiences teaching online (doctoral dissertation). Retrieved from ProQuest Dissertations and Theses database (UMI No. 3379753).

Shulman, L. S. (1986). Those who understand: Knowledge growth in teaching. *Educational Researcher*, 15(2), 4–14. Retrieved from JSTOR database.

Ward, C. L., & Benson, S. N. K. (2010). Developing new schemas for online teaching and learning: TPACK. *MERLOT Journal of Online Learning and Teaching*, 6(2), 482–490.

Wiggins, G., & McTighe, J. (2005). *Understanding by design* (expanded second ed.). Alexandria, VA: Association for Supervision and Curriculum Development.

CHAPTER 5
Diminishing Distance and Being There

...at any moment there may be a multitude of theories all addressing the same issue. Each might be consistent with the observed facts and be as plausible as the next one.
—Sir Ken Robinson, *Out of our minds: Learning to be creative*

CONCEPTUAL FRAMEWORK FOR QUALITY INSTRUCTION

Among the criteria for quality online instruction, interaction with an active and vibrant community of scholars figures prominently. Moore (1989) was among the first to address interaction in distance education, describing learning as a three-way interaction of learners with instructor, content, and other learners. Looking at distance education as a pedagogical concept, he noted the need to bridge the transactional distance caused by psychological and communications space (1993). His work in this area stimulated further interest in interaction and related issues in online learning (Garrison & Cleveland-Innes, 2005, p. 134).

The Sloan Consortium cites interaction with content, instructor, and other students as the key to quality online learning and advocates building communities of inquiry that promote student collaboration with instructors and other students (Lorenzo & Moore, 2002). The regional accrediting commission's guidelines for distance education/online learning specify: "Course design and delivery supports student-student and faculty-student interaction" (Middle States Commission on Higher Education, 2011, p. 9). The National Association of Schools of Music (NASM) notes that, in distance learning programs, technologies are used to deliver and support student/instructor interactions (NASM, 2013). Two of the seven principles for good practice in undergraduate education

(Chickering & Gamson, 1987) specifically emphasize interaction: encouraging student/faculty contact and developing reciprocity and cooperation among students.

Garrison & Anderson (2003) built their community of inquiry framework upon a "collaborative constructivist" view of teaching and learning (p. 12) that consists of the integration of social, teaching, and cognitive presences. And Harasim (2012) has proposed online collaborative learning as a new learning theory for the information age. It is similar to constructivist theory, but it emphasizes collaborative learning and involves a process of discourse, collaboration, and knowledge building. There are various appropriate uses of both cooperative and collaborative learning in the music subdisciplines. In music theory, for example,

> ...if the topic is the principles of notation or some other well-established aspect of musical vocabulary, cooperative learning is appropriate because students can work in groups to reinforce an understanding of existing concepts. If the topic is improvisational or compositional creativity, then students can actively create their own assessment. (Don, Garvey, & Sadeghpour, 2009, p. 88)

As Robinson (2011) noted, there may be multiple theories that address the same issue, in this case, online learning. Each one proceeds from a particular perspective, and each may be useful for explaining online learning and for deriving appropriate instructional practices for the online environment.

Transactional distance

The concept of transactional distance was developed by Moore (1993) to describe the dynamic relationships between instructors and students in distance education: The separation of instructor and learners creates a psychological and communications space to be bridged. It is this space that constitutes the transactional distance, which is understood not simply as geographical distance, but also as a pedagogical concept. It is a gap that must be bridged if understanding and learning are to occur. The theory of transactional distance was proposed as a way to define distance education, but it applies as well to online learning. However, there is some transactional distance in any educational setting, face-to-face instruction included, and the degree of distance varies from learner to learner. Three key elements related to teaching and learning and their interaction determine the extent of transactional distance: structure, dialogue, and learner autonomy (Moore, 1993, p. 24). Structure and dialogue are key considerations in the design of online courses for meaningful learning. Structural aspects include course design, organization of learning experiences, and use of various communications media. Dialogue or interaction can be synchronous or asynchronous and may involve communication between and among students and instructor. Dialogue and interaction bear certain similarities; however, there is a distinction between the two. Instructional dialogue implies positive interaction that promotes student understanding; interactions can be positive, negative, or neutral. Multiple factors affect the extent and quality of dialogue that occurs in any specific course, including the instructor's teaching philosophy as embodied in the course design, the personalities of the instructor and the students, the nature of the subject matter, and the communications media used in the course. Learner autonomy is the extent of self-directedness in terms of goals, learning experiences, and evaluation in a course. It depends on the amount of structure and the type of interaction. A highly structured course with little interaction would not provide opportunity for learner independence; a lightly structured course with appropriate levels of interaction would promote learner independence.

Communications media and dialogue

The medium of communication has been a central organizer in descriptions and definitions of distance and online education, and it is still a point of focus in discussions of quality in online learning as compared with face-to-face learning. The interactive nature of the communications medium directly impacts the amount and quality of dialogue and its effect on transactional distance. One-way media such as recorded lectures do not support dialogue/interaction and therefore do not significantly reduce the transactional distance, although some authors point out that students may carry on a virtual or internal dialogue in these cases (Moore, 1993, p. 24). For example, a recorded lecture, podcast, or performance provides one-way communication from instructor to learner, but offers no opportunity for two-way dialogue with the instructor, although the learner may engage in internal dialogue with the content—a virtual dialogue. This would maintain a certain degree of transactional distance, as there would be no two-way interaction.

The selection of media that support two-way interaction can effectively increase dialogue while decreasing transactional distance: Interactive media do support dialogue and therefore have potential to reduce transactional distance. Discussion boards provide asynchronous communication, and web conferences or videoconferences provide synchronous communication. Both formats enable a two-way dialogue and consequently reduce the transactional distance between instructor and learner. However, simple use of these media does not guarantee that two-way dialogue will occur with an accompanying reduction in transactional distance. An instructor who uses interactive media primarily to deliver lectures is not maximizing the interactive potential of the medium, and therefore the transactional distance is not effectively bridged. Web conferencing and videoconferencing opportunities designed into learning experiences can reduce the degree of transactional distance experienced by learners, but the extent to which this actually occurs depends on the appropriate use by instructors and students alike. These uses highlight the relative affordances and constraints of specific technologies. For example, podcasts afford creation and delivery of lectures and other presentations that students can access at any time, but they simultaneously constrain interaction and may detract from building an online community if they are used as the primary means of conducting classes. On a related note, some authors point out that they represent "older forms of pedagogy" (Palloff & Pratt, 2007, p. 90). On the other hand, even if the instructor does provide discussion opportunities, a particular student may be hesitant or unwilling to participate in these discussions.

Context also affects transactional distance: Different degrees of dialogue and interaction are possible and appropriate in certain disciplines and at particular academic levels. Graduate-level seminar courses may involve a high degree of interaction among instructors and students with a resultant decrease in transactional distance. Undergraduate courses that may require more direct instruction and allow for less interaction would maintain a certain degree of distance between instructor and students. For example, a graduate-level music education seminar might incorporate extensive discussion while an undergraduate music theory course might involve more direct instruction with less interaction. Some media that represent earlier generations of distance learning may still be used effectively in current online learning environments, as they provide additional options for interaction. For example, the correspondence model may come into play when an instructor reviews or critiques a student's research proposal and returns a word-processed document with comments and suggestions. This technique involves high instructor/learner interaction. Current options for providing recorded lectures are reminiscent of televised instruction, as they offer one-way learner/content interaction. Web conferencing tools support learner/learner interaction for discussion of readings or lectures. However, they can also be overused for lecture presentations with little to no opportunity for learner/learner interaction, mirroring the face-to-face lecture model and missing the kind of interaction these media are designed to support.

Course design

From the standpoint of transactional distance as influenced by communications media, course design determines the way media affect the degree of structure in a course, the extent of dialogue and interaction, and the resultant degree of transactional distance. An optimum online course design provides a balance between availability of structured learning materials, either print or recorded, and opportunities for relatively unstructured dialogue and interaction using various web conferencing tools. This kind of interaction can reduce transactional distance and increase learner independence. Design considerations bring into play the components of the TPACK framework—the interaction between and among subject matter, pedagogy, and technology within a specific context that influences all three elements. In the TPACK design process, instructors consider the context of the learning situation, including subject matter, level, and learner characteristics. Using an appropriate technology, they deliver content via learning materials that they designed or created and that reflect their educational philosophy and pedagogy. Content may also be created or contributed by students.

Bridging the psychological gap

As noted previously, transactional distance may be understood as a psychological and communications space, a gap caused by the separation of instructor and learners. This gap is related to social presence, the perception of people as real in the online environment, and it can be bridged by course activities designed to promote dialogue and interaction. It is also a pedagogical concept that can be addressed through the use of various communications media. Immediacy behaviors (i.e., verbal behaviors such as sharing of personal information, use of humor, addressing course participants by name, referring to the class as "us," quoting and remarking on others' posts, and asking questions related to other participants' posts) can lessen the psychological distance, as well as motivate students to learn. All these immediacy behaviors can occur in text-based communications in which participants project their personalities into their posts, as well as in web conferences or videoconferences.

Learning as a three-way interaction

Moore (1989) attempted to clarify the definition of the term "interaction," which he felt was used too generally and imprecisely to be practical as a concept in discussions of distance education. He proposed that at least three levels of interaction are needed for effective learning to occur: learner/content interaction, learner/instructor interaction, and learner/learner interaction. A fourth level, learner/interface interaction, was later proposed as one of four dimensions of transactional distance particular to web-based instruction (Hillman, Willis, & Gunawardena, 1994; Chen, 2001).

Learner/content, learner/instructor, learner/learner

Learner/content interaction occurs between the learner and the subject matter or content to be learned: It is an essential requirement for learning to take place. According to Moore, learner/content interaction is a process of intellectual interaction with content that results in learning. It represents an internal conversation in which students individually reflect on and deliberate about information and ideas they have encountered through lectures or texts. In online music learning, this kind of interaction might be achieved through the use of written or recorded lectures prepared by the instructor, videos that provide demonstrations, performances, or modeling of skills. Learner/content interaction might also be provided through textbooks and various other web-based resources. Instructor interaction or feedback is not a feature of this kind of interaction; therefore, it is more self-directed and general rather than tailored to the needs and interests of each individual student.

Learner/instructor interaction, a second essential type of interaction, occurs between the student and the instructor, who has probably prepared the content and learning materials to be used. This type of interaction begins with course design, and it involves motivating students to learn, giving presentations, organizing learning experiences in which students work with information and ideas or practice skills they are learning, designing assessments, and providing feedback to students on their progress. In an online music course, the presentation might include written or recorded lectures, as well as videos of performances or skills demonstrations. The communication with and feedback from the instructor in this kind of interaction are especially important in helping students apply new knowledge appropriately and effectively.

Moore introduced learner/learner interaction as a new and challenging element of distance education in the 1990s. He suggested e-mail and synchronous chats as ways to support this kind of interaction. However, learner/learner interaction is now expected due to the current emphasis on collaborative learning and the availability of web 2.0 technologies that support interaction.

Proposed learner/interface interaction

Hillman, Willis, & Gunawardena (1994) pointed out that all interaction in distance learning involves mediation through some technological means that serves as a gateway to any kind of interaction. Because of the increased complexity and growing use of communications technologies in education, they proposed a fourth kind of interaction: learner/interface interaction. This kind of interaction is "a process of manipulating tools in order to accomplish a task" (p. 34): Students must interact with the technology in order to interact with the content, instructor, and other students. For example, a student must successfully deal with communications protocols in order to post to discussion boards or take part in an audio or video web conference. Others later pointed out that students "interact with the hardware, the software, the process, and each other" (Palloff & Pratt, 2007, p. 91) and suggested that interaction with the process includes cognitive presence and teaching presence, while interaction with each other refers to social presence.

THE COMMUNITY OF INQUIRY THEORETICAL FRAMEWORK

A basic difference between online learning and the traditional face-to-face model is the separation of instructor and learners, and a major task for the online instructor is to design a way to bring everyone together. The community of inquiry theoretical framework (Garrison, Anderson, & Archer, 2000; Garrison & Anderson, 2003; Garrison, 2011) proposes that effective learning occurs in a community of teachers and students through the interaction of social, teaching, and cognitive presences. Presence in general is defined as "a sense of being or identity created through interpersonal communication" (Garrison, 2011, pp. 22–23). It is further refined through definition and description of the three subcategories of social, teaching, and cognitive presence.

Underlying this framework are two key principles: interaction (the construction and sharing of meaning) and continuity (the capacity for further learning). A transactional view suggests that instructors and students share both responsibility for and control of learning. Although it is the instructor's responsibility to define goals and content and to determine learning activities and assessments, students are brought into the dialogue about these elements and are given certain choices when it is deemed appropriate. Having a voice in the learning process provides students with a sense of control, which motivates them to take responsibility for the outcomes. And similar to Moore's three-way interaction (learner with instructor, content, and other learners), learning takes place at the intersection of the three presences (figure 5.1).

Community of Inquiry

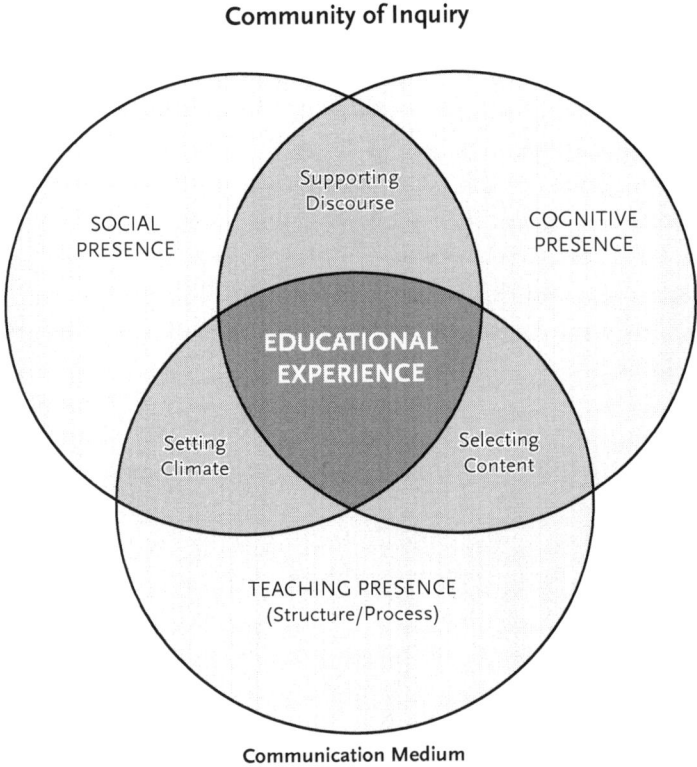

Communication Medium

Figure 5.1 Community of Inquiry
Republished with permission of Taylor and Francis Group LLC Books, from *E-learning in the 21st century: A framework for research and practice*, Garrison, D. R., second ed., 2011; permission conveyed through Copyright Clearance Center, Inc.

Learning community

A community of inquiry is defined as "a group of individuals who collaboratively engage in purposeful discourse and reflection to construct personal meaning and confirm mutual understanding" (2011, p. 15). The individuals include instructors and students, who interact with each other to facilitate understanding, construct meaning, and pave the way for further learning. The learning community is characterized as "a fusion of individual (subjective) and shared (objective) worlds" (p. 20). These two functions represent the purposes of the learning community in encouraging social interdependence through purposeful discourse concurrently with cognitive independence through reflection. These processes result in creation of a collaborative constructivist learning experience, one that has personal value for the members of the learning community.

Conceptual framework

The community of inquiry model is a conceptual framework that defines presences associated with online learning—social presence, cognitive presence, and teaching presence—each of which must be considered in the design and implementation of online learning. It provides a setting in which students have opportunities to take responsibility for and control of their learning through dialogue and critical thinking, to develop both social interdependence and cognitive independence.

Online presence can be defined most simply as being there. It is sometimes defined as the degree of person-to-person awareness or the extent to which a person is perceived as real in a mediated environment, specifically in the context of asynchronous text-based communication. Online presence includes projection of one's personality and one's ideas. It can be considered a perceptual "illusion of non-mediation" (Lombard & Ditton, 1997) that occurs when people are able to transcend a communications medium or ignore its existence and communicate as they would in person. In this kind of situation, the technology seems to disappear, and participants focus on their interactions with each other. Within the community of inquiry model, presence has been divided into three related and overlapping categories, each of which is crucial to a successful online learning experience: social presence, cognitive presence, and teaching presence.

Social presence: Perception of "real" people

Social presence was first defined as "the ability of participants in a community of inquiry to project themselves socially and emotionally, as 'real' people (i.e., their full personality), through the medium of communication being used" (Garrison, Anderson, & Archer, 2000, p. 94). It has sometimes been equated with the human touch or humanizing the online course. A more recent definition casts it as "...the ability of participants to identify with the group or course of study, communicate purposefully in a trusting environment, and develop personal and affective relationships progressively by way of projecting their individual personalities" (Garrison, 2011, p. 34). Both definitions are applied in this framework to asynchronous text-based communication, which presents specific challenges to the establishment of social presence. Clearly, the use of audio or video web conferencing would not present identical challenges.

Social presence is further subdivided into the categories of interpersonal communication, open communication, and cohesive communication. Interpersonal communication sets the stage for other types of communication by creating a supportive climate of respect and trust along with a sense of belonging to the group. Indicators of interpersonal communication in an asynchronous text-based environment include affective expressions such as emoticons, personal information conveyed through short profiles or autobiographies, and use of humor. Because humor can be easily misunderstood in this kind of environment, it should be used with care, probably after participants have become fairly well acquainted. This supportive climate diminishes the psychological distance inherent in this context, and it establishes a necessary foundation for the other dimensions of social presence: open communication and cohesive communication. Open communication is established through a process of acknowledging the contributions of others in the group, and it develops on the basis of the respect and trust that are established through the various forms of interpersonal communication. Indicators of open communication include recognizing and replying to others' posts, making direct reference to others' ideas, perhaps by quoting portions of their posts, and elaborating on them. This kind of open communication suggests engagement in the processes of reflection and dialogue, and it contributes to the building of a community of inquiry. Interpersonal communication and open communication promote development of cohesive communication, the primary goal of social presence. Cohesive communication includes practices such as addressing participants by name and referring to the group as "we" or "us." These kinds of expressions contribute to the cohesiveness of the group and afford a strong basis for collaboration.

The reason for emphasizing development of social presence is its contribution to the establishment of a community of inquiry and the kind of reflection and dialogue associated with it. This requires a balance between social interaction and its specific role in this educational context (i.e., development of professional relationships that promote a high-quality learning experience). The instructor plays a key role in its development by modeling the communications and behaviors indicative of social presence and by steering social interactions toward critical thinking, reflection, and dialogue, which are elements of cognitive and teaching presence.

Cognitive presence: Constructing meaning

Cognitive presence refers to "the intellectual environment that supports sustained critical discourse and higher-order knowledge acquisition and application... facilitating the analysis, construction, and confirmation of meaning and understanding within a community of learners through sustained discourse and reflection" (Garrison, 2011, p. 42). An asynchronous text-based environment requires and supports both reflection and dialogue. Reflection underlies the critical thinking that informs dialogue in this context, and social presence creates the conditions in which dialogue or discourse can occur.

Critical thinking and practical inquiry (experience)

In the community of inquiry theoretical framework, critical thinking is defined in terms of practical inquiry, which in turn is grounded in experience. Indicators of cognitive presence are framed within four phases of practical inquiry: a triggering event, exploration, integration, and resolution. Conceptualization of a problem or issue constitutes a triggering event; it could involve presentation of information designed to stimulate questions and promote discussion. The exploration phase involves seeking additional information and ideas relevant to the problem or issue at hand. The search for information might include brainstorming, relating personal experiences or anecdotes, agreeing or offering contradictory experiences, and remarking on the relative value of contributed ideas or information. The integration or third phase involves moving the discussion forward toward a solution. At this point, participants connect the ideas and information explored in the second phase, elaborate on those ideas, and move toward agreement and a potential solution to the problem or issue. Resolution, the fourth and final phase of the practical inquiry model, involves application and evaluation of the proposed solution. This could be achieved in a direct way through implementation of an individual or group project, or indirectly through presentation and critique of hypothetical applications.

Achievement of cognitive presence and its associated outcomes requires expert facilitation, shaping the discussion so that it proceeds from the initial and exploratory phases that emphasize inductive reasoning and divergent thinking toward the integration and resolution phases, which emphasize problem-solving through convergent thinking and deductive reasoning. Facilitation is a primary function of teaching presence. "What is most required to create cognitive presence . . . is a moderator who can assess qualitatively the nature of the discourse and then proactively shape it following the critical thinking cycle" (Garrison, 2011, p. 53).

Teaching presence: Role of the instructor

Garrison highlights the nature of the community of inquiry framework as "a learn*ing*-centered approach rather than a learn*er*-centered approach . . . a unified process where teachers and students have important, complementary responsibilities" (2011, p. 54), in which students and teachers collaborate to achieve educational outcomes. He also emphasizes that this presence is called *teaching* presence, not *teacher* presence, and while the role of the teacher is indispensible, students may also act in this capacity (2011, p. 62). Teaching presence suggests a collaborative approach to the teaching process in which students may sometimes assume a teaching role, perhaps as co-facilitators or discussion moderators.

Teaching presence is defined as "the design, facilitation, and direction of cognitive and social processes for the purpose of realizing personally meaningful and educationally worthwhile learning outcomes" (Garrison, 2011, p. 55). Each of these factors constitutes a role that the instructor plays in the online learning environment. Teaching presence begins with instructional design, and in that sense, the instructor is present throughout the course. It includes facilitation of discussions, as well as direct instruction, with all roles targeted toward achievement of designated learning outcomes. These roles describe in a general way the actions an instructor takes, bringing together social and cognitive presences in order to create a community of inquiry. These actions move the role of the instructor beyond the somewhat clichéd and artificially opposed roles of "guide on the side" versus "sage on the stage" (King, 1993) to a multifaceted role that includes both functions but also adds the more encompassing role of director of learning. Garrison states that "[t]hese roles are integrative in the sense that teaching presence must bring together the cognitive and social in purposeful and synergistic ways" (p. 56).

Design and organization, facilitation, direct instruction

Design and organization are concerned with the overall structure and process of a course of study. Challenges include course design or redesign that takes into account the online context, transition to an inquiry format that emphasizes dialogue, and familiarity of potential students with online learning. Design refers to decisions about course structure that are determined prior to its beginning. Organization, although it involves similar decisions, refers here to changes made once the course is in process. In this collaborative constructivist framework, design and organization need to be flexible in order to accommodate student input regarding content and how it is approached. Design and organization indicators include determining course content overall, identifying weekly topics as the course progresses, explaining the goals of each week's discussion, designing instructional strategies, providing guidelines for participation, and setting time limits on participation or cutoff dates for submissions. As the community of inquiry framework focuses on asynchronous text-based communication, these indicators appear as statements in instructor discussion posts or announcements.

Facilitation of reflection and dialogue is central to the online learning experience: It requires attention to both social and cognitive matters. The primary tasks in this role are creating and maintaining a community of inquiry in order to achieve the learning outcomes of the course. Facilitation includes setting the tone for the discussion, encouraging participation through skillful prompts or questioning, acknowledging insightful student posts, weaving threads of the discussion to point out areas of agreement, identifying areas of disagreement, moving the discussion toward consensus, and pointing out tangents that move off topic. The instructor models posts appropriate to critical discourse and contributes enough to keep the discussion on track while taking care not to dominate the discussion and consequently dampen student participation. If students are given the opportunity to contribute to teaching presence as co-facilitators or discussion moderators, they may take greater ownership of the online discussion and contribute more effectively to the achievement of learning outcomes.

Direct instruction brings into play the instructor's content expertise and scholarly leadership. It represents a proactive approach that moves beyond facilitation to provide both initial and continuing direction with regard to content issues, learning activities, and the progress of the discussion. Direct instruction includes presenting content and posing questions to be explored, focusing on particular issues, summarizing the discussion, shaping it and moving it forward, enhancing understanding through feedback, clarifying misconceptions, and contributing additional knowledge or directing students toward further resources about topics of discussion.

Proposed learning presence

Development of a separate learning presence emerged from an interest in expanding upon the role of learners in the community of inquiry framework and explicating how people learn online (Shea & Bidjerano, 2010; Shea, et al., 2013). Learning presence consists of online learners' self-regulatory behaviors, which complement and elaborate social, cognitive, and teaching presence. Online learner self- and co-regulation are defined as "the degree to which students in collaborative online educational environments are metacognitively, motivationally, and behaviorally active participants in the learning process" (Shea & Bidjerano, 2010, p. 1723). Metacognitive traits that constitute learning presence include self-explanation, self-monitoring, and self-reflection. Behaviors associated with those traits include forethought and planning, monitoring and adapting learning strategies, and reflecting on results.

Self-efficacy, the strength of students' beliefs about what they can do, is a central factor in self-regulation. While students may overestimate or underestimate their actual capabilities, on the positive side, self-efficacy promotes the use of more effective learning strategies. Within the community of inquiry framework, expanded teaching presence that engages students in teaching responsibilities such as co-facilitation, together with positive social presence that offers feedback from others, supports self-efficacy. This kind of learner self- and co-regulation should result in achievement of a higher level of cognitive presence. Learning presence, then, consisting of metacognitive, motivational, and behavioral traits and activities under the control of successful online learners, can serve as a complementary element of the community of inquiry framework.

Swan (2004) displayed relationships between Moore's interactions (learner with content, instructor, other learners, and interface) and the community of inquiry model (figure 5.2).

The overlapping areas of the model demonstrate in a general way the relationships among interaction types and presences and how they contribute

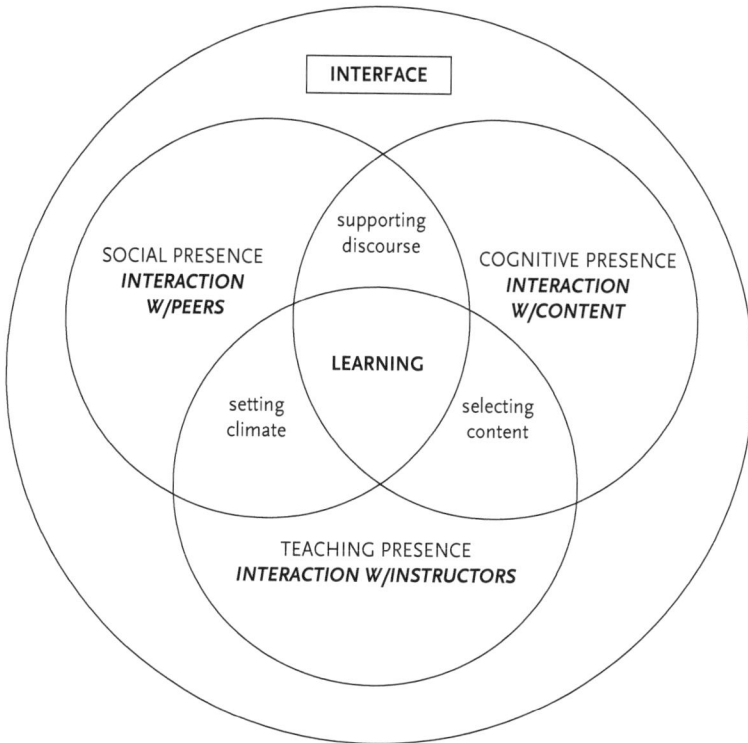

Figure 5.2 Interactions and Online Learning
Republished with permission of Sloan-C, from *Relationships Between Interactions and Learning in Online Environments*, Swan, K., 2004.

to content, educational climate, and discourse. However, the diagram cannot fully reveal the richness of the relationships. For example, teaching presence is paired with interaction with instructors, but students can also provide teaching presence (Garrison, 2011, p. 62).

Teaching and learning guidelines

As noted previously, the goal of the community of inquiry framework is for participants to fully engage in the collaborative construction of meaningful knowledge. Collaboration, as a key component of a community of inquiry, must include purposeful discussion that incorporates reflection. These two processes are integrated, with reflection supporting informed discussion and informed discussion promoting further reflection. Both are central to a meaningful educational experience. Creating the conditions for a meaningful learning experience "demands content expertise, but it is what the teacher does pedagogically that determines the degree to which students assume responsibility for their learning" (Garrison, 2011, p. 11). The community of inquiry model as a framework for online teaching and learning in higher education emphasizes the collaborative nature of online learning while highlighting the central role of the instructor in this setting. Achievement of the goal of collaborative knowledge construction requires a strong and active teaching presence:

> The instructor...plays a key role throughout the e-learning experience—even when the discourse and activities are largely regulated by the students. The instructor is an ever-present and key person, managing and monitoring the process. There is always a need for an instructor or facilitator to structure, shape, and assess the learning experience, if it is to be more than an informal or fortuitous learning experience. (p. 83)

The teaching and learning guidelines were developed in order to provide a coherent, practical perspective on the interrelationships among social, cognitive, and teaching presence within the community of inquiry framework (p. 83). Because teaching presence links social and cognitive presence through its sub-functions of design, facilitation, and direct instruction, the guidelines are aligned with these sub-functions and are focused on how to address issues of social and cognitive presence within each sub-function. And although both synchronous and asynchronous technologies may be used concurrently and in complementary ways in the online environment, much online teaching still relies upon written communication. Therefore, the guidelines emphasize asynchronous text-based discussion. Design determines how students approach these goals; facilitation sustains community and promotes meaningful engagement in discussions; and direct instruction provides academic expertise and scaffolding of subject matter.

A successful online experience depends on thoughtful design and organization that account for all the interrelated elements; anything that is to be achieved in the course must be designed into it from the outset. In the case of a community of inquiry, the foremost design and organization concerns are collaboration and a constructivist approach. Because social presence is essential to a collaborative online experience and a critical element in establishing cognitive presence, it must be designed into the course in the context of educational issues. This issue is particularly important in preparation for the first session, which sets the tone for the course. Planning how to sustain that balance through the progression of the course is another critical consideration in the design and organization phase. Design issues for establishing social presence include building a sense of trust and belonging, a sense of control and accomplishment, and the dispositions needed to participate and contribute to the discussion. Suggested ways to achieve these goals include sending an introductory welcoming e-mail, posting student biographies, and discussing students' expectations for the course. These strategies create a foundation for the establishment of cognitive presence, which builds upon and is supported by the relationships established through social presence. The major design issue for the development of cognitive presence is considering the phases of inquiry and planning activities to help students progress systematically through them by defining problems, exploring related issues, integrating ideas into potential solutions, and applying and evaluating the solutions. A related issue is balancing the amount of content to be covered with the amount of time required for reflection and discussion, so that activities are congruent with goals. Recommended activities include early brainstorming followed by problem-based activities that promote reflection.

Sustaining community through social presence and promoting reflective discourse are the tasks of facilitation. At this point, it is difficult to separate social and cognitive presence, as they are integrated factors in this collaborative/constructive approach. If students do not feel part of the group, they may hesitate to engage in critical inquiry. Therefore, in terms of social presence, the initial goal is establishing a climate that will motivate and promote participation, as well as reflective discussion. Techniques for establishing a climate for inquiry include replying to student biographical posts with a welcome message, inviting student questions about content and the nature of the discussion process, posing interesting questions based on assigned readings, and clarifying the expectation that students will explore the questions further to identify some key issues. In terms of cognitive presence, the goal of facilitation is to keep the discussion on track and foster progress through the phases of inquiry; instructor modeling is important here. Instructors also need to maintain a balanced presence in the discussion, neither dominating it nor appearing to be absent from it, but rather managing the process and monitoring student understanding. Strategies include providing productive questions, identifying issues raised in student posts, contributing additional information and insights, giving objective feedback, identifying misconceptions, shaping the discussion through the phases of inquiry, and concluding the discussion at an appropriate stage.

The focus of facilitation is managing process; the focus of direct instruction is providing subject matter expertise and scholarly leadership. In terms of social presence, direct instruction involves maintaining a climate in which students feel free to pose questions or challenges. The strategies can resemble facilitation—shaping but not dominating the discussion, providing constructive feedback on student posts, and being open to student questioning. On the cognitive presence side, instructors provide content expertise by giving direct responses to student questions, clarifying misconceptions, and explaining or illustrating difficult concepts. They offer scholarly leadership by first pointing out key concepts that constitute a framework for the course, guiding students through activities designed to achieve specific learning outcomes, summarizing the discussion upon its conclusion, and proposing the next steps or further study.

Media and presence

Different media offer different opportunities for interaction, dialogue, and learning. If multiple communications technologies are to be used within a course, the instructor must determine why, how, and when each type is to be used. For example, the spontaneity of synchronous communication heightens social presence and therefore eases the beginning of discussions, while the more reflective discourse supported by asynchronous communication optimizes cognitive presence and better supports the expansion and problem-solving aspects. These decisions then become part of the course design, and they must also be communicated to course participants. The instructor therefore designs the course to accommodate these media and informs course participants of the functions of each kind of technology.

Reflection and discourse lie at the heart of the educational experience and are the integrated components of inquiry in higher education (Garrison, 2006, p. 25). Reflection informs discourse, which in turn may promote further reflection. Although the face-to-face classroom with its synchronous communication affords immediacy and spontaneity in discussions, it simultaneously constrains reflection, although reflection may precede a face-to-face discussion if students prepare in advance. The online environment, on the other hand, particularly with the use of asynchronous text-based communication as featured in the community of inquiry framework, does afford reflection. It also supports a greater flow of communication, as students can post their ideas, read and reflect on others' posts, and respond to others' contributions at any time. They are not constrained by time to wait their turn to speak, as would be the case in the face-to-face setting. Although it is not a prominent feature of the community of inquiry model, desktop audio/videoconferencing can provide a synchronous environment for more spontaneous interaction.

Garrison pointed out that "[n]ew possibilities of approaching the teaching and learning transaction open with the flexibility of utilizing and merging synchronous and asynchronous technologies" (2006, p. 25). Although concurrent use of both synchronous and asynchronous modes can bring more spontaneous dialogue into the online environment, creating a form of blended online learning (Power, 2008; Power & Vaughan, 2010), and current applications tend to use multiple forms of synchronous and asynchronous communication (Means, et al., 2010, p. 1), there will still be a certain amount of asynchronous communication in online learning. The guidelines put forth in this framework therefore emphasize the specific requirements of that mode, but they can apply in synchronous settings as well.

A theory of online learning?

The community of inquiry framework, a collaborative constructivist view, was first described more than 10 years ago (Garrison, Anderson, & Archer, 2000; Garrison & Anderson, 2003). Since then, it has been widely researched, with results confirming the community of inquiry structure. Additionally, research on the interrelationships among the presences has led to increased understanding of a community of inquiry as dependent upon the dynamic relationships among social, cognitive, and teaching presences, and it has underscored the validity of the framework. Although this framework was first applied to computer conferencing and online learning, it has been extended to both blended learning (Garrison & Vaughan, 2008) and the broader category of e-learning, defined as "electronically mediated asynchronous and synchronous communication for the purpose of constructing and confirming knowledge" (Garrison, 2011, p. 2). Garrison argues that the research-based evidence suggests that the community of inquiry framework constitutes a theory: "We believe it is the most coherent theory to date in guiding the research and practice of e-learning and that it has enormous potential to design, guide, and assess e-learning approaches, strategies, and techniques" (p. 29).

ONLINE COLLABORATIVE LEARNING THEORY

Harasim (2012) cites the pervasive nature of online learning and its increasing integration into more traditional approaches that include classroom and distance programs. She notes that because there are limited theory- or research-based guidelines to help educators develop pedagogies specifically tailored to online environments, they have tended to use trial-and-error approaches when implementing new technologies, and in many cases, they have simply mirrored face-to-face teaching practices in online settings—20th-century pedagogies in 21st-century environments. Such practices include using the web and web-based tools for transmission of lectures via presentation software, podcasts, and videoconferences; for communication between students and teachers (and not students with other students); and for administration and grading of tests. She advocates reflecting on our theory of learning and reassessing our pedagogical approaches in relation to the opportunities afforded by online technologies. She therefore proposes online collaborative learning (OCL) as a learning theory for the 21st-century knowledge age, "a new theory of learning that focuses on collaborative learning, knowledge building, and Internet use as a means to reshape formal, nonformal, and informal education for the Knowledge Age" (p. 81). While acknowledging a developing body of literature on how to design and moderate online courses, Harasim suggests that online collaborative learning can enhance that work by providing a theoretical structure to focus those activities.

Harasim identifies some limitations of 20th-century models, including constructivist approaches, and notes that active learning as currently defined and practiced does not adequately address social issues. While acknowledging that both constructivist and collaborative online learning theories reflect a constructivist epistemology, she states that "OCL theory differs from constructivist learning theory, by locating active learning within a process of social and conceptual development based on knowledge discourse" (p. 13). In the OCL model, the teacher plays a central role as a connection to the knowledge community, whereas in the active learning model, the teacher is often considered another participant or a "guide on the side" (King, 1993; Harasim, 2012, p. 94). Constructivist approaches such as reflective practice and collaborative discussions as mentoring have been implemented in music teacher preparation; however, they do not seem to have been extended to online environments. The research appears to have been carried out in traditional classroom settings (Webster, 2011a). OCL theory focuses on learners of all ages as participating members of 21st-century knowledge communities in a variety of settings (p. 13), but it appears to be particularly relevant to adult learners in formal institutions of higher education and, by association, to traditional and non-traditional age learners of music in higher education.

An online learning theory for the 21st century

OCL theory may provide a practical basis for knowledge-age designs and pedagogies, and the designs must emphasize collaborative discourse, knowledge creation, and the use of online communication technologies (p. 81). As Harasim points out:

> The 21st-century Knowledge Age signals the need for a theory of learning that emphasizes knowledge work, knowledge creation, and knowledge community. Whereas the 20th-century Industrial-Age learning theories and pedagogies focused on narrow individualistic tasks with simple sets of rules and clear destinations, the 21st-century Knowledge Age emphasizes creative, conceptual work where there is no clear right or wrong answer, or where there may be many right answers, requiring the knowledge workers to collaborate to identify or create the best option. The role of the instructor or moderator becomes mediating between the learners and the knowledge community, which serves as the state of the art in that discipline. (pp. 83–84)

Harasim states, "Ours is a knowledge-creating age and our theories and practice of learning are challenged to move beyond didactic and even active learning approaches to enable learners to become knowledge builders" (p. 89). Learning in the knowledge-age OCL theory encourages active learner engagement, and that idea is expanded to accommodate conceptual learning as well. The theory consists of three processes: discourse, collaboration, and knowledge building. These processes highlight a distinction between collaborative learning and cooperative learning. In collaborative learning, both the process and the product are collaborative, whereas in cooperative learning, each person may make an independent contribution to a final group product.

Collaborative discourse supports and drives knowledge-building activities. It consists of three types of discourse: idea generating, idea organizing, and intellectual convergence, with possible social applications, all facilitated by an instructor. Idea generating, including brainstorming and sharing of ideas, represents divergent thinking within a group. Idea organizing, by clarifying ideas, grouping them according to relationships to each other, and eliminating less salient ones, constitutes conceptual change and movement toward convergence. Intellectual convergence involves a group contribution to a shared understanding, which does not imply a homogeneous result, but allows for both consensus and agreement to disagree. At the point of intellectual convergence, a conclusion or a final position follows: a solution to a problem, a project, or even a work of art (p. 93). The process is "one of continued growth or advance based on a feedback spiral" (p. 94) (i.e., idea generating or brainstorming might lead directly to idea organizing or analysis, but it might also yield additional brainstorming). Likewise, a conclusion reached in the intellectual convergence stage may lead to a practical application or to further discussion, analysis, and refinement.

Online collaborative learning pedagogy

There is a growing body of literature on designing and teaching online courses, and these resources are valuable for the kind of information that they provide. Nevertheless, "how-to" literature and collections of activities and tips for online instruction fall short of providing a firm foundation for online teaching and learning. Procedures and activities need to be carried out within a framework that guides their use, and OCL theory has potential to serve that purpose. As Harasim argues, it can serve as a guide to design, implementation, and assessment: "OCL theory can enrich or contribute to the above pedagogical activities by providing a theoretical framework to help design and inform activities . . . OCL theory can also help in assessing conceptual change" (p. 94). Her statement parallels Garrison's argument regarding the potential of the community of inquiry framework in designing, guiding, and assessing e-learning (Garrison, 2011, p. 29).

In OCL pedagogy, conceptual change and learning occur as students proceed through the stages of idea generating, idea organizing, and intellectual convergence. Pedagogical activities such as group discussions, seminars, debates, or problem-solving activities are connected with conceptual processes that are mediated by a teacher and that promote increased understanding and knowledge. In the OCL model, the teacher is neither a "sage on the stage" nor a "guide on the side" (King, 1993), both of which at best oversimplify the teacher's role and at worst tend to disparage or diminish the overall contribution of the teacher. Rather, in the OCL model, the teacher plays several critical roles, as facilitator and representative of the knowledge community or discipline, inducting students into a knowledge community and helping them engage in the discourse of a discipline. For example, students in a music psychology course must learn the professional or analytical language of music psychology and use "music-psychology-speak" to engage in discourse about music psychology—identifying issues, discussing various perspectives on those issues, and developing an informed position. The role of the teacher is to help students develop fluency with the language of music psychology and engage them in the discourse and activities typical of that discipline. The teacher also facilitates the process by presenting a topic or problem to be discussed, determining the kinds of activities to be carried out, and establishing the procedures to be used in the discussion.

Online collaborative learning technology

A distinction is made between types of online technologies and the roles they play within the OCL theory. Online tools support learning tasks, while online environments support learning processes, and they are defined quite precisely in light of these purposes. Online learning tools are "web tools that can facilitate or enable particular tasks in a learning activity" (p. 98); they can be either generic or education-specific web tools. An online learning environment is "web-based software that is designed to host or house the learning activities" (p. 98); it is the online counterpart of a physical classroom. Generic online tools (search engines, e-mail, blogs, wikis, and podcast authoring tools) and education-oriented tools (websites that offer information on discipline-specific content such as assessment) can enhance discourse by enabling or expediting tasks within learning activities, and they are useful for those purposes. In music history and music theory courses, selected assignments that emphasize critical thinking, active learning, and group problem-solving have been designed as collaborative learning projects using wikis and blogs (Folio & Kreinberg, 2009/2010; see box 5.1).

The instructors note: "Although wiki and blog assignments may not be appropriate for every assignment in music history or music theory, these Collaborative Learning tools have the potential to invigorate traditional teaching" (p. 173). Additionally, these kinds of collaborative assignments can work well in both blended courses and fully online courses.

These online tools are significant components of a collaborative approach, but the learning environment itself is even more important to online collaborative learning. Online learning environments should not be considered as venues for transmitting information (e.g., podcasting lectures), but rather as places where learners can discuss, collaborate, and build knowledge. Like a physical classroom, the space itself does not contain content; rather, content consists of the discourse produced by the learners. Group discussion software such as discussion forums, bulletin boards, and web conferencing systems support the OCL process and can be organized in various ways—topic-based forums, activity-based forums, full group and smaller group forums. Ideally, an OCL environment is a space designed and structured specifically to support the processes of collaborative discourse

For a music history wiki project, students worked in five groups of five, with each group member assuming a specific role (leader, scribe, multimedia expert, fact checker, proofreader). They read a book chapter, discussed it with their group either in person or online, and responded as a group to some open-ended questions about the reading. Following a designated period of collaboration within assigned groups, the groups shared their collective results. Finally, after reading all group responses, each student submitted a short individual paper reflecting on the project and the process.

For a music theory assignment emphasizing analysis, students contributed to two class blogs, which replaced study questions intended as preparation for class discussions. Students responded to two questions of their choice from approximately 10 questions or commented on another student's response. Questions ranged from specific inquiries, such as questions about form, to more open-ended questions about the meaning of a song text and text painting.

and knowledge building. Harasim notes that few such environments are currently available but that the open-source movement holds potential for such development, although that potential has yet to be realized and presents significant challenges (p. 102).

Characteristics of discussion forums

OCL environments, particularly discussion forums, support discourse that is place-independent, time-independent, many to many, text-based, and Internet-mediated (p. 102). Each characteristic both supports and challenges discourse in specific ways, or to use the terminology of the TPACK framework, presents both affordances and constraints. The constraints also suggest development of practices to minimize their effects. Place-independent discourse removes discussion from the confines of the traditional classroom, providing access for learners in more remote geographical areas, for working professionals with family and other responsibilities, and for those with disabilities that might preclude on-campus attendance. It enables guest experts to address the class and contribute to the discussion. In an online music curriculum design course, for example, students might use a textbook whose author is later invited to present a short lecture and comment on student designs. Challenges associated with place independence include creating an appropriate learning space in the home and developing sensitivity to conversational style differences such as formality/informality or succinctness/talkativeness.

Time-independent discourse suggests asynchronous discussion, although synchronous meetings via videoconferencing and audioconferencing technologies (e.g., Skype) may also be used. Asynchronous discussion translates to availability 24 hours a day, seven days a week, creating a continuous conversation. Learners can contribute at any time that is convenient or conducive relative to work schedule or other responsibilities, and with asynchronous discussions, time zones are not an issue. Time independence provides for both immediate feedback and thoughtful, reflective, even research-based preparation of responses. A high school choral director might read recent discussion posts at home in the evening, process the ideas over the following day, and post his own response in his school office during a preparation period or a break prior to an evening rehearsal. One challenge associated with the possibility of immediate feedback is the expectation of it. Students can become anxious or frustrated while awaiting a response, especially from the instructor, and the discussion may stall if too much time elapses between responses.

Group (many-to-many) discourse, the foundation of collaboration and knowledge building, is well supported by online discussion forums, which were developed precisely to support group discussions. Current online forums provide supportive environments for divergent processes such as brainstorming and explaining ideas; however, they do not specifically support convergent thinking. The instructor or moderator must weave the threads of the discussion, organize it, structure it, keep it on track, and move it forward toward convergence or a conclusion.

Although audio and video may be used for various online activities, as well as for synchronous discussions, discourse in the OCL environment is predominantly text-based. Harasim observes, "Writing is thinking made visible, whereby it is subject to consideration and comment" (p. 105) and points out that written conversation is a critical component of knowledge building. Put simply, we don't know what we think until we see what we say (write). Students can take whatever time is needed to formulate and refine their responses, and even use a grammar or spell-checker to ensure accuracy. An advantage of online text-based communication is that it results in an archive, an accurate record that learners can access in any place at any time to review new posts, analyze the discussion, and respond to comments or questions. Likewise, with text-based discussion, instructors can see what students are learning and can intervene to clarify or correct when necessary. Given the contemporary predilection for texting, text is a familiar and even preferred mode of communication, although discussion posts must admittedly be more extensive than typical text messages. There are few challenges involved in text-based discussion (non-native speakers have the advantages of time and access to a dictionary if necessary) and it can be enhanced with the use of multimedia.

The final characteristic of OCL forums, Internet mediation, is perhaps the most powerful trait, given the broad spectrum of resources that can be integrated into or linked to discussion posts. For example, a music psychology student reflecting on the relationship between language and music might add a link to a short YouTube video of Aniruddh Patel (author of *Music, Language, and the Brain*) lecturing on that topic and then point out some key issues for further discussion. Visualization software can be used in a music research course to enhance data-intensive discussion posts with illustrations such as pie charts or other representations. However, in this context, Internet resources must be used to support, not substitute for, thoughtful and well-reasoned responses.

In summary, OCL theory is presented "as a theory and as a framework for pedagogical and technological design" (p. 102), and perhaps it could be adapted to become a distinct theory of online collaborative music instruction. It appears as appropriate to online learning in the more "academic" music disciplines as it is to learning in other disciplines. It provides a framework that accommodates interaction (Moore, 1993) within a learning community and its associated presences (Garrison, 2011). With its emphasis on online collaboration, it may be adapted to work with online applied instruction and online collaborative music-making.

REFERENCES

Chen, Y-J. (2001). Dimensions of transactional distance in the World Wide Web learning environment: A factor analysis. *British Journal of Educational Technology, 32*(4), 459–470.

Chickering, A. W., & Gamson, Z. F. (1987). Seven principles for good practice in undergraduate education. *AAHE Bulletin, 39*(7), 3–7.

Don, G., Garvey, C., & Sadeghpour, M. (2009). Theory and practice: Signature pedagogies in music theory and performance. In R. A. R. Gurung, N. L. Chick, & A. Haenie (Eds.), *Exploring signature pedagogies: Approaches to teaching disciplinary habits of mind* (pp. 81–98). Sterling, VA: Stylus Publishing.

Folio, C., & Kreinberg, S. (2009/2010). Blackboard and wikis and blogs, oh my: Collaborative learning tools for enriching music history and music theory courses. *College Music Symposium, 49/50*, 164–175.

Garrison, D. R. (2006). Online collaboration principles. *Journal of Asynchronous Learning Networks, 10*(1), 25–34.

Garrison, D. R. (2011). *E-learning in the 21st century: A framework for research and practice* (second ed.). London: Routledge/Taylor and Francis.

Garrison, D. R. & Anderson, T. (2003). *E-learning in the 21st century: A framework for research and practice*. London and New York: RoutledgeFalmer.

Garrison, D. R., Anderson, T., & Archer, W. (2000). Critical inquiry in a text-based environment: Computer conferencing in higher education. *The Internet and Higher Education 2*(2/3), 87–105.

Garrison, D. R., & Cleveland-Innes, M. (2005). Facilitating cognitive presence in online learning: Interaction is not enough. *American Journal of Distance Education 19*(3), 133–148.

Harasim, L. (2012). *Learning theory and online technologies*. New York: Routledge.

Hillman, D. C. A., Willis, D. J., & Gunawardena, C. N. (1994). Learner–interface interaction in distance education: An extension of contemporary models and strategies for practitioners. *American Journal of Distance Education, 8*(2), 30–42.

King, A. (1993). From sage on the stage to guide on the side. *College Teaching, 41*(1), 20–35.

Lombard, M., & Ditton, T. (1997). At the heart of it all: The concept of presence. *Journal of Computer-Mediated Communication, 3*(2). Retrieved from http://onlinelibrary. wiley.com/enhanced/doi/10.1111/j.1083-6101.1997.tb00072.x/

Lorenzo, G., & Moore, J. C. (2002). *The Sloan Consortium report to the nation: Five pillars of quality online education*. Retrieved from http://sloanconsortium.org/ publications/freedownloads

Means, B., Toyama, Y., Murphy, R., Bakia, M., & Jones, K. (2010). *Evaluation of evidence-based practices in online learning: A meta-analysis and review of online learning studies*. Center for Technology in Learning, U.S. Department of Education. Retrieved from http://www2.ed.gov/rschstat/eval/tech/evidence-based-practices/ finalreport.pdf

Middle States Commission on Higher Education. (2011). *Distance learning programs: Interregional guidelines for the evaluation of distance education (online learning)*. Retrieved from http://web.njcu.edu/programs/vision2015/Uploads/ msche_guidelines-for-the-evaluation-of-distance-education.pdf

Moore, M. G. (1989). Editorial: Three types of interaction. *American Journal of Distance Education, 3*(2), 1–7.

Moore, M. G. (1993). Theory of transactional distance. In D. Keegan (Ed.), *Theoretical principles of distance education* (pp. 22–38). New York: Routledge.

National Association of Schools of Music. (2013). *Handbook 2013–2014*. Retrieved from http://nasm.arts-accredit.org/index.jsp?page=Standards-Handbook

Power, M. (2008). The emergence of a blended online learning environment. *Journal of Online Teaching and Learning, 4*(4). Retrieved from http://jolt.merlot.org/ vol4no4/power_1208.htm

Power, M., & Vaughan, N. (2010). Redesigning online learning for international graduate seminar delivery. *Journal of Distance Education, 24*(2), 19–38. Retrieved from http://www.jofde.ca/index.php/jde/article/view/649/1103

Robinson, K. (2011). *Out of our minds: Learning to be creative* (rev. ed.). Chichester, UK: Capstone Publishing.

Shea, P., & Bidjerano, T. (2010). Learning presence: Towards a theory of self-efficacy, self-regulation, and the development of a communities of inquiry in online and blended learning environments. *Computers & Education, 55*, 1721–1731. Retrieved from http://www.sunyresearch.net/hplo/wp-content/uploads/2012/08/ Shea-and-Bidjerano-2010.pdf

Shea, P., Hayes, S., Uzuner-Smith, S., Vickers, J., Bidjerano, T., Gozza-Cohen, M., Jian, S., Pickett, A., Wilde, J., & Tseng, C. (2013). Online learner self regulation: Learning presence, viewed through quantitative content- and social network analysis. *International Review of Research in Open and Distance Learning*, 14(3) 427–461. Retrieved from http://www.sunyresearch.net/hplo/wp-content/uploads/2013/07/Online-Self-Regulation-Shea-2013.pdf

Swan, K. (2004). *Relationships between interactions and learning in online environments.* Needham, MA: Sloan-C. Retrieved from sloanconsortium.org/publications/books/pdf/interactions.pdf

Webster, P. R. (2011a). Construction of music learning. In R. Colwell & P. R. Webster (Eds.), *MENC handbook of research on music learning: Volume 1: Strategies* (pp. 35–83). New York: Oxford University Press.

PART THREE

Teaching and Learning in the Online Classroom

CHAPTER 6

Course Development

Fully Online Courses

... the technology sets the beat and creates the music, while the pedagogy defines the moves.

  —Terry Anderson & Jon Dron, *Three generations of distance learning pedagogy*

INTRODUCTORY CONSIDERATIONS

Research on online learning provides evidence that it produces outcomes that are at least as good as traditional modes of instruction, often equated with the "no significant difference" phenomenon. Additionally, accrediting agencies stipulate that online courses must be equivalent to on-campus courses. At this point, it is time to change the representation of online learning from "as good as" what it is not to "high quality" for what it is. To achieve that goal, we cannot simply take face-to-face approaches and put them online. A simple change of delivery mode does not make a high-quality online course; pedagogy is a major determinant of quality. Designing online courses provides an opportunity to innovate, but we cannot innovate if we continue to do the same thing in the same way. We need to rethink our existing approaches in light of current theories and technologies. Theories of online learning emerge from a specific context (e.g., education, music education, or communication), so there may be reason to consider several theories, as each provides a different perspective and addresses a different part of the design puzzle. We also need to take advantage of Internet capabilities and design or redesign our courses and approaches to adapt to these technologies.

Thoughtful design and organization of the online experience are crucial to the success of an online course: Whatever is to be achieved in the course must be built into the design from the outset. If you believe that vital discourse within an online community of learners is at the heart of online learning, then your design efforts will be targeted toward various ways to create and sustain that community. Course design for online learning is a creative process, and seemingly it should be all the more so when it involves design for online learning in music. Any subject can be designed and taught creatively, but perhaps a creative design and creative processes are particularly well suited to the subject matter of music courses, whether approached from a historical, analytical, or pedagogical standpoint. Online course design, particularly when you are redesigning a course you have previously taught face to face, presents an opportunity to revisit and rethink both musical content and its pedagogy in light of the online environment and associated technologies, and to discover or develop fresh ways to illuminate the subject matter for 21st-century students.

Because online and face-to-face environments are considerably different, designing for the online learning environment requires more than simply transferring practices that are effective in the face-to-face setting directly to an online setting. It requires attention to the nature and context of the media with which we are working. Sir Ken Robinson states: "Whatever the media, there is an intimate relationship between the ideas that form and the media through which they take shape. . . . Creativity is a dialogue between the ideas and the media in which they are being formed" (2011, p. 153). In the case of online music course design, that dialogue includes sensory media (sound), cognitive media (words and music notation), and digital media (tools and environments). Online course design also takes into account research, frameworks, and theories that directly inform online pedagogy. Just as working within the constraints of a form does not inhibit a composer's creativity but rather provides a structure for it, working within a theoretical framework provides structure for creative online course design. Various frameworks and structures have been presented in previous chapters, and each has something to contribute to the course design process, from broad overall considerations of teaching with technology to development of specific course components and processes.

As you embark upon design or redesign, you will want to consider some preliminary questions, such as what factors besides delivery medium affect student outcomes. You will want to identify those factors and incorporate them into the design and development of your course. Those elements include curriculum materials, instructional approach, the instructor's facility with the technologies used, and student learning styles or preferences. For example, rather than discourage certain students from taking online courses, perhaps because they don't like the descriptions given in the "Is online learning for you?" sections of some student orientations, you will want to think about how you can design your course so that it "speaks" to students with diverse learning styles and preferences. To build that diversity into your course, you will need to include specific elements—media, technologies, and asynchronous or synchronous structures—that help create rich online learning experiences in the music disciplines. By using a variety of presentation modes and both asynchronous and synchronous elements, you can address the different styles and needs of various students.

The TPACK framework provides a global approach to thinking about and designing online courses. It takes into account the interactions among content, pedagogy, and technology within a specific context. It was pointed out previously that online courses need to be designed specifically for the online environment, and that redesign of courses previously taught face to face requires consideration of how to represent the content online, how the pedagogy will work online, and what technologies within or outside of a learning management system will support the pedagogy and facilitate learning the content: "The incorporation of a new technology or new medium for teaching suddenly forces us to confront basic educational issues because this new technology or medium reconstructs the dynamic equilibrium among all three elements" (Mishra & Koehler, 2006, p. 1030). A few specific factors are the variety of media for content presentation and the use of asynchronous and synchronous discussion forums for participation and discourse. With a grasp of the major elements involved in the course design—content, pedagogy, and technology—the instructor or designer can proceed to details of design within a specific structure.

Creating an online learning community

As noted previously, interaction with an active and vibrant community of scholars is one of the hallmarks of quality online instruction. In order for that interaction to occur, there must be a sense of respect and trust among course participants that supports an open exchange of ideas and perspectives. The Sloan Consortium advocates building communities of inquiry that promote collaboration among students and instructors (Lorenzo & Moore, 2002), and the National Association of Schools of Music (NASM) alludes to technology-supported interactions in distance learning programs (NASM, 2013). There are various definitions of an online learning community, some quite general and others associated with a particular theory or theoretical framework. The definition of learning as a three-way interaction of students with content, the instructor, and other students addresses the notion of interaction in distance learning (Moore, 1989). The community of inquiry (CoI) theoretical framework features three types of online presence (social, cognitive, and teaching presences) that support interaction and collaboration among students and instructors (Garrison, 2011), and online collaborative learning (OCL) theory focuses on a collaborative approach within a knowledge community (Harasim, 2012). There are certain similarities, as well as differences, between these two models. CoI focuses on development of a learning community through the interaction of social presence, cognitive presence, and teaching presence. OCL theory focuses on the processes through which learning takes place in an online environment—discourse, collaboration, and knowledge building—with discourse as the means by which learners are brought into a knowledge community. Both theories provide useful guidance for the design and development of online courses, as they present different windows onto the structure and processes of online learning. However, both theories involve building multiple opportunities for interaction into the course design, opportunities that create a supportive climate and foster group cohesion while balancing social interaction with development of the professional relationships needed for a high-quality learning experience.

Developing online presence

"I thought I would have done better if I had a real teacher." This student response to an inquiry about how they thought they did in their first online music course highlights the importance of establishing an online presence—the human touch. With its focus on the teacher and lack of any reference to other course participants, the remark also suggests assumptions about education in general and online learning in particular. Because of the physical separation of instructor and students in online learning, a primary task in online course design is creation of an online learning community. Online community building depends to a great extent upon development of a sense of social presence, which has been described as the extent to which a person is perceived as real in a mediated environment (Palloff & Pratt, 2007; Garrison, 2011). The concept applies to instructors and students alike, both of whom need to be perceived as really being there for the course. Social presence involves identification with a group, purposeful communication in a trusting environment, and development of personal relationships, all for an educational purpose. Social presence establishes conditions amenable to the discourse that constitutes cognitive presence and contributes to a high-quality learning experience.

Because of its contribution to the establishment of a learning community and the discourse associated with it, presence is a critical component of online course design, and it can be embedded throughout the design, in the content, pedagogy, learning experiences, and supportive technologies. The design process must take into account the specific music discipline, the content of the course, and the processes of engaging with that content. A music education curriculum design course, for example, might be process-oriented, with students in small groups or teams working together to complete specific curriculum-building tasks. Participants might be assigned to asynchronous forums designated for specific topics. Members of each forum would make their presence felt by sharing ideas with the group and responding to ideas posted by others, finally completing their task collaboratively and reporting back to the group at large in a full class forum. A music history period course might be more content-focused, with students engaged in discussion of social and cultural issues that influenced compositional practice within a particular musical era and their significance for our own times. Individual students might contribute selected points to an instructor-moderated synchronous discussion, which offers greater immediacy and a more vivid sense of presence than an asynchronous one.

COMPOSING THE COURSE

Online course design can be considered a kind of composition. Sometimes, this might involve creating a new course specifically for the online environment. At other times, it might involve redesign of a course previously taught face to face; this might be comparable to orchestrating an existing work for a different ensemble. Redesign for the online environment entails more than moving face-to-face practices online with a few adjustments like PowerPoint presentations to replace in-person lectures and discussion board postings to parallel classroom discussions. Just as re-orchestration involves careful consideration of the capabilities of the instruments and the size of the ensemble, redesign for online learning requires consideration of the capabilities of the technologies available and their pedagogical affordances and constraints. The dynamic relationships between and among content, pedagogy, and technology within the online context, together with development of an online learning community, present complex challenges that, at a minimum, require rethinking and recreating traditional practices. In light of these factors, redesign presents an opportunity to engage in a creative process, to begin with the realities of 21st-century learning, and to bring an entirely new perspective to familiar courses. Like a musical composition, an online course has a beginning, a middle, and an end: The structures and processes could be compared to sonata form. The beginning or exposition provides an introduction or overview and presents all the main and secondary themes. In the middle or the development, the themes are expanded, explored, worked through, combined, connected, or juxtaposed. At the end or recapitulation, the themes reappear, but they are understood differently because of the working through, and resolution or consensus is reached. And as is the case with experiencing a musical composition, each participant gains something different based on their previous experience and their level of engagement with the subject matter.

One could also liken the design process to the work of a curator, who organizes works of art according to a point of view to provide a unique experience for patrons who encounter the artworks. The curator, an expert in the art field, has insight into the artworks, sees new connections among them, organizes exhibits to convey those insights, writes descriptions of the works, and explains the connections. Visitors read the narrative, experience the art in a new way, and take away something unique from the experience. There are several similarities in the expertise and professional activities of professors and curators. Both are experts in their disciplines, and both probably hold advanced degrees. Professors and curators alike conduct research in their areas of expertise, and both interpret artistic works for less knowledgeable audiences. In preparing an exhibition, the curator selects and organizes the works to be shown according to a specific perspective, creates labels, and writes essays for display or publication that explain the works in the context of the chosen perspective and ideally lead to a greater or transformed understanding of familiar works. Often, a guided audio tour is available for in-depth interaction with the exhibit. The curator might additionally develop related activities such as "brown-bag, lunch-and-learn" events, book clubs, or lectures that provide individual and group opportunities for further exploration of the topics of the exhibit. Similarly, the professor determines course content and organizes it according to a particular perspective. He or she selects a textbook and other readings and may develop additional explanatory material such as study guides, sample analyses of research articles or musical works, and case studies. The professor may also create audio or video lectures, possibly with the assistance of a design team. Related activities might include exploration of supplementary web-based materials, including articles and videos relevant to course topics. Perhaps thinking as a curator, stepping out of one's familiar role as professor and into a new role, might provide a fresh perspective on familiar subject matter and generate creative ideas for ways to present and engage with it.

From a logistical standpoint and for the benefit of both students and instructor, it is important to design your online course as a whole, to have all details worked out and clearly delineated from the start of the course, including subject matter, learning objectives, assessments, learning experiences, and teaching strategies. Specifics of assignments, discussion questions, expectations for discussion contributions, times for any synchronous meetings, and due dates are not to be overlooked. Online courses allow little opportunity for the kinds of spontaneous changes that on-campus courses might afford on a weekly basis. Online students are frequently busy professionals like in-service music educators, who like to plan their work in advance around the published schedule. Any deviations from that schedule are likely to cause conflicts, as well as student confusion. It is best to have your course completely developed from the outset so that when classes begin, you can focus your attention and efforts on instructional processes and not on development of the next module or assignment. It is advisable to create your basic content first, emphasizing the essentials or most important concepts at the outset and providing important but supplementary content or simply interesting items later. Of course, when you add items, you also need to inform your students that new material is available and where they can view it. And because of the time and space separation inherent in an online course, the design and organization need to be clear.

Published online course design rubrics can be useful here, as they emphasize that kind of internal integrity and can be used as a kind of design roadmap. Two well-regarded rubrics for online course design (outlined in chapter 9) are the *Rubric for online instruction* (2009) developed by California State University, Chico, and the *Quality Matters*™ rubric standards developed by MarylandOnline, Inc. Both rubrics emphasize alignment of important course elements—goals, learning objectives, learning activities, assessments, instructional materials, technologies, and student engagement—such that all these elements directly support and lead to achievement of the learning objectives or outcomes.

Framing the elements

At this point, it can be helpful to reconsider your content and pedagogy in light of the online environment context and in terms of the technologies you will have at your disposal—to look at the whole picture in terms of the TPACK framework from a broad level to more finely grained stages. First, analyze your course elements and their intersections on a broad, general level, remembering that content, pedagogy, and technology choices are designed with particular subject matter and specific educational contexts in mind. Second, consider the major outcomes and the specific technologies at your disposal. Third, develop each of the major outcomes in detail. Because of the dynamic intersections and interactions inherent in the

---

Box 6.1

You may be teaching a graduate-level on-campus music psychology course, and you want to redesign it as an online course. "Online/ graduate-level/music psychology" constitutes the context, which remains constant throughout the design process. At a macro or general level, the goal of the course is for students to explore ideas in music perception, cognition, and affect, using transdisciplinary studies in philosophy, linguistics, and medicine to investigate the fundamental question of how music works. The content encompasses acoustics, psychoacoustics, music cognition, theories of learning, music and emotion, musical skills, and musical behaviors. You want to use an interactive, collaborative learning approach, and you will deliver the course through the learning management system (LMS) in use at your institution.

Box 6.2

Major outcomes, stated in terms of what students will know and be able to do upon completion of the course, might include the following: (1) List and describe some processes involved in the production of sound (basic musical acoustics) and explain their significance for music professionals and amateurs; (2) explain how music is processed in the brain; (3) describe human responses to music, including affective responses, aesthetic responses, and physiological responses; (4) describe relevant theories of learning and music learning, and design applications of selected theories for your own use; (5) describe ways in which people perceive and learn music over time, including cognitive development, music cognition and development, and development of specific musical skills; and (6) explain how people find meaning in music, and develop practical strategies to help people maximize their musical experiences. Course tools available in your LMS may include announcements, e-mail, learning modules, discussion boards, web conferencing, blogs, and wikis. These tools provide some asynchronous and synchronous options that can support your interactive, collaborative pedagogy.

TPACK framework, you will most often be dealing with content, pedagogy, technology, and context concurrently.

First, you will consider the scope of your subject matter, the best ways for students to learn it, the technologies that can support your pedagogy, how your pedagogy will work online, and, overall, how you can bring your content to life in the online environment (see box. 6.1).

At the second level, you identify the major objectives or outcomes of the course and note the tools available to you in the LMS (see box 6.2).

The third level represents a further expansion of the learning objectives. At this level, you select each of the major outcomes, list subtopics related to the main topic, identify sources of information on the subtopics, determine how you want your students to engage with those topics, and identify what technologies will support that interaction (see box 6.3).

Box 6.3

Outcome 5 deals with music cognition and musical skill development. Subcategories may include, among others, Gestalt principles of cognitive organization as they relate to music perception, music memory, and music and language. Each topic can be developed in much greater detail. A more comprehensive examination of music and language might begin with the question of whether music is a language. It might include an anthropological approach focusing on earliest known uses of music, comparison of musical and linguistic sound systems, analysis of musical and linguistic syntax and semantics, and consideration of what music communicates and how it communicates. For each of those topic areas, you identify resources for student use. If you are using a textbook, there will undoubtedly be at least one chapter devoted to this topic. You may also be familiar with Leonard Bernstein's Harvard lectures, specifically *The Unanswered Question* (Bernstein, 1976), in which he explains music phonology, musical syntax, and musical semantics. The lectures, which were published in book form, are also available on YouTube—a convenient option for online students. You may also be familiar with the work of Aniruddh Patel, author of *Music, Language, and the Brain*, and his podcast lecture on that topic in the Library of Congress's series on music and the brain. Both sources are excellent supplements that can enrich basic readings on the topic of music and language. You want your students to become familiar with evidence and arguments for and against music as a language and to be able to explain what and how music communicates. To refine their thinking and strengthen their arguments, you want them to identify and discuss the issues and come to some group consensus on the topic.

Goals and objectives

Goals and objectives or outcomes are likely to be the same whether you teach the course face to face or online, but the way you achieve them differs in the online environment. Goals and objectives address two simple questions: Where are you going, and how will you get there? Goals are broad, general statements that project the overall purpose of the course—where you're going. Objectives are specific statements that describe what students will know and be able to do upon completion of the course—how they'll get there. The backward design process, described in connection with the taxonomy of significant learning (Fink, 2013), brings assessment into the equation with the question of what performance will demonstrate that students have achieved the objective—how you will know if you have arrived. With goals, objectives, and assessments formulated, you then move on to development of learning experiences, activities, and assignments that will help your students achieve the objectives. Congruence among course goals, objectives or outcomes, content, activities, assignments, and assessments is a global characteristic that drives course design and development and promotes student achievement of stated outcomes. Alignment of course goals, learning objectives, learning activities, and assessments is emphasized in the previously mentioned course design rubrics and standards. These rubrics can be useful as guidelines or checklists for course design.

Developing content for the online environment

Covering the content is an issue in any face-to-face or online course. We want students to grasp the essence of the subject matter and the structure of the discipline, to develop a deep understanding of the essential concepts, and to be conversant with a wide range of topics. But we have to bear in mind that we cannot convey in one course our own accumulation of years of research and scholarship. This does not imply lowered standards or diluted content. It does suggest that we need to be realistic about the amount of content that students can absorb during a single course and the extent to which breadth of coverage influences depth. If you espouse a collaborative pedagogical approach and want your students to engage in reflective discourse, you may need to limit the breadth of your content in favor of in-depth exploration. For the first iteration of your online course, especially if you are the sole designer/developer/instructor, you will need to establish curricular priorities, focusing first on essential content, then on important but less essential content, and finally, on content that you might consider to be enrichment. For your first online course design or redesign, you may be daunted by the seeming magnitude of the task of content development. However, some materials you have used in your face-to-face approach will still work, while other materials will not lend themselves to the online environment though they might be reworked. Again, it is a good idea to develop the most important or basic materials first and add supplementary or enrichment materials when this primary level of content is complete.

Textbooks, lectures, and beyond

Traditional textbooks can be used in an online course and e-books are sometimes an option, especially as library resources. Just as in a traditional classroom, you may design your course around the structure provided in the textbook, or you may organize the course in your own way and use selected chapters or sections of the textbook as they relate to your course. You can record audio or video lectures yourself or with the assistance of a campus media center. When you upload the audio or video file, you may also be able to attach a transcript for those who may not be able to see or hear the lecture. Video lectures provide an immediacy that can help establish your presence online and make you seem real to your students. Short videos or micro-lectures, about 10 minutes in length and scripted with a well-chosen narrative, can convey the essence of a topic or the main concepts associated with it in a memorable way, as shown in the Khan Academy (educational website created by Salman Kahn, featuring short, focused tutorials) or TED (Technology, Entertainment, Design; short talks on "ideas worth spreading") models. Brief is better. Regardless of how enthusiastic you are about the topic and how well you convey your excitement in your video, if it is too long, students may not watch it in its entirety, and a segmented viewing is likely to result in loss of momentum. Your own enthusiasm is not the main event; the purpose is triggering and sustaining your students' interest in the topic. Short video presentations can be effective in almost any online music course. They can be particularly effective in music technology courses for equipment demonstrations or brief software tutorials. They can also be effective in music education methods courses or applied music studies for demonstrations of correct embouchure, posture, bowing, and so on.

You can also incorporate published podcasts or YouTube videos. For example, as mentioned previously in connection with the topic of music and language, a textbook may include chapters or sections that address music and language or music as communication. If the book includes a CD with multimedia examples relevant to that topic, you can assign those as listening examples. Presuming that you have taught this course previously in a face-to-face setting, you might have collected web-based materials like Library of Congress podcasts that include short talks by experts on the topic of music and language. In your face-to-face class, you might have played part or all of these lectures in class. For the online version of your course, you can create a link to these podcasts with instructions for students to either subscribe to the series or listen to the relevant lectures. Assigning recorded lectures such as these might also help to document direct instruction time associated with contact or credit hour policies, as the length of the podcast is published along with the title.

Pedagogy for the online environment

It is not the delivery mode that produces the outcomes; it is the pedagogy. In particular, it is what pedagogy is appropriate for the particular subject matter, the way people learn now, and the online environment. There is not just one way to learn, but in our present knowledge age, our pedagogical approaches must harmonize with its emphasis on knowledge communities and knowledge creation. Our approaches must support creative work in which there may be multiple right answers—answers that emerge from interaction among learners who collaborate in order to discover the best or most promising options. There is a place for information delivery, and there is a place for testing; however, both need to be adapted to a pedagogy for our time. Immersed as we are in digital technologies, the Internet, the web, and social media, OCL theory seems to make sense, and it provides a reasonable theoretical framework for online learning. As noted previously, it has potential as a theory of pedagogical and technological design, and it appears to be appropriate to online learning in many music courses. Collaborative pedagogical approaches (such as instructor-mediated group discussions, debates, seminars or webinars) and problem-solving activities incorporate the processes that lead to increased understanding and knowledge. Generally speaking, OCL can serve as a guiding structure with its emphasis on knowledge building through discourse—idea generating, idea organization, intellectual convergence—and collaboration.

CHOREOGRAPHING LEARNER-CENTERED EXPERIENCES

Creation of learning experiences is like choreography: We create ways to guide students through the steps of learning activities. And these learning experiences emerge logically from our pedagogical approach; in other words, "the pedagogy defines the moves" (Anderson & Dron, 2011, p. 81). The focus is on engaging students with subject matter in multiple ways. A learning experience consists of a sequence of related activities that ultimately culminates in new or increased understanding and knowledge.

To return to the example of music and language, one learning objective is for students to become familiar with evidence and arguments regarding music as a language and to be able to explain what and how music communicates. The task is to work out the steps that will take them there (see box 6.4).

Box 6.4

You feel that exploration of the functions of language and music constitutes a first step toward an informed discussion of music as communication. In your own study of this topic, you may have consulted sources in anthropology, the work of Noam Chomsky, and Aniruddh Patel's work on music, language, and the brain. You may have read Leonard Bernstein's *The Unanswered Question*. You may also have searched for online resources and found the Library of Congress's podcast series *Music and the Brain*, as well as some YouTube videos on the topic. And the textbook you have chosen includes sections on the universality of music, the acquisition of language, music and language, and music as language or poetry. All of these resources are pertinent to the topic of music and language; the challenge is to use them selectively to create a reasoned learning experience. What would serve as a good introduction to the topic? Do they need to read Chomsky's work or will the references in Bernstein's and Patel's lectures provide sufficient information for purposes of the discussion? In terms of musical semantics, what will help them distinguish between musical meaning and musical expression? Here is a sequence of activities that progresses from acquiring information to synthesizing knowledge and incorporates both collaborative and reflective activities:

Reading: Textbook selections on acquisition of language, music and language

Listening: Patel podcast: *Music, Language, and the Brain*; Bernstein lecture: *Musical Semantics*

Hands-on/analysis: Individual students or small groups explore structural connections between music and language by analyzing a short musical work from the common practice period in terms of musical patterns that resemble speech patterns.

Presentation: Based on their analyses of the short piece, participants present their findings/conclusions about prosody in music using presentation software.

Discussion: Based on the textbook readings and salient points from the podcasts, participants first identify the central concepts and explore similarities and differences between linguistic and musical structures. Then they explore distinctions between musical meaning and musical expression, finally reaching consensus on music as a language and what it communicates.

Building an interactive online classroom

It was pointed out in an earlier chapter that a pedagogy for 21st-century online learning should emphasize the development of an online learning community that engages in collaborative discourse, and that this type of pedagogy is appropriate to many kinds of online music courses. The online learning community has been characterized as "a fusion of individual (subjective) and shared (objective) worlds" (Garrison, 2011, p. 20), which suggests a linking of reflection and discourse, of cognitive independence and social interdependence. Both elements are integral to the creation of an interactive online environment, and as such, must be incorporated into the design of the course. The sample learning experience on music and language included opportunities for communication, collaboration, and reflection. The following sections suggest design features to create the structure in which these activities can be accomplished.

Communication and collaboration

Wikis and discussion forums, both asynchronous and synchronous, are obvious choices for communication and collaboration. Using both types of forums results in a type of blended online design. You can create asynchronous forums for discussions that involve extended exploration and development of ideas. In the music and language example, an asynchronous discussion of linguistic and musical structures allows participants to develop their own ideas and react to those of their classmates. An asynchronous forum would work equally well for the second part of the discussion, which involves the same kind of exploration but adds the further step of coming to consensus on the nature of musical communication. A class wiki could support the same kind of collaborative development and accommodate both parts of the discussion: musical and linguistic structures and music as communication. It could prove to be even more effective than asynchronous discussion forums for this activity. You can consider synchronous meetings for activities that benefit from the immediacy and energy of live interaction (e.g., student presentations of their conclusions about prosody in music).

To emphasize the importance of collaborative discussion and the value that you place on it, you will want to require it, allot a significant percentage of the grade to discussion participation, and inform students of your expectations for discussion posts. Rubrics that are tailored to your teaching style and published in the syllabus inform students of the standards for the online discussion and provide you with concrete grading criteria. A simple rubric might list characteristics of timeliness, responsiveness to the assigned discussion questions, evidence of understanding of relevant assignments, substantial comments that advance the discourse, and evidence of having read other participants' comments. Some instructors like to include issues of grammar, usage, and spelling as additional characteristics of quality work. Required and graded work, together with concrete expectations as expressed in a rubric, can help motivate quality discussion participation.

Reflection

Asynchronous discussions and blogs accommodate reflection that ideally informs discourse. Asynchronous discussions provide time for development of considered responses, and the previously listed criteria for a discussion forum rubric imply reflection. Blogs provide a parallel structure for individual reflection. You can create a blog for each student within the LMS or, alternatively, you can assign students to create blogs on a public site, which itself can serve as a motivator for creation of thoughtful posts.

COURSE DELIVERY

After rethinking your course and redesigning materials and experiences for the online environment, you need to make the course available to your students. Making it available includes arranging it in such a way that it makes sense to students and provides a roadmap or guide to the course. You can think of the organization process as orchestration or arranging your course—within the structure of a learning management system.

Learning management system (LMS)

Good organization is key to designing a course that works well. A learning management system, while not always ideally matched to the instructor's pedagogical style, can help organize course objectives, contain materials, and support learning and management processes with built-in communication and grading tools. Although learning management systems tend to replicate a more traditional instructional model and may sometimes seem to constrain your creativity, they provide a structure that can be helpful to instructors for management purposes, as well as to students for ready access to course materials and activities. Your LMS probably provides multiple options for creating content, such as learning modules that might contain a table of contents, objectives, content, and learning activities. Learning modules can be an effective way to organize a single topic, and they can also be used to organize multiple topics within a single weekly folder. Multimedia integration, including the ability to insert text, images, audio, and video, is usually supported as well. Here are general LMS arrangements that some online instructors find effective.

Assignment folders

Organize the course by week. Create an assignment folder for each week of the course to make it easy for students to know where to go to find materials and assignments. You can identify each folder with an appropriate label (e.g., "Class 3: Mind, Brain, and Body"). If you think it will help your students, you can include dates; however, you will need to change each date with subsequent offerings of the course if you move the content each time you teach the course. Alternatively, you can coordinate class numbers in LMS folders with class dates on a course schedule in the syllabus, which then serves as a guide to the course site.

Learning guides

Because you can't be with each student to guide them through the week's assignments and answer any questions they might have, it is a good idea to create a roadmap or learning guide in each week's folder. If students open the weekly folder and find only a collection of materials and links, they may be at a loss for where to begin, how to proceed, and what to focus on in the readings and other activities. If that is the case, then you are likely to receive multiple e-mails with the message: "I'm confused. What do you want us to do?" Rather than waste time trying to clear up the confusion you caused, be proactive and try to anticipate the questions. Provide context for the topic of the week (e.g., a brief description of where this topic fits within the course as a whole). If your LMS provides a voice authoring tool, you might consider creating an audio introduction to draw your students in. Add learning objectives for the week together with instructions for reviewing content, engaging in learning experiences and discussions, and completing and submitting any assignments as individual items. Alternatively, you can create a learning module to contain all elements relevant to a particular topic (see box 6.5).

Box 6.5

The following outline would appear in a weekly assignment folder:

INTRODUCTION TO CLASS 3

Last week, we discussed the universality of music in world cultures. This week, we will expand on that notion and begin exploring the idea of music as a language.

LEARNING OBJECTIVES

When you complete this week's work, you will be able to identify and explain some similarities and differences between the structures of language and music, and describe what music communicates and how it does so.

READINGS

First, please read chapter 3 in our textbook, with particular attention to the acquisition of language.

VIDEOS

Listen to podcast 18, The Music of Language and the Language of Music, from the Library of Congress series *Music and the Brain* (18 minutes). The podcast is by Dr. Aniruddh Patel, author of *Music, Language, and the Brain*. Note particularly his explanation of linguistic and musical grammars and how they are processed in the brain, the centrality of rhythm, and how studying musical behaviors helps us learn more about brain function.

https://itunes.apple.com/us/itunes-u/music-and-the-brain/id38601 8026?mt=10

Listen to two YouTube videos of Leonard Bernstein's 1973 Harvard Lectures *The Unanswered Question*. In Lecture 2: Musical Syntax, think about how well the syntax analogy holds up. In Lecture 3: Musical Semantics, note the differences between meaning and expression, and where feeling comes into the picture.

http://www.youtube.com/

DISCUSSION

Please address the following questions in the discussion forum. Please post your responses to both questions by Thursday of this week. Then respond to one other participant who has taken the other side of

(continued)

Question 1 by Monday of next week. This will ensure that we all express our ideas before we conclude this discussion.

Question 1: How are musical and linguistic grammars similar? How are they different? Please choose one side of this issue and explain your thinking.

Question 2: What is it that music actually communicates: a message, the composer's feelings? How do you gain meaning from the music you listen to?

Discussion forums

Organize discussion forums by week so that they parallel your weekly assignment folders, again making it easy for students to find them. You can create a link to the discussion forum within the weekly folder to serve as a reminder to contribute to the discussion of the week. You can also help jog your students' memories by including a brief description of the topic for each discussion within the folder title: "Class 3: Please post your thoughts on music and language here." It is a good idea for you to create the first post to start the discussion and set the tone. Having participants reply to your original post organizes all subsequent posts in the same thread.

Course menu

Customize the course menu or course navigation to reflect the items in your course (e.g., Syllabus, Assignments, Weekly Folders, Discussions, Live Meetings, among others). Display only the areas and functions you are using and make any others unavailable. These techniques will create an accurate map of your course and give an uncluttered appearance to the site. It will also prevent confusion among students.

Backup

Create a mirror site on your computer using a comparable filename structure as both a backup and a way to ease future updates and revisions.

Whereas the LMS distributes your materials in a structure appropriate to student use, your mirror site provides a compact version you can review at a glance and readily access and revise.

Social media

While many authors call for a move toward participatory learning activities, opinion is divided on the use of social media like FaceBook and Twitter within online courses. Some instructors use social media effectively and consider it a worthwhile component of their courses (e.g., a FaceBook group used as a component of a popular music studies course), allowing students to develop highly personalized profile pages and share resources via mobile access. Others question whether these media add genuine value to a course and feel that wikis and blogs provide better ways for students to collaborate and share their ideas and work.

CHALLENGES AND SOLUTIONS

Designing and developing a first-time online course is challenging and involves multiple steps: covering the content, developing materials appropriate for online use, and building in opportunities for communication, development of a learning community, and collaboration. To keep the tasks manageable, place reasonable limits on the amount of content you intend to cover. Focus first on the essential knowledge and add supplementary materials as feasible. Seek out published materials such as podcasts from respected sources.

Developing rich online learning experiences is desirable; however, you want to create an optimum balance—enough activities to explore an issue thoroughly and resolve it or come to consensus in a discussion, but not so many that students become confused or overwhelmed. And like all other parts of the course, learning experiences need to be worked out before the start of the course. Visualizing your students carrying out the activities you design can provide the insight you need to keep learning experiences manageable for them.

Achieving this kind of balance also applies to course tools within the LMS. How many tools are too many? When do they distract from, rather than support, learning? With a plethora of tools at your disposal, it can be tempting to incorporate as many as possible in order to create what would appear to be a rich learning experience. But just as you are selective about content and the activities that constitute your learning experiences, you also want to be selective about course tools. You can consider, for example, how a new tool for synchronous discussions might foster student engagement in a particular assignment or student presentation. You want to use the right tools, the ones that will engage students with topics and support the development of reflective thought and thoughtful discourse, the ones that will promote development of a learning community and collaboration.

Designing and developing an online course is a large-scale undertaking, but a systematic plan together with knowledge of your potential students and consideration of some of the challenges will help you create a high-quality course with great promise for success.

REFERENCES

Anderson, T., & Dron, J. (2011). Three generations of distance learning pedagogy. *The International Review of Research in Open and Distance Learning, 12*(3), 80–97.

Bernstein, L. (1976). *The unanswered question: Six talks at Harvard.* Cambridge, MA: Harvard University Press.

Fink, L. D. (2013). *Creating significant learning experiences: An integrated approach to designing college courses* (rev. ed.). San Francisco: Jossey-Bass.

Garrison, D. R. (2011). *E-learning in the 21st century: A framework for research and practice* (second ed.). London: Routledge/Taylor and Francis.

Harasim, L. (2012). *Learning theory and online technologies.* New York: Routledge.

Lorenzo, G., & Moore, J. C. (2002). *The Sloan Consortium report to the nation: Five pillars of quality online education.* Retrieved from http://sloanconsortium.org/publications/freedownloads

Moore, M. G. (1989). Editorial: Three types of interaction. *American Journal of Distance Education, 3*(2), 1–7.

National Association of Schools of Music. (2013). *Handbook 2013–2014.* Retrieved from http://nasm.arts-accredit.org/index.jsp?page=Standards-Handbook

Palloff, R. M., & Pratt, K. (2007). *Building online learning communities. Effective strategies for the virtual classroom.* San Francisco: Jossey-Bass.

Quality Matters™ rubric standards 2011–2013 edition with assigned point values. Retrieved from https://www.qualitymatters.org/

Robinson, K. (2011). *Out of our minds: Learning to be creative* (rev. ed.). Chichester, UK: Capstone Publishing.

Rubric for online instruction. (2009). California State University, Chico. Retrieved from http://www.csuchico.edu/roi/

CHAPTER 7

Course Development

Blended Courses

...there will come a time when the blended learning distinction will dissolve as a useful label.... Blended learning will just be the way learning occurs.

—D. Randy Garrison & Norman D. Vaughan, *Blended learning in higher education: Framework, principles, and guidelines*

INTRODUCTORY CONSIDERATIONS

Blended learning is seemingly one of the most accessible types of online learning, and yet perhaps one of the most elusive. Various definitions or descriptions have been put forth. Allen & Seaman (2013) describe a blended course, sometimes referred to as a hybrid course, as one that "blends online and face-to-face delivery. Substantial proportion of the content is delivered online, typically uses online discussion, and typically has a reduced number of face-to-face meetings" (p. 7). The portion of content delivered online is estimated at 30 to 80 percent. Garrison & Vaughan (2008) define it as "the organic integration of thoughtfully selected and complementary face-to-face and online approaches and technologies" (p. 148). Garrison explains that "blended learning can include the blending of individual and collaborative activities, modes of communication (verbal and written), and a range of face-to-face and online courses that constitute a blended program of studies" (2011, p. 76). And Harasim (2012) notes a variety of uses of the term:

...it typically refers to a mix of face-to-face and online learning. However, blended learning can also be used to describe a pedagogical mix of distance education or courseware applications with online collaborative activities such as group discussions, seminars, debates, research or group projects. Blending may also be institutional, as in the case of a degree program offered by two or more institutions, or instructional, to refer to a course with team teaching. (p. 29)

Based on contemporary associations with the term "hybrid" (e.g., hybrid car), McGee & Reis (2012) make a distinction between blended and hybrid, with a preference for blended: "Hybrid suggests that one mode is unused while the other is used. Blended suggests that there are no perceivable notifications when modes shift, if they do at all" (p. 8). They propose a definition of blended courses that more accurately describes what constitutes a blend:

> Blended course designs involve instructor and learners working together in mixed delivery modes, typically face-to-face and technology-mediated, to accomplish learning outcomes that are pedagogically supported through assignments, activities, and assessments as appropriate for a given mode and which bridge course environments in a manner meaningful to the learner. (p. 9)

It is evident from these descriptions that blended learning is not merely an enhancement of traditional classroom practice, a simple joining together of diverse technologies or a straightforward combination of the best of both worlds. Rather, it is a fundamental structural redesign that calls for a rethinking of existing pedagogical approaches. Just as there is no single model for either face-to-face or online courses, likewise there is no single model for blended courses, no rigid prescription regarding the percentage of time and the type of activity allotted to online or face-to-face learning experiences: "...blended learning should be viewed as a pedagogical approach that combines the effectiveness and socialization opportunities of the classroom with the technologically enhanced active learning possibilities of the online environment, rather than a ratio of delivery modalities" (Dziuban, Hartman, & Moskal, 2004, p. 3).

Rethinking and redesign are major endeavors that are not undertaken without reason, and the question of why one would want to do that often arises. Recent research-based evidence for improved learning outcomes as a result of using blended approaches may provide some motivation for adopting a blended learning model. A U.S. Department of Education meta-analysis and review of online learning studies revealed the advantages of blended learning and some factors that influenced its effectiveness: "In recent experimental and quasi-experimental studies contrasting blends of online and face-to-face instruction with conventional face-to-face classes, blended instruction has been more effective, providing a rationale for the effort required to design and implement blended approaches" (Means, et al., 2010, p. xviii). The report emphasizes that these results are not to be taken as evidence of the superiority of the medium. Rather, it is the combination of elements—additional curriculum materials, aspects of pedagogy, additional learning time—that together account for the advantages. In addition, blended learning is a design in tune with current communication trends and technologies, and it incorporates these technologies as significant course components, not simply as occasional supplements to a more traditional approach. Although the Internet and communication technologies have transformed everyday social interactions, they have not had the same effect on higher education. Blended learning has the potential to bring that kind of transformation into the college classroom due in part to the relative ease of implementing it in an already familiar classroom environment.

A report on blended learning, based on three years of responses to a national survey of over one thousand colleges and universities (Allen, Seaman, & Garrett, 2007), revealed that blended courses were considered at least as promising as fully online ones and that blended learning was a distinct choice, not part of a planned transition to fully online learning. Possible configurations for blended programs included all blended courses, a combination of face-to-face and fully online courses, or another variation on the two approaches. Over the time period covered by the report (2003–2005), the percentage of blended courses declined slightly while the percentage of online courses showed continued growth. However, identifying all the blended courses taught at a particular institution was found to be problematic. Blended courses generally use the same campus services as face-to-face courses, so there is no need to differentiate them for institutional recording purposes. In this report, business and liberal arts and sciences showed the highest percentages of blended courses, nearly 48 percent. As might be expected, music was not specifically named among the disciplines surveyed.

The current state of blended learning and its future prospects were the focus of an online meeting of the EDUCAUSE Learning Initiative (Diaz & Brown, 2010). Participants reported that over a period of 10 years, "blended learning has matured, evolved, and become more widely accepted by institutions of all types" (p. 2). Among other issues discussed was the percentage of face-to-face and online meetings, the mix of face-to-face and online activities, and the mix of synchronous and asynchronous activities among institutions; these factors vary depending on context. Participants pointed out the need to reassess and redesign existing courses in order to integrate the face-to-face and online elements, and they noted that both face-to-face and online meetings can be interactive and collaborative. They emphasized the importance of developing a clear understanding of blended learning in order to avoid the phenomenon of the course-and-a-half that results when online elements are simply added to a face-to-face course, rather than integrated in a complementary way into the fabric of the course. Several participants highlighted the opportunity to learn from the experience of rethinking and redesigning courses. Several institutions represented at the meeting were documenting student satisfaction with blended courses. Findings included "slightly more" satisfaction with blended courses than with fully online ones, with satisfaction increasing as students take more blended courses. Dissatisfaction involves reduced face-to-face meetings, technology issues, and increased workload (p. 11). Challenges of blended learning were organized into theme areas of logistics and administration, research and quality assurance, faculty development, and course design. Faculty development challenges included motivating a comprehensive redesign of courses and creating a faculty development program for blended learning. Course design challenges included defining a quality blended course (e.g., by accreditation standards or rubrics such as Quality Matters™) and effective use of technology.

A qualitative meta-analysis of research and resources on blended learning (McGee & Reis, 2012) resulted in a collection of effective practices for the design process, pedagogical strategies, classroom and online technology use, assessment strategies, and course implementation. The authors advise that, because of the variety of blended learning models, the practices may be more useful as broad generalizations than as specific guidelines. The major findings and recommendations follow. Redesign of existing courses is emphasized, with an eye toward creating ways to achieve objectives using multiple media and delivery modes, because not everything translates literally from one mode to the other. The primary pedagogical consideration is integrating face-to-face and online components, followed closely by using varied interactive activities and providing prompt feedback. Practices regarding technology focus on its use in support of learning. There is a recommendation to make technology integral to the face-to-face environment, as well as online. The only tools specifically recommended are discussion forums and wikis. Assessment is not widely represented in the literature, and there is a tendency in blended courses to use traditional objective assessments even though assignments tend toward non-traditional types, such as project-based learning. Course implementation recommendations concentrate around online work, probably because that is the factor that initiates the blend. It is important that instructors inform students about blended design processes and expectations. For example, instructors need to explain the role of online discussions as a critical component of the course and underscore their importance by continuing the discourse in face-to-face meetings. Fostering community building for the duration of the course and giving prompt and specific feedback are also recommended.

Integrating online and in-class work

Online experiences are filtering down to face-to-face courses in a natural way. Many traditional music courses already include some online activity, and learning management systems (LMS) are frequently used as a convenient means of accessing course materials, submitting assignments, and providing feedback on assignments. In music courses that involve research, electronic databases and web-based music reference materials are the tools of choice. Online library-supported music services are often used to provide access to selections for in-class and out-of-class music listening. However, the transformative potential of this kind of online activity should not be overlooked, as it can open the door to fully integrated blended learning. The use of digital technologies in face-to-face classes can serve as the first step in a transition to a blended course. A blended approach offers an alternative to an instructor for whom it is not feasible to teach a fully online course, who is not comfortable doing so, or who prefers to teach in the face-to-face classroom but understands and appreciates the pedagogical potential of the Internet and communication technologies. By choosing a blended model, this instructor can merge the strengths of online learning with those of face-to-face learning. The appeal of a blended model can be attributed in part to its simplicity and adaptability: It builds upon a familiar environment, the face-to-face classroom, and each blended course is unique to its discipline and subject matter.

As stated previously, simple enhancement of a face-to-face learning experience with supplementary online activities does not constitute a blended learning design. Rather, the key issue is "full integration of face-to-face and online activities" (Garrison, 2011, p. 75). This full integration involves replacing a portion of "seat time" (Dziuban, et al., 2004, p. 2) or, in some instances, an entire class meeting with online experiences. In any case, both face-to-face and online activities are integral parts of the course, both are required, and both are graded. What is done online

In a music history course, small groups of students might conduct online research on dwindling audiences for classical music, analyze the issues, and develop summary statements to be presented in the face-to-face class, followed by brainstorming of possible solutions—ways to interest contemporary audiences in classical music. In a blended course, similar experiences would be interspersed strategically throughout the course.

is brought back to the face-to-face class and informs in-person activities and experiences (see box 7.1).

Learning experiences like these need to emerge from consideration of the course as a whole, how face-to-face and online elements complement each other. The online part must be integral, a necessary part of the learning experience, not something extra that can be eliminated without detriment to the learning experience.

"Tuning the blend" is an expression used to describe the process of determining an optimum balance of online and face-to-face activities within a blended course (Schaffhauser, 2012b, p. 22), and the blend will be different for each course. Some instructors already incorporate a number of digital technologies in their face-to-face courses, notably use of the institution's LMS to place syllabi and handouts online and to create a collection of resources such as websites and videos relevant to course content. Others make choices based on efficient use of class time: Quizzes and some asynchronous discussions are completed online, while complex assignments are first introduced and explained in a face-to-face session. One instructor experimented with class debates in both settings and found that, although the energy and excitement of the face-to-face debate was undeniable, the online responses were superior, possibly due to increased time to reflect on arguments.

Preparing and extending class discussion

A blended design can bookend face-to-face class time by providing a structure through which students prepare class discussion and continue or extend it beyond the time limits of the face-to-face meeting. Preparation can include listening to an instructor-created audio introduction, reading textbook selections on the topic, viewing a video, listening to a musical recording, analyzing a score, and noting significant musical events that distinguish the work. Small working groups can discuss preliminary findings that they will then bring to the face-to-face discussion. The online advance preparation provides some assurance that students will arrive at the face-to-face meeting acquainted with the issues and ready to discuss various perspectives or arguments—ready to maximize class time. Face-to-face discussions can be dynamic, generating considerable interest and energy, but sometimes the class period ends before the discussion is concluded. Unlike face-to-face class meetings, asynchronous online discussions do not run out of time, so they provide an ideal way to extend classroom discussion and give each student an opportunity to speak. The asynchronous nature of these discussions offers an additional advantage: Students have time to think about what they want to say and develop a considered response.

Making the most of class time

There are several ways of thinking about making the most of class time: We can consider efficiencies (online quizzes free up class time; wikis support asynchronous collaboration) or we can consider strengths and optimum conditions (an asynchronous online discussion provides time for reflection and thoughtful response). Instructors are frequently advised not to lecture in the face-to-face class, as that can be achieved in other ways, such as short audio lectures posted online for pre-class listening. A question that predates web-based instruction still arises: What will you do in class if your lectures are posted online? Interaction and discussion make better use of the time when the group is together. Face-to-face meetings are an ideal venue for brainstorming and organizing ideas, while online asynchronous discussions are well suited to expanding and developing the ideas generated in the face-to-face meeting. It can be a good idea to begin and conclude discussions in the face-to-face class and to use online asynchronous discussions in a way that maximizes their strength in supporting reflective discourse. By beginning the discussion face-to-face, the instructor can explain or clarify the assignment, offer some prompts, and engage students immediately with the issues. By ending the discussion face to face, the instructor can ensure a satisfactory and timely conclusion, and can move on or connect to the next topic.

COMPOSING THE COURSE/CHOREOGRAPHING THE EXPERIENCES

Designing a blended course is different from designing a fully online one, as it involves integrating online and face-to-face experiences; however, many design considerations hold for both types of courses. Both online and blended designs require more than a simple transfer of face-to-face practices to the online environment. In terms of design and pedagogy, both are informed by the various frameworks and theoretical models previously presented. As pointed out in connection with online course design, "[t]he incorporation of a new technology or new medium for teaching suddenly forces us to confront basic educational issues because this new technology or medium reconstructs the dynamic equilibrium among all three elements" (Mishra & Koehler, 2006, p. 1030). The rebalancing of content, pedagogy, and technology is an even more salient factor in blended learning because of the concurrent, integrated use of two delivery mediums. Considering content and experiences—composition and choreography—in tandem may be the most productive approach to this redesign venture.

Course goals and objectives are likely to remain the same as for the face-to-face version of the course, as will the need for congruence among course goals, objectives or outcomes, content, activities, assignments, and assessments. Objectives require close attention in blended courses because they influence delivery mode, pedagogy, integration of face-to-face with online activities, and time allotted to face-to-face and online activities. As for the design of any course (face-to-face, fully online, or blended), start with course objectives and be sure they align with activities, assignments, and assessments.

Many of your existing materials may work for your blended course, but you will probably develop some new materials. It is important to review your current face-to-face syllabus and determine what elements of that class could be handled online. An effective redesign requires that you rethink content and learning activities: what content lends itself to online work and what is better suited to face-to-face work, which activities make best use of face-to-face class time and which ones can be carried out effectively in an online environment. You will consider some overarching questions: What are the strengths of face-to-face learning; what are the strengths of online learning; and how can you connect the two for a coherent, cohesive, integrated learning experience? You will need to consider the general characteristics of learning activities and tools, and then determine how the tools and activities you are currently using can be redistributed or adapted to maximize the advantages of face-to-face and online environments. Experimenting with new tools can help you develop new pedagogical strategies as well.

There are various ways to analyze course activities, tools, and materials. One workable approach is to consider these components in terms of time (synchronous or asynchronous), place (face-to-face or online/LMS), and engagement style (group/collaborative or individual/reflective). For example, discussions (group/collaborative activity) can be held face-to-face (synchronous) or online (asynchronous or synchronous). A wiki is an online tool that supports asynchronous collaboration. A blog is an online tool that supports individual reflection, although class blogs can be set up for group reflection and comments (asynchronous). This kind of analysis is a first step toward making decisions about what will happen in the face-to-face classroom and what will happen online. The goal is to develop a continuum of engaging, complementary face-to-face and online activities, and determine how you will connect them. A course outline that includes major objectives and types of learning activities (when, where, and how the activities will occur) can be a useful planning tool. This kind of map helps you weave individual activities into the kinds of cohesive learning experiences that constitute a blended course. Table 7.1 displays a sample learning experience designed to achieve one objective in a blended music

Table 7.1 BLENDED LEARNING EXPERIENCE

Objective

Students will be familiar with evidence and arguments for music as a language and will be able to explain what and how music communicates.
(Objective may be divided into two segments: music as language and music as communication.)

Activity	Delivery mode	Connections
Lecture/Introduction: Music, language, communication	Face-to-face	Instructor introduction & explanation
Discussion: Brainstorm instances of music as communication	Face-to-face	Initial organization of ideas; follow-up/continuation with textbook & audio lectures
Reading: Textbook selections on music and language	Textbook	
Listening/audio lectures: Patel (*Music, Language, and the Brain*); Bernstein (*Musical Semantics*)	Online/LMS link Asynchronous	Instructions for listening, points to think about posted by instructor
Application project: Analyze a short piece, identify musical/speech patterns	Face-to-face	Application of principles from audio lectures
Group discussion: Conclusions about music as language	Face-to-face	Based on listening & responses to guide questions

psychology course. A variety of media and activity types is used to ensure that different learning styles will be accommodated.

On the basis of your course outline, in which you list face-to-face and online activities and how they connect, you can develop a syllabus that explains the blended format, how the course works, and expectations for participation in the entire range of activities. Because students may not have experienced a blended course before, it is important to help them understand how it works. If they have taken courses in which enrichment materials were provided online, they may consider the online portion of your blended course as supplementary. You need to proactively disabuse them of this notion. In your blended course, the online and face-to-face portions are integrated components of the course as a whole. One is not more important than the other: They are complementary, and to be successful in the course, students need to complete all the activities. Your syllabus should include a statement that informs them of these procedures and expectations.

Models for blended/hybrid courses

In line with the idea of disappearing distinctions between online and face-to-face instruction, online and face-to-face courses are each expanding to include elements of the other. Blended learning has become a rather fluid category, and it is evolving in a natural way. Some may wonder if a blended course is a face-to-face course with online elements, or an online course with face-to-face elements. Although the answer cannot be framed in either/or terms, the final determinant for institutional purposes may well be the primary locus of attendance. As noted previously, online and face-to-face courses are treated differently for purposes of institutional services: Face-to-face and blended courses require schedules and classrooms, while online courses do not rely on these services. There are multiple ways to structure blended courses, and they differ by course and context. Each blended design is unique, developed to suit a particular course within a particular disciplinary structure using its own signature pedagogy, and designed to achieve specific educational goals (see box 7.2).

The flipped or inverted classroom model is a type of blended learning that uses technology to reverse the conventional approach of in-class lecture and discussion followed by out-of-class assignments in which students work with and apply the concepts covered in class. Instead, students watch videos or screencasts outside of class and participate in learner-centered activities during class meetings. Face-to-face meetings focus on questions

A face-to-face music history course with three weekly 50-minute meetings may be redesigned to consist of two weekly meetings and an hour of online synchronous discussion participation or an hour devoted to wiki collaboration. A two-hour music psychology course may be reconfigured as a one-hour face-to-face meeting and an hour-long online synchronous collaborative session.

In a 14-week graduate music research and bibliography course, the instructor may choose to meet face to face for the first two sessions, alternate every other week with participation in online asynchronous consultations, and hold the last class face to face. In any case, the first meeting should be held face to face so that the instructor can provide an orientation to the blended format.

Fully online applied lessons can be particularly challenging due in part to audio and video quality and other issues. However, a blended approach to applied lessons, consisting of in-person applied instruction together with online activities, can result in a richer and more comprehensive experience for students in applied studies. The online component might feature a module devoted to learning how to practice, with assignments that include readings from research on effective practice techniques, use of those techniques in individual practice sessions, and reports on their effectiveness noted in a blog/practice journal. An asynchronous discussion might accommodate student suggestions based on their experience with various practice techniques. It might provide an area for exchange of performance videos posted by students and annotated by the professor. Finally, it might include instruction in the pedagogy of the instrument, with small teaching experiences documented in an individual or course blog.

and issues that arise online. Videos or screencasts are typically used for recorded lectures that present an overview of some content, supplementary mini-lectures that focus on specific concepts, or software tutorials that provide procedural guidance. They might be instructor-created or accessed from a public site. For example, in a music psychology course, students might watch a video of Aniruddh Patel, author of *Music, Language, and the Brain*, in preparation for an in-class exploration of music as a language, what it communicates, how it communicates, and how we understand it. In a music technology course, students might watch demonstration videos or view screencasts of music software procedures so that class time may be devoted to work on individual projects with targeted assistance from the instructor. Some recent research has shown that students typically vary in the way they use these resources (i.e., they may watch a video in its entirety or simply browse) and that the videos help them gain a deeper understanding of the material (Green, Pinder-Grover, & Millunchick, 2012). Learning management systems typically provide a means of tracking students' viewing patterns of videos if that is a concern.

COURSE DELIVERY

For blended courses, the syllabus and course delivery are closely connected. Because of the mixed media format, advance planning is critical: You need to visualize the student experience and anticipate questions that will arise because of use of an unfamiliar structure. You do not want to hear the dreaded words "I'm confused," which lead to lost class time, extended explanations on your part, and sometimes even greater confusion on the part of students. It is best to prevent confusion in the first place by including a clear and comprehensive orientation to the course in your syllabus and by reinforcing that orientation during the first face-to-face meeting. In the syllabus, you will need to explain what a blended course is, how it works, and why you are using a blended model. Provide a guide to procedures that includes a class meeting schedule, time allotments for face-to-face and online activities, expectations for participation in all activities, and an introduction to the learning management system. Grading would be included in any syllabus, but you will want to be sure students understand that all activities, face-to-face and online, are required and graded. Suggestions for time management are useful for helping students organize and accomplish the activities. And because online work is an integral part of the course and the grade, you will want to include contact information for academic and technical support.

Learning management system (LMS)

The synthesis of effective practices for blended learning mentioned previously (McGee & Reis, 2012) revealed divided opinion on the necessity of an LMS. Nevertheless, an LMS can provide convenient access to many online materials, particularly those developed by the instructor, as well as to discussion forums and other course tools. If you are already using an LMS to post your syllabus and some content materials, you have a head start on building an online site to support your blended course. Having all or most course materials located in one place can help head off student confusion about where to access the materials and tools for each component of the blended course. Use an organization scheme that matches the structure of your course; organization by week works well regardless of where the meetings take place, in your face-to-face classroom or online. Weekly folders make it easy to locate course materials and assignments, and a learning guide (chapter 6) can provide a clear map for the activities. The guide includes learning objectives and directions for proceeding through the assignments. Additionally, it reinforces the connections among the assignments, whether carried out online or face to face. Likewise, discussion forums should align with the weekly structure. A customized course menu that displays only the areas and tools used for the course provides a roadmap at a glance and prevents confusion.

Social media

Well-chosen social media can make sense in a blended course if they are philosophically consistent with the course. Social networking sites can be used successfully in blended popular music studies courses as a way for students to create micro-blogs, share resources, and document trends. In blended music education courses and seminars, development of personal learning networks using Twitter, blogs, wikis, and other resources can be used as one component of 21st-century teacher preparedness.

CHALLENGES AND SOLUTIONS

Some challenges noted for online learning apply as well to blended learning. However, helping students understand how the blended approach works and ensuring their participation in all activities regardless of delivery medium is a particular challenge and a crucial issue with blended courses. In your syllabus, you will stress that one is not more important than the other and that they're all connected. An additional concern with blended courses is creating a mix of rich and varied face-to-face and online learning experiences without overwhelming or confusing students. Mapping out your objectives and associated learning activities provides you with an informative guide. A related challenge for you as the designer/instructor is determining how online and face-to-face activities will mesh. Again, creating a course roadmap helps, as it shows you how the components align. Calculating the time for combined face-to-face and online activities can help you create a reasonable workload for students. It can also provide you with the information you may need in order to document contact hours, particularly if you are substituting online work for face-to-face class meetings.

The lines between online and face-to-face learning continue to blur as instructors incorporate more technology and online activities and experiences into their face-to-face classes. For that reason, blended learning is also among the most promising approaches to online learning.

REFERENCES

Allen, I. E., & Seaman, J. (2013). *Changing course: Ten years of tracking online education in the United States.* Babson Survey Research Group and Quahog Research Group, LLC. Retrieved from http://sloanconsortium.org/publications/survey/index.asp

Allen, I. E., Seaman, J., & Garrett, R. (2007). *Blending in: The extent and promise of blended education in the United States.* Sloan-C™. Retrieved from http://sloanconsortium.org/publications/survey/index.asp

Diaz, V., & Brown, M. (2010). *Blended learning: A report on the ELI focus session* (White paper). EDUCAUSE. Retrieved from http://net.educause.edu/ir/library/pdf/ELI3023.pdf

Dziuban, C. D., Hartman, J. L., & Moskal, P. D. (2004). *Blended learning.* Boulder, CO: EDUCAUSE Center for Applied Research. Retrieved from http://www.educause.edu/ecar

Garrison, D. R. (2011). *E-learning in the 21st century: A framework for research and practice* (second ed.). London: Routledge/Taylor and Francis.

Garrison, D. R., & Vaughan, N. D. (2008). *Blended learning in higher education: Framework, principles, and guidelines.* San Francisco: Jossey-Bass.

Green, K. R., Pinder-Grover, T., & Millunchick, J. M. (2012). Impact of screencast technology: Connecting the perception of usefulness and the reality of performance. *Journal of Engineering Education, 101*(4), 717–737.

Harasim, L. (2012). *Learning theory and online technologies.* New York: Routledge.

McGee, P., & Reis, A. (2012). Blended course design: A synthesis of best practices. *Journal of Asynchronous Learning Networks, 16*(4), 7–22. Retrieved from http://sloanconsortium.org/jaln/v16n4/blended-course-design-synthesis-best-practices

Means, B., Toyama, Y., Murphy, R., Bakia, M., & Jones, K. (2010). *Evaluation of evidence-based practices in online learning: A meta-analysis and review of online learning studies.* Center for Technology in Learning, U.S. Department of Education. Retrieved from http://www2.ed.gov/rschstat/eval/tech/evidence-based-practices/finalreport.pdf

Schaffhauser, D. (2012b). Tuning the blend. *Campus Technology, 26*(4), 22–24.

CHAPTER 8
Teaching and Learning

To an experienced educator, teaching is much like jazz performance: a well-practiced fusion of careful, creative planning and spontaneous improvisation.

—Judith B. Harris, *TPCK in in-service education: Assisting experienced teachers' "planned improvisations"*

HIGH-QUALITY ONLINE TEACHING

A key issue in implementing online learning in music and in teaching music online is the need for appropriate instructional models and practical teaching approaches. Because of the rapid growth of online learning, online instructional theory is not yet clearly defined. However, several design frameworks and theoretical models have been put forth, each of which provides perspective on online teaching and learning (see chapters 4 and 5). These theories both describe online learning and prescribe practice, and they can be helpful in the design of online music courses. Because instructors new to online teaching often do not have a clear idea of how to use online technologies to best advantage, they turn to strategies that have been successful in face-to-face classes with the expectation that these strategies will also work in the online environment. However, theories and practices developed for the face-to-face environment do not translate directly to the online environment. When teachers and students are not physically together at the same time and place, the techniques and strategies that rely upon that kind of presence are unlikely to be successful. Therefore, the approach to achieving course objectives needs to be reconsidered in light of features and potentials of the online environment. Additionally, faculty development has typically focused on use of learning management systems (LMS) and associated tools. Generally speaking, it has not adequately addressed the larger issue of interaction with students online.

Transitioning from face-to-face teaching

Moving from face-to-face to online teaching involves moving out of one's comfort zone. In their professional and personal lives, music instructors may frequently be online using the Internet for their own research, as well as for non-work-related purposes. When we want to know something, we go to the Internet. However, teaching online is different from being online, and for some professors, the idea of teaching online is a foreign concept. They may wonder exactly what online teaching is, how they can present their subject matter—music education, music history, music theory—online with educational and artistic integrity, how they can engage with students in the online environment, and even why they might want to teach online. But there are certain similarities with face-to-face teaching that may ease the transition. There is no single model for either face-to-face instruction or online instruction. Online courses, like face-to-face courses, differ from each other in a variety of ways, including course design, pedagogical style, and implementation. In both face-to-face and online environments, there is content and communication: Subject matter is presented and participants interact with the subject matter and each other. Teaching with technology can be a first step toward online teaching, as it may help an instructor develop a comfort level with some of the technologies that will be used in an online course. For some, it may be a natural progression rather than a transition. Using the TPACK framework to design online assignments, employing a flipped classroom model, or experimenting with a blended design in their face-to-face course can help instructors move toward fully online teaching. Basic online assignments might consist of researching musical genres using the *New Grove Dictionary of Music and Musicians Online* or creating and sharing harmonizations in a cloud-based notation program for feedback from other students. A flipped classroom model might involve out-of-class video lectures and web research on teaching popular music in K–12 classrooms in preparation for a class discussion and demonstration of potential strategies. In a blended approach, the instructor of a music research and bibliography course might reallocate the time of a typical two-hour class meeting so that class meets for an hour for instruction and student presentations, and students complete substantial online activities like detailed research journals or blogs on their own.

Excellent online teaching

Because excellent teaching may be considered an art, some faculty and prospective online instructors wonder whether it is possible to go beyond effectiveness and convey the art of teaching—the energy, excitement, and inspiration of in-person learning experiences—in the online environment. A closer analysis of excellent and inspiring teaching would reveal that the instructor is an expert in his or her discipline, has attained a certain mastery of the craft of teaching, and is able to focus on engaging students with the subject matter, much like a performing musician has attained a level of expertise and technical mastery of his or her instrument and is therefore free to focus on the artistic expression that engages the audience. Excellent online teaching is responsive to context, which varies with each online course, with different groups of students, and with different technologies. The answer is found in the pedagogy, not the delivery mode. The key is development of the craft of online teaching to the extent that musician/teachers are able to design and develop online courses that support the kinds of compelling and inspirational experiences they wish to provide for their online students.

THE ONLINE INSTRUCTOR: A ROLE FOR ALL REASONS

The role of the online instructor is complex and multifaceted, but it has been presented in simplistic ways—the professor is no longer the "sage on the stage" but rather a "guide on the side"—a comparison reminiscent of the pitting of one delivery mode against another in the research on online learning. These terms create clever caricatures of professors and yield catchy sound bites. However, they also convey a stereotypical and marginalized view of teaching professors and their roles in both online and face-to-face environments. The instructor's roles and responsibilities do not fundamentally differ between online and face-to-face environments, but their implementation varies depending upon the context. The role of the online instructor is far more nuanced than these glib either/or catchphrases imply. The pedagogical role is foremost: The online instructor is a teacher and a representative of an academic discipline, but he or she also fulfills a social role and takes on the roles of evaluator, advisor, technologist, and administrator (Bawane & Spector, 2009).

Beyond "guide on the side" and "sage on the stage"

This terminology first appeared in an article that compared a transmittal model of instruction with constructivist pedagogy (King, 1993). King emphasized that in the constructivist model, the professor

...functions as a "guide on the side," facilitating learning in less directive ways. The professor is still responsible for presenting the course material, but he or she presents that material in ways that make the students do something with the information—interact with it—manipulate the ideas and relate them to what they already know. (p. 30)

She further described the facilitator as one who "orchestrates the content, provides resources, and poses questions to stimulate students to think up their own answers" (p. 30). She suggested that for every concept a professor presents, he or she also develops an active learning experience that engages students with the concept and requires them to use their own words and experiences to construct meaning about the concept. Clearly, the idea was not for the professor to merely stand aside, abandon direct instruction, and simply guide students according to their own interests.

King's language has been co-opted and oversimplified in some literature on online learning, sometimes with the implication that the professor's function is merely to moderate or facilitate student discussion. And this language persists—it makes a clever sound bite, but it paints a distorted picture of the online teacher, whether that person is the sole instructor in a small to medium-sized class, a lead instructor of a larger class, or one of several facilitators in charge of a section of a large class. An online instructor may sometimes act in the capacity of a "sage," but not necessarily "on the stage," although the art of teaching has sometimes been described as a performance. He or she may sometimes function as a "guide," not simply "on the side," but in a more proactive way, scaffolding concepts, perhaps based on assessment of discussion posts that indicate students' understanding of complex concepts. The reality of the online instructor's multifaceted role cannot be captured in stark contrasts.

Director of learning: Conducting the course

An online instructor might better be considered a director of learning, one who has overall responsibility for the course and the interactions that take place within it—creating the overall design, pointing students toward a path through the subject matter, and highlighting key issues and topics throughout the course. This view of the online instructor appears in two theoretical models previously presented. In the community of inquiry (CoI) framework, the instructor is described as "an ever-present and key person, managing and monitoring the process," one who is needed "to structure, shape, and assess the learning experience" (Garrison, 2011, p. 83). Online collaborative learning (OCL) theory likewise highlights the "critical" roles of the professor as facilitator and, perhaps more important, as representative of the knowledge community or discipline, inducting students into a knowledge community and helping them engage in the discourse of a discipline (Harasim, 2012, p. 94). Other authors are also beginning to emphasize the central role of the instructor. Some sources invoke artistic references: "To continue the theater metaphor, the faculty mentor is the director of learning experience, not a sage on the stage transmitting knowledge or a guide on the side with minimal input into the learning experience" (Boettcher & Conrad, 2010, p. 25), and "...online instructor as conductor or leader of a band of learners who knows how, when, and to what degree to bring out the music, the strengths, and depths of various sections" (Heuer & King, 2004, p. 3). These views provide a more balanced and realistic description of the roles of online instructors. They imply related responsibilities and concomitant actions. They also trigger a return to the question of whether the art of teaching can be conveyed online. One author has framed this question in aesthetic terms:

> Since great teaching is often considered an art, there are relevant aesthetic issues to consider here as well. Namely, can online music education be offered in a manner that is truly tasteful and inspiring, or must it inevitably pale in comparison to the excitement of a live learning experience? As artist-scholars, this question is a legitimate one, for we surely want our instruction to not only be effective, but also uniquely compelling and inspirational for students. Can the art of teaching be adequately conveyed online? (Hebert, 2008b, p. 102)

The answer to that question subsumes the frameworks and theories presented previously—TPACK, the CoI framework, and OCL theory. The specific dispositions and actions parallel those of a director or conductor.

The conductor studies the score, knows it well, and identifies the points in it that will be troublesome or challenging. He or she selects techniques that will overcome those challenges and develops a rehearsal schedule that will bring work on the composition to completion at an optimum time prior to the performance. A major task for the conductor is developing the ensemble and ensuring that all members of the group work together and listen to each other in order to maintain the appropriate balance within the ensemble. The conductor directs the entire group while being attentive to individual instrument voices and cueing solos. The online instructor (director of learning) reviews and rethinks the content, pedagogy, and technologies appropriate to the course in the online setting in light of the challenges that environment presents (TPACK). Like the conductor, he or she selects techniques to address those challenges—activities and learning experiences that will engage students with the subject matter within a course schedule that will bring the course to completion at the appropriate time. A major task for the director of learning is developing an online learning community (CoI) and ensuring that all students are actively participating, with no single voice overshadowing the others. The online instructor oversees the general flow of discussions, attends to and encourages expression of individual ideas, and ensures that participants work collaboratively toward their common goals and objectives (OCL).

Thoughtful course design, development of appropriate activities and learning experiences, and organization within a course schedule all contribute to setting the stage. However, the course comes to life only when students enter. There is in fact an aesthetics of online teaching, and a skilled, well-prepared instructor can teach online in an artistic and inspiring way. Like a director who steps up to the podium to begin a rehearsal, the director of learning greets the class with a welcoming introductory message that signals the beginning of the course. As director of learning, the instructor establishes a weekly rhythm, conducts the course, maintains the beat (pace), keeps the group on track, and highlights important themes, sections, transitions, and connections. Establishing a weekly rhythm helps students feel comfortable with the online environment and course procedures that include accessing weekly assignment folders, contributing to asynchronous discussions, participating in synchronous meetings, submitting assignments, and receiving feedback. The following tasks and techniques provide guideposts for the prospective director of learning that can smooth the process of conducting online classes effectively and artistically.

Establishing and modeling online presence

At the most basic level, presence means being there, being visible, and being perceived as real in a mediated environment, in this case, the online classroom. Establishing presence is the first step in building an online learning community. In a face-to-face class, you are ordinarily present in the classroom when students enter. You may have prepared explanatory handouts or worksheets that are available as students enter the room, and you may provide a brief overview of the objectives or agenda for the class. However, in the online environment, you are invisible unless you are communicating, most often by posting to discussion forums. Students will not see the instructor and the instructor will not see the students unless all participants are contributing to discussion forums. The instructor, as director of learning, is responsible for setting the pace—modeling the online behavior expected of students and demonstrating how online learning is done.

Announcements and logging in

You can make your presence felt and remind students that you are there by logging in regularly, creating announcements on a regular basis, and checking in to comment briefly on the progress of discussions. A welcome announcement alerts students that the course is about to begin, directs them to important materials, and informs them of some class procedures (see box 8.1).

E-mailing, as well as posting this kind of announcement to the course site, should eliminate uncertainty among students and ensure that they begin the course on schedule. Regular reminders about concluding current discussions and beginning new ones remind students that you are there to help them stay on track. When you discover relevant articles or other resources you wish to share with students, brief informal announcements can be an effective way to pass them on. Connecting course content with current events enlivens discussions and makes the content more memorable. These kinds of informal communications also assure students that you are engaged with the course and are working along with them (see box 8.2).

Box 8.1

Hello and Welcome
　Hello, and welcome to this course.
　Our course site is now available, and it looks like there will be 21 people here this semester. In the Syllabus link, you'll find our syllabus, which describes the course and class procedures in detail. The Assignments link includes weekly assignment folders and a form for submitting the final project.
　As soon as you post a short biography to the Class 1 Discussion forum, we can all see who is in the course and get to know each other. Our live meeting night is Tuesdays at 7:30–8:30 p.m., and our first meeting will be next Tuesday, January 8th.
　See you soon.

Box 8.2

Current events and Music and the Mind

Hello everyone,

You may be interested in some news about how Gabrielle Giffords is improving her speech with the assistance of a music therapist—along with an article describing her recovery process. You'll find them in Web Resources in the Gabrielle Giffords folder. Both are relevant to some topics we will be discussing soon. Just click the link in the announcement on our course site.

Posted and e-mailed announcements of agendas for synchronous meetings serve as reminders of the meeting and the expectation that students will prepare for the discussion.

Creating an effective online syllabus: Setting the stage

A syllabus for an online course is not drastically different from a syllabus for a face-to-face course. Some elements, such as the course description, major goals of the course, course objectives, and some assignments, will remain the same as for a face-to-face class. However, class procedures and other elements that affect how students are to achieve the objectives will differ from those used in face-to-face courses and even in online courses taught by another instructor. To ensure that students know how the course will proceed, how they are expected to participate, and how they will be graded, you need to provide detailed descriptions and instructions that explain these features. The following syllabus excerpt offers concise descriptions of some requirements, expectations, and procedures (see box 8.3). You could provide more extensive, detailed explanations, but sometimes brevity is clearer than wordiness.

Conveying content

Content should be organized in a consistent way within the LMS (e.g., in weekly assignment folders) so that students can locate and access it without difficulty. Having accessed the materials, students need a map of some kind to guide them through the ideas and concepts under consideration. An effective

Box 8.3

ASSIGNMENTS

This is an online course; materials are available on the course site as listed in the following section. Because we meet weekly online on Tuesdays, the course operates on a weekly schedule, from Tuesday to the following Tuesday. In our Live Meetings (Live Classrooms) on Tuesdays, we will discuss the topics and readings listed on the Course Schedule for that date. Therefore, you will want to prepare the readings and post any comments to the Discussion Board prior to the Live Meeting. In Live Meetings, we will expand upon/clarify issues from the discussion forums, and further explore the topics of the week.

Assignments include the following:

- Readings and related activities from textbooks and other sources
- Study/discussion questions related to the readings
- Participation in Discussion Forums and Live Meetings
- Individual Special Topic & presentation
- Individual Learning Portfolio

READINGS

Readings from the textbooks provide basic information; other activities supplement and enhance the readings.

STUDY/DISCUSSION QUESTIONS

Study/discussion questions are provided for each week's topic to help you focus your reading. The questions are intended to stimulate your thinking and call attention to some important points in each chapter. You should not limit yourself to simply answering those questions, as individual insights are most valuable, but you would not want to overlook the points they highlight.

PARTICIPATION

You will address several of these questions in a general way in each week's Discussion Forum. Discussions provide opportunities to explore and share ideas related to the weekly topic. Your work here begins with posting your ideas on the study questions. The next step is contributing further to the discussion by reading and responding to the insights and comments posted by other course participants. For that reason, a significant amount of credit is allotted to participation.

(continued)

Box 8.3 (CONTINUED)

Live Meetings on a weekly basis supplement asynchronous discussions (Discussion Board) and provide opportunities for real-time brainstorming and idea exchange. Please prepare the topic and assignments of the week for discussion at this meeting so that our time together is as productive as possible. You can access the meeting by clicking Live Meetings on the navigation bar in our course site. The Live Meeting night for this course is Tuesday, 7:30–8:30 p.m. We will meet every week beginning Tuesday, January 8th. Live Meetings entail audio communication and also allow for text-based chat. It is recommended that you use a headset (with integrated headphones and microphone) for best audio quality.

INDIVIDUAL SPECIAL TOPIC

This assignment consists of a brief overview (1,000-word essay) and annotated reading list (8–10 resources) on a topic of your own choice. You will present highlights (2 or 3 top points) of this topic during the last two Live Meetings, and you will post an abbreviated version to the Special Topics Discussion Forum so that we can benefit from each other's findings. The full version will be part of the appendix to your Learning Portfolio.

LEARNING PORTFOLIO

This is the final project for the course. The purpose of the Learning Portfolio is for you to reflect on and synthesize your entire learning experience in this course. By the date stipulated on the Course Schedule, you will submit a document in which you describe and illustrate the meaning of your learning experience. The document should include two parts: (1) a well-written narrative statement, and (2) an appendix containing materials that support your narrative comments.

ATTENDANCE

Participation in online discussions is crucial to the learning process because you are not visible in the class unless you are making your presence known by posting your ideas to the discussion board. As in the assignments, we progress through a series of topics relevant to the course material we are covering at the time and the assignments that we are developing. You are required to contribute to the asynchronous Discussion Board, which you may do at any time during each week of the course. You are also expected to participate in Live Meetings at a specified date and time (Tuesdays, 7:30–8:30 p.m.), although unforeseen conflicts with professional responsibilities may occasionally preclude your participation.

(continued)

In an online course, you must remember to log on, just as you must remember to attend a face-to-face class at a given time, so it is best to create a study schedule that works for you. Whatever your schedule, here is a suggested work order.

- To get started, go to the course site and click on the Syllabus link: download, read, and print out the Syllabus. Using the included Course Schedule and the Reading and Discussion Assignments list as a guide, go to Assignments and select the folder that corresponds to the class date. Folders are labeled by week and contain all the materials you will need for the week's work.
- Please prepare all readings for the day for which they are listed on the Course Schedule; this corresponds to our Live Meeting day. Complete any readings and post your thoughts and comments to the Discussion Forum by Monday of each week so that we may have time for an exchange of ideas on these topics during our Live Meeting on Tuesdays. Check the Discussion Board periodically during the week to view any posts made since your last visit so that we can keep the conversation going. Each week's discussion concludes on Tuesday at the Live Meeting.

The final grade is based upon quality and on-time completion of assignments and projects, as well as on participation. Your grade will be based on these components:

- Weekly discussion posts and live meeting participation: 25 percent
- Individual Special Topic and presentation: 25 percent
- Learning Portfolio: 50 percent

way to provide this map is with the use of a learning guide, which could be posted as a separate "Read Me First" file or integrated into the structure of the weekly assignment folder. The learning guide includes an introduction to the week's topics together with learning objectives. It can list an optimum order for reviewing the materials and incorporate salient points in individual readings, as well as connections to be made among readings and other media like podcasts or videos. It also includes discussion questions and related assignments. In the online environment, it is most effective to divide content into small, accessible segments or chunks. This type of organization can easily be accommodated within subdivisions of a learning guide file or in the weekly folder itself with the use of subfolders for the various topics. Digital formats are most likely to be used and are preferred by online students. Library research and supplementary materials that are available online (e.g., digital references, full-text articles, and e-books), provide convenient access to these resources, a particular concern for students who are working professionals like in-service music teachers. By using different forms of digital content, you can provide a comprehensive experience with content and concepts. Possibilities include brief word-processed lecture summaries or reading guides; PowerPoint files in various formats, including PDFs that students can use for note-taking; audio narrative in PowerPoint files; links to web resources such as lectures, performances, and tutorials on YouTube; and high-quality published podcasts, available through the iTunes Store or iTunes U, to which students can subscribe. Original brief audio or video mini-lectures, five to 10 minutes in length, can provide concise overviews of concepts with immediacy not achievable with print materials. Video also helps project your presence online. You can make all content available at the beginning of the course or choose to release it on a timed basis. Many students choose online courses because of the flexibility they offer for working ahead, which meshes well with busy schedules that sometimes conflict with course responsibilities. Students who are high school band directors, for example, might want to complete coursework that is due the week of their scheduled concert in advance. Having materials available beforehand provides the flexibility needed for that purpose.

Engaging students, creating community

You set the stage by designing and developing the course and by uploading your content, but the course only comes to life when students enter and interact with each other. Icebreaker activities are useful at the beginning of the course to promote social presence and development of community—to help students get to know each other and establish a comfort level that will support open communication. A getting-to-know-you discussion can be an effective and enjoyable icebreaking exercise: Each participant posts a short autobiography that includes professional information and personal interests, as well as their special interests in the course. It can be a good idea to provide a few suggestions about the kind of personal information to post (e.g., the person's name and perhaps the way they prefer to be addressed within the class, their hometown, their undergraduate school, degree major or major instrument, where they are teaching and in what academic areas). Sharing these and other common areas of interest (pets and favorite sports) helps to build community. An open forum can accommodate general student questions, informal exchanges, and links or other resources that students want to share with the group. Use both asynchronous and synchronous activities to create a balance between the energy of in-person interaction such as brainstorming and the possibility of immediate feedback with opportunities for outside research, reflection, and thoughtful written response. Asynchronous discussions make it possible for everyone in the class to contribute; time does not run out as it does in face-to-face classes and synchronous discussions. And asynchronous discussions provide a written record that students and instructors alike can revisit to observe the development of students' thinking over time. Both kinds of communication are effective and important for online learners.

Facilitating asynchronous discussions

Advance planning is key to a productive asynchronous discussion, including discussion forum organization that matches the organization of the course, well-constructed discussion questions that provide clarity and prompt full participation, and a structure or schedule for posting. For a course organized by week, a clearly labeled discussion forum for each week informs students of the location of that week's discussion and other activities. For example, an assignment folder labeled Class 1 links to a corresponding discussion forum labeled Class 1 Discussion. Questions should be specific but open-ended, neither answerable with a "yes" or "no" nor so broad that the replies are unfocused. For example, a question like "Do you think music is a language?" could elicit either a one-word reply or a tome. Questions can be based on textbook readings together with your guiding questions and perhaps links to relevant websites. When there are several related questions on a single topic, you can ask students to respond to one that seems most relevant to their experience. For example, "Please address one of these questions: Based on our readings about practice techniques and your own experience, what techniques seem most effective? Given some effective practice techniques, how can you get your beginning instrumentalists to use them consistently?" It is advisable for the instructor to begin the discussion and all major threads with a starter message to which students are instructed to reply rather than start new threads. This first post initiates the dialogue and establishes a structure that should keep responses organized. It also establishes your presence in the discussion forum and sets the tone of the discourse. Students are likely to take their cues from you. If you adopt an informal but professional style, they are likely to reply in a similar manner.

To promote timely discussion participation and to avoid a pileup of contributions at the end of the week, specify a schedule for contributions. For example, within the first two days, all participants should reply to your original post. During the next three days, they should read and respond to at least one other student's post. Check on the progress of the discussion regularly and post some brief comments to show that you have been there. Ask additional probing questions to deepen and extend the discussion, or provide clarifications of confusing points. Be aware, however, that instructor posts can be perceived as more important than those from other students. You don't want to dominate the discussion so that it devolves into a two-way conversation between you and individual students or into a lecture. Rather, you want to encourage and support discussion between and among students. A poke-your-head-in approach establishes your presence and allows you to provide input as another participant in the discussion. "Amy, your remarks on music and language were right on target. Does anyone else want to comment on this? I'd like to hear from you, so please post your thoughts by the end of this week." Conversely, you can also uncover misconceptions early in the discussion, clarify them, and steer the discourse in a more productive direction. By the end of the week, all should have contributed, and you will summarize or otherwise conclude the discussion.

Moderating synchronous meetings/chats

Successful synchronous meetings also require advance planning and preparation to avert both technical problems and academic issues. An announcement of the meeting specifying the day and time can serve as a preventive measure. Although your syllabus undoubtedly specifies the details of synchronous meetings, students sometimes forget to log in since they do not have to go to a physical classroom. Your announcement serves several purposes: It reminds students of the meeting time, informs them of the agenda or topics for the meeting, and advises them to do a browser check prior to the session. You too can avoid technical issues by performing a browser and equipment check prior to the meeting, as updates can affect the performance of chat software. At the same time, you can upload any materials (e.g., PowerPoint files) for display during the synchronous session.

On the day of the synchronous meeting, you will want to arrive early, perhaps 10 minutes prior to the start time, so you are there to greet students as they enter, much as you would in a face-to-face class. The time while students are arriving provides a good opportunity for some brief socializing. Again, this is like entering the classroom, greeting everyone there, carrying on an informal conversation while people assemble: "How are you tonight?" "How was your day?" "Are you still in rehearsals for the school musical?" and so on. When all have arrived, you can conclude the informal chat, remind students of the agenda, and perhaps point out any persistent confusion in the asynchronous discussion and clarify it. For example, in one possible scenario, students in a graduate music education course are studying Howard Gardner's theory of multiple intelligences, and from their posts, you recognize that some are equating the intelligences with learning modalities. To highlight the differences, you might pose a series of questions that challenge the students to recall the criteria for musical intelligences, to define a learning modality, to distinguish between the two, and to come to a satisfactory conclusion. Chat software typically includes management tools such as icons that indicate questions, comments, agreement, and so on. By using these tools, you can maintain order during the session and also ensure that everyone who has a question or comment has the opportunity to speak. When students select a raised hand icon, for example, you can call on them in the order in which the icon appeared.

Moderating synchronous meetings includes keeping the discussion on track and moving it forward. Sometimes a break in the conversation may be warranted, for example, in order to proceed to the next topic or explain a term or idea. At other times, however, the discussion may veer off into tangents that are not relevant to the topic at hand. These can delay or derail the discussion and may be better handled through an alternative means, perhaps a personal e-mail. You can redirect these kinds of topics with a brief remark and return promptly to the primary dialogue. In addition to supporting general group discussions, synchronous meetings can be an ideal venue for student presentations. In this case, students contribute the content and field questions about the topics of their presentations. You will also want to record and archive synchronous sessions so that students (and you) can review them if necessary, and so that students who may have been unable to attend due to a schedule conflict or technology glitch may listen and add their own comments to an asynchronous forum created for that purpose.

Coordinating collaborative activities

A class wiki can be a particularly engaging kind of collaborative activity, one in which students contribute course content. All class participants contribute to the wiki, and all have the capability to edit each other's contributions. You can make the wiki available at an appropriate time during the online course with a specific cutoff date for contributions. You would want to look in on the wiki periodically to check on progress and also to ensure that all students have begun participating by the start date you specified. You can track contributions and editing by accessing a history section, and you can add comments if necessary using a comments feature. If contributions seem to lag, you can post a brief friendly reminder to the announcements on the course site. In addition, a short announcement providing positive feedback about in-progress contributions can sustain and encourage continued participation while serving as a reminder to those who may have forgotten about their ongoing responsibility in this collaborative effort. Following is a syllabus description and instructions for a class wiki within a graduate-level music education philosophy course (see box 8.4).

Providing feedback

Feedback is always important, regardless of delivery medium. Giving prompt feedback is one of the seven principles for good practice in undergraduate education (Chickering & Gamson, 1987; see chapter 9). Students are rightly concerned with their achievement in any course: They want and need regular feedback on their progress, particularly on assignments that constitute part of their grade. In the online environment, prompt and frequent feedback is especially important to assure students that they are on the right track and keep them motivated. You can set the pace for feedback at the beginning of the course, with a response to individual students' first posts, the autobiographical profiles that include professional and personal information along with their interests in the course. As you reply with a welcome message in a music psychology course, for example, you can acknowledge a student's prior experience with special learners and point out its relevance for other course participants. Poking your head into discussion forums and making brief comments to the group about the quality of postings provides ongoing feedback on the direction of their thinking. If questions arise that require instructor input, you will want to respond promptly, perhaps within a day, in order to maintain the momentum of the discussion. Students especially need timely feedback on graded assignments, and much student anxiety can be avoided if you inform them of when they can expect feedback and grades (e.g., within a week of the due date of the assignment).

Students' feedback to the instructor on their course experiences can be useful early in the term when you have the opportunity to adjust aspects of the course that do not seem to be working for them or add elements they would find useful. You can create a survey using the survey tool in your LMS or one of the free commercial survey tools. To conduct an informal

Box 8.4

MUSICAL ROLES WIKI

The purpose of this group project/wiki is to collaboratively explore the idea of musical intelligence and its expansion into musical roles as expressed by Bennett Reimer, while adding ideas and insights of your own. Our goal is to develop a broader understanding of what it means to be musically intelligent and specifically how that plays out in our chosen professions or roles. To achieve this goal, you will read some basic literature on the topic, summarize what you read, and add your own thoughts to the mix. You can comment on additions made by others, and you are also free to edit the entries of other participants.

This is a public wiki, open to all course participants, where you will all work together—everyone will see everyone else's contributions. It can have as many pages as you want. Everyone can create, edit, and delete content within the wiki—the History section of the wiki keeps track of all contributions. You can also post comments on the material in the Comments space. You'll begin working on this project by Monday, March 21st. The cutoff date for submissions is Friday, April 8th.

CONTENT WRITING/EDITING TASKS

1. From the reading, choose at least three of the musical roles and add to the definitions and characteristics of each one. Feel free to change the very brief definition at the top of each page; it is only a starter and is not intended to be a permanent component of the page.
2. Add your own thoughts on each of the roles you selected. You might consider incorporating some components of the roles as expressed in the Reimer text.
3. Explore ways we can develop and incorporate roles that are not our primary role. For example, if you are a music teacher, then how can you integrate the thinking of the musicologist and the improviser into your teaching? If you are a performer, how can you integrate the thinking of the music theorist and the music educator into your major role?
4. Try to extend the application of these ideas to an exploration of how we can teach for role-based intelligences.
5. You are also free to propose additional musical roles. You can start a new page to accommodate a proposed musical role.

survey, you can set up a discussion forum with anonymous posting for constructive feedback about course processes that students feel are working or not working, and for any suggestions they may have. The student input then calls for feedback from the instructor (e.g., an announcement or a reply to the feedback forum in which you describe changes you are making to the course based on their input).

Online assessment

Effective assessment begins at the course design level with alignment of objectives, outcomes, and assignments—what the outcomes are and how students will demonstrate that they have achieved those outcomes. There are multiple techniques for assessment in online learning. There are also concerns about assessment in online learning. Forms of assessment frequently used in online courses include automated tests and quizzes, graded discussion posts, research papers, projects, learning portfolios, and proctored exams. Each type may be useful for certain purposes; however, the assessments used in the online course must be in alignment with the kind of instruction provided in the course. For example, in a course that emphasizes practical applications of pedagogical concepts to elementary music education, a series of lesson plans would be a more appropriate assessment than a multiple-choice test on pedagogical terminology. Many online instructors find that authentic assessments like projects are the most effective way to assess student learning. Learning portfolios or e-portfolios may contain such artifacts, as well as journals or reflections. They provide a picture of the individual student's learning process and overall growth.

Many issues about assessment in the online environment concern academic integrity (e.g., verifying that the person who is registered for the course is the same one who is participating in discussions, taking quizzes, and writing papers, and ensuring that students are not plagiarizing or cheating on quizzes and exams). There are proctoring services that address the issue of identity verification for students taking tests and exams. Test creation tools within learning management systems can usually provide a question pool and randomization of test questions, which should yield different sets of questions for test takers. Some instructors are concerned that students may have books open during a test. It is best to create questions that cannot be copied from a book or article (e.g., questions that require application of concepts rather than repetition of definitions). However, there are ways to prevent such situations from arising, particularly with smaller classes. You can use a series of written assignments like short essays, as well as frequent discussion contributions, to help you get to know your students' typical work and writing styles, so that an abrupt change in writing style or vocabulary would alert you to a potential issue of this kind. Larger projects created in small increments, such as music education research proposals that are created in sections, revised, and resubmitted, result in the same familiarity with a student's style, so that any kind of ghost writing or plagiarism would probably be evident to you.

THE ONLINE STUDENT

Your students may or may not have previously taken an online course. If not, they may be apprehensive about online learning. And even if they have already experienced online learning, they may not be familiar with your teaching style. A well-designed course can convey the illusion of non-mediation, in which the technology becomes transparent to the extent that people ignore or forget about it and simply communicate with other people. Your design can foster this perception, helping students to develop an online presence and take an active role in the course.

Student presence

Online students, like online teachers, establish their presence by posting professional and selected personal information to an introductory discussion forum and by communicating with other course participants. If they are not posting, they are not visible. As the instructor, you can create the conditions that will help your students develop online presence, first by helping them acclimate to the online environment. A well-prepared orientation to your course can ease concerns about technology while it provides important information about course procedures. The orientation will probably be included in your syllabus, but it is worth repeating in a welcome announcement or in a section of the course site devoted to introductory information as well. Here your own modeling of online presence sets the tone for your students. An explanation of the technologies you will be using and the reasons for using them informs students from the outset about the kinds of technologies they will be expected to use (e.g., asynchronous discussions for extended discourse and problem-solving, synchronous meetings for brainstorming and project presentations, a wiki for a group project that requires various perspectives on an issue, published podcasts for supplementary and detailed explanations of topics under discussion, and YouTube videos for lectures on current topics by noted experts in the field). This information provides a preview of their class experience and an indication of the level of technological expertise they will need in order to be successful in the course. A few words about support, both instructional and technical, should ease concerns that inhibit the development of online presence, and promote a confident beginning.

Student roles: Learner, presenter, content creator, discussion moderator

Online students, like online instructors, can take on a number of roles in the online class that contribute to the richness of the learning experience and provide a sense of ownership of the course. Students can give individual presentations on topics they have researched. Student presentations make good use of valuable time in synchronous meetings and promote student/student interaction when question/answer periods are included. Students can serve as discussion moderators, leading the conversation and summarizing themes and comments. As director of learning, you can assign such leadership roles to them while maintaining your own role as conductor, somewhat like designating section leaders within an ensemble. An effective online learning environment also provides opportunities for students to take on additional teaching roles, such as contributing original content. Class wikis, for example, provide ample opportunities for all students to create and share content. Extending these teaching roles to students also promotes ownership and responsibility for the course.

WHEN THINGS GO WRONG: TROUBLESHOOTING

Sometimes, despite our best efforts and diligent preparation, Murphy's Law prevails and whatever could go wrong does go wrong. Being alert to potential problems over which you have some control and taking steps to prevent them is the first line of defense. Sometimes, however, nature steps in—storms take out power and Internet service, computers crash, and LMS updates cause glitches. Although these incidents can be disruptive, they are not fatal, and perhaps the online instructor is best advised to stay calm and carry on. The best solutions to the problem of things going wrong are prevention, having a plan B, technical support contacts, and sharing this information with students.

Preventing problems

It is better to be proactive and avoid problems in the first place than to scramble for solutions to situations that could have been prevented. Both academic and technical snags have potential to disrupt the flow of the course, and they are frustrating for instructors and students alike. Accurate technical information must be available and easy to find so that students can prepare their computers and other equipment prior to the beginning of their courses. They need accurate login and password information in order to access courses. In the case of fully online programs, many of these issues may be addressed by the institution, as well as by the college or department offering the program. When only selected courses are offered online, as in hybrid or blended programs, there may be less formal support of this kind and more responsibility on the individual professor to provide important information about academic and technical issues. Overall, online instructors need to be aware of potential pitfalls and plan accordingly. And although institutions typically provide general technical information for online learners, duplication of the requirements in your syllabus can be helpful. Sometimes, however, despite careful planning and preparation, problems arise: Updates to an LMS cause unexpected breakdowns and chat software crashes due to large numbers of users. Having a plan B is always a good idea.

Student orientation

Some general information targeted toward both prospective and current students may be provided in an area of the institution's website devoted to institution-wide online learning. The area for prospective students typically aims to answer some basic questions about online learning, such as what online learning is like, the quality and rigor of the online program, what kind of interaction they can expect with faculty and other students, and what kind of academic and technical support is provided. This kind of information is intended to help prospective students decide whether to enroll in an online course or program. The area for current students may include a new student orientation with information about how online learning works, how to be a successful online learner, academic resources such as library services for online students, and an overview of the institution's LMS. Often this area includes detailed information about a variety of technical issues that include technology requirements such as an appropriate computer and a high-speed Internet connection, operating system requirements, synchronous communication technology, and software and other applications that may be needed by most online students. Links to appropriate personnel and offices like library, writing, or tutorial centers and technical support are ordinarily provided along with this information.

Practice assignments

In addition to this general orientation to online learning, you can help your students by providing an orientation to your particular course and your own style of online teaching. Your syllabus will contain introductory information such as class procedures, location of course materials, and expectations regarding participation. To ensure your students' successful online experience, you may want them to demonstrate their understanding of how the class works and their ability to navigate the LMS. A few initial practice assignments can be useful for this purpose, and they can often be included within orientation assignments such as posting a short autobiography to the discussion forum. For example, an introductory discussion forum assignment might involve both an original post and a reply that requires students to read and respond to other students' posts (see box 8.5).

For students new to online learning, submitting assignments through an LMS may be challenging. For example, if they upload an assignment but forget to click a submit button, you will not receive it. Low-stakes assignments designed to help familiarize students with these assignment features can alleviate the uncertainty and potential anxiety about assignments being properly submitted and received. In a music research course, a first assignment might consist of writing a short essay on a topic in music history and submitting the file using an assignment form or uploading it as part of a discussion forum post. This kind of assignment serves the dual purpose of providing the instructor with a writing sample and ensuring that students are able to submit assignments or upload files.

Box 8.5

Please post a short autobiography to the discussion forum. Tell us a little about yourself and include your particular interests in this course. Also post a reply to at least one other participant who may have interests similar to yours, noting your common interests. If you know of resources that are relevant to someone else's interests, feel free to mention those.

Announcements and reminders

Students who are accustomed to attending face-to-face classes at a specific time and place may forget to log in to their online courses, with the result that they fall behind in discussions and miss assignment due dates. Timely announcements can be an effective way to remind students of synchronous and asynchronous discussion assignments, due dates, new content posted to a weekly folder, and other matters specific to your course.

Solving student issues

Prevention is the best strategy, but even planning ahead and proactively addressing potential issues will not preclude the occasional glitch, which can involve pedagogical issues, time management issues, or technical problems. Students new to online learning may need to adjust to a different instructional style that emphasizes discussion and collaborative learning. An explanation of course procedures in your syllabus can prepare them and help them make the transition. They may also need assistance with time management issues such as remembering to log in regularly, posting to discussion forums, returning to discussion forums to continue the discourse, creating a timeline for completion of large-scale assignments like research papers, and using instructional resources. These matters are well within your purview as instructor. For example, you can direct students to an online calendar provided within the LMS, or alternatively, you can advise them to schedule course activities on their mobile device calendars along with alerts to remind themselves of course responsibilities. For synchronous sessions, having students perform a browser test prior to logging in can prevent delays and last-minute requests for help from the instructor. If a student's technical issue is relatively uncomplicated and you have experienced or resolved the same problem previously, then you might help a student in a specific instance. However, you should be aware that doing so may set a precedent that could result in erosion of your instructional time. The primary contact for technical problems should be technical support personnel.

Navigating the LMS

A learning management system can be somewhat confusing for new students, and they may become frustrated in their attempts to locate materials, enter discussion areas, and submit assignments. You can eliminate some of the confusion by removing links to areas or functions you are not using, so that every link takes students to some relevant part of the course. You can also design assignments that lead students through various areas of the LMS so that they become familiar with it before any assignments are due or discussions begin. As noted previously, basic navigation tasks can often be integrated into initial practice assignments.

Accessing materials

"Where can I find the readings for this week?" If you organize your content in a simple and consistent way, you may never hear this question from students. Clearly labeled weekly folders located in an assignments area make course content easy to find. Place all materials and links for each week in the weekly folder, and include a link to the discussion forum as a reminder to contribute to the week's discussion.

Completing activities, submitting assignments

"Didn't you receive my assignment? I sent it through e-mail." Students need precise instructions on how to submit assignments. Clear instructions can ease the process and any anxiety about their submitting and your receiving assignments. It is advisable to have students submit assignments using an assignment form available in the LMS, as all assignments are sent to one location. Assignments sent to your e-mail can be overlooked or not credited properly. Stipulating a naming convention for submissions, such as "yourlastname_topic1," ensures proper crediting of assignments. This is another area where repetition may be warranted: You may state it in your syllabus and repeat it along with assignment descriptions.

Troubleshooting technical problems

Generally speaking, technical problems are best handled by technical support personnel who deal with such issues on a daily basis and whose responsibility it is to provide technical support. However, in order to teach online, you need a certain degree of expertise with computer equipment, some familiarity with network connections, and awareness of software and browser compatibility, as you will undoubtedly need to troubleshoot your own technical issues at some point. When you have achieved a level of comfort and proficiency with technical matters, you can convey that to your students, who should also be able to perform some basic troubleshooting functions. Instructors and students alike need to check their equipment against the technical requirements for online learning provided by the institution and install updates and upgrades as necessary. A reliable high-speed Internet connection is a necessity for online learning in order to access many materials and participate in synchronous sessions. An incompatible browser and plug-ins that have not been updated will make it difficult, if not impossible, to function in an online course. Everyone can avoid problems by keeping operating systems up to date, installing updates, and checking for updates to plug-ins required for applications such as synchronous chat software.

Finding help

When things go wrong—students can't access the synchronous meeting, the course site is down—they need to know whom to contact for what kind of problem. It is a good idea to list contact information for technical support or a help desk and other common resources in your syllabus, where students can readily access it. If you have experienced and resolved some common technical issues, such as updates that affect synchronous communication technologies, you might be able to advise students on correcting these issues. However, it is usually preferable to direct these kinds of questions to technical support specialists. Generally speaking, faculty should remain focused on instructional responsibilities and not take on the role of technical support.

FACULTY DEVELOPMENT

As pointed out previously, the instructor's roles and responsibilities are not fundamentally different between online and face-to-face teaching. Nevertheless, there are differences in how those roles and responsibilities are carried out, particularly in the ways that instructors engage and communicate with students.

Professors are undoubtedly aware of some differences (e.g., conveying subject matter in interesting ways and stimulating and sustaining class discussions when a class is not physically present and instructors cannot observe students' reactions directly). However, awareness of the differences does not directly translate into knowing how to adapt one's instruction to accommodate them online, any more than familiarity with technology automatically confers the ability to teach with technology. This situation is presented as one of several challenges in the most current *Horizon Report*, which highlights emerging technologies and their impact on higher education (Johnson, et al., 2013; see chapter 10). First, despite the importance of digital media literacy in all disciplines and professions, it is rarely included in K–12 teacher education or music teacher education and is essentially nonexistent in the preparation of higher education faculty. Second, although institutions may provide professional development opportunities targeted toward online teaching or teaching with technology, many professors who have not had training in technology-supported teaching techniques do not participate in these offerings, possibly due to lack of time or lack of an awareness of its importance. Other classic barriers include factors like promotion and tenure issues that affect candidates' teaching and research decisions, and professors' overall educational philosophies and established teaching practices.

Higher education

At this time, most higher education institutions house a teaching center—variously titled Center for Teaching, Center for Teaching and Learning, Center for Teaching Excellence, Center for Teaching and Faculty Development—an educational technology division, and possibly an online learning division. Each of these divisions may provide workshops or other types of presentations related to online teaching and learning. The offerings typically focus on the general features and use of a course management system, use of specific tools within a course management system such as blogs and wikis, and options for lecture capture. These kinds of technology-intensive workshops are useful; however, this kind of knowledge can also be acquired individually through the use of print or video tutorials. Information about how to think about online learning and presentations regarding educational approaches that are effective in the online environment are more important and more relevant to learning to teach online. In addition, workshops are most often designed for a multidisciplinary audience rather than tailored to a specific discipline. Presenters are typically instructional technology specialists who may have teaching experience in one or more disciplines. If they know in advance who will be attending a given workshop or presentation, some presenters may prepare examples relevant to the expected audience. However, the music disciplines are particularly challenging and can even be opaque for non-musicians, presenters, and attendees alike, so it is often up to music instructors to draw their own practical, targeted applications from the general information.

Formal and informal programs

Formal programs tailored to online music teaching are rare. Informal programs are also uncommon. And even when opportunities are available, such as the occasional summer institute or three-day intensive workshop, it is difficult for music faculty to find or make the time to attend, much less undertake the ensuing task of building their own online course. And unless these events are specifically targeted toward music instruction, issues of greatest concern to music instructors are unlikely to be addressed in a useful way unless the presenters also have significant background in music instruction in higher education. Professors generally seem to prefer brief one-on-one sessions that directly address their own concerns and resolve immediate difficulties. Because of their already demanding schedules, they have less tolerance for longer presentations that seem only peripherally related to their issues and interests. It sometimes falls to knowledgeable practitioners or early adopters to informally assist or mentor those instructors who might teach online but are wary for various reasons, from concerns about quality to uncertainty about how to teach in this environment. Undoubtedly, the best guidance would come from colleagues who have already dealt with the specific demands of teaching music online, experimented with a variety of techniques and strategies, created rigorous and challenging courses based on an appropriate theoretical framework, and experienced some degree of success in online instruction. Their experience on the path to finding what works would be invaluable to someone just beginning that journey.

Mentoring and coaching

There is some evidence in recent research for the effectiveness of a coaching model, a collaborative approach in which colleagues work together to solve problems or instructional challenges. Instructors who learn from or with peer coaches and mentors develop confidence in the use of technology that enables them to design effective technology-based learning environments: "Coaching support for teachers is a powerful means of both modeling and harnessing the potential of technology to improve teaching and learning" (Beglau, et al., 2011, p. 3). The success of the peer coaching model results from the personalized assessment and support that it offers, along with three factors: focus on what the instructor can use immediately, relevance to what the instructor is currently teaching, and ongoing support for the instructor (p. 7). This model has been implemented formally and used successfully in multiple K–12 school districts (pp. 13–18). However, it can be equally effective in higher education settings even if only used on an informal basis, as this kind of coaching begins with a conversation between the coach and the colleague and is tailored specifically to the colleague's needs and interests. Although peer coaching may present challenges involving the coordination of busy schedules, it appears to be a useful format for working with higher education faculty.

ISTE NETS for Technology Coaches (NETS•C)

The International Society for Technology in Education (ISTE®) is a professional society whose mission is to help prepare teachers, students, and administrators to effectively use technology in PK–12 education and teacher education. As part of that mission, ISTE® developed sets of National Educational Technology Standards (NETS) for teachers, students, administrators, and technology coaches. The standards for coaches are intended "to benchmark what coaches should know and be able to do to effectively help teachers develop their confidence and effectiveness in designing and supporting technology-rich environments that maximize student learning" (Beglau, et al., 2011, p. 5). The NETS for Coaches (NETS•C) consist of the following six general standards

1. Visionary Leadership
2. Teaching, Learning, & Assessments
3. Digital-Age Learning Environments
4. Professional Development & Program Evaluation
5. Digital Citizenship
6. Content Knowledge and Professional Growth (ISTE, 2011)

Each standard is followed by a number of performance indicators that describe what technology coaches should know and be able to do in each of the major categories. These indicators serve as benchmarks that coaches can use to help instructors design and support effective technological environments that maximize student learning. Among the standards most relevant to online learning in higher education, pre-service teacher preparation, and most useful within a peer coaching model is Standard 3: Digital-Age Learning Environments and several of its indicators:

(c) Coach teachers in and model use of online and blended learning, digital content, and collaborative learning networks to support and extend student learning as well as expand opportunities and choices for online professional development for teachers and administrators

(e) Troubleshoot basic software, hardware, and connectivity problems common in digital learning environments

(g) Use digital communication and collaboration tools to communicate locally and globally with students, parents, peers, and the larger community (ISTE, 2011, p. 2)

These indicators provide some broad guidelines for peer-to-peer coaching and mentoring, as they represent some of the most basic and immediate questions posed by instructors embarking upon some form of online learning. Addressing these issues at the outset goes a long way toward easing some of the instructors' initial concerns.

Being your own faculty developer

If no formal or informal professional development options are available, or if they are available to you on a limited basis because, for example, an equally busy faculty colleague is serving as an informal coach, you may need to take charge of your own development. Organizations such as The College Music Society and the Association for Technology in Music Instruction offer many opportunities to explore techniques of online learning, including annual conferences that feature presentations, demonstrations, and special interest groups, as well as opportunities to network with others who have similar interests. For an overview of accreditation requirements that affect online learning, review the general and music accreditation standards outlined in chapter 2.

To engage in some do-it-yourself professional development, try conducting a brief self-assessment: What course would you like to teach online? What is your current level of technology expertise? How could you get started? Scan your syllabus to see which topics or activities might work well online and sketch out a few ideas. Would a flipped classroom approach in which students view an instructional video outside of class in preparation for an in-class discussion make for a more productive class meeting? Would an online discussion forum extend your customary classroom discussion and ensure that all students have the opportunity to contribute? Would blogs or online journals make reflective assignments more engaging? Would a class wiki produce more in-depth student thinking and research? Consider these ideas in light of the TPACK framework (see chapter 4) to determine how these technologies and techniques would affect the way you represent and teach your subject matter online. Review the external rubrics outlined in chapter 9—Quality Matters™ and the *Rubric for online instruction*—for their usefulness to you as guidelines or course design checklists. And on a practical basis, experiment with selected online assignments in your face-to-face classes. Any of the techniques just mentioned would provide practice with tools and techniques you can use in an online course. Try a blended approach in one of your courses, and perhaps take advantage of the summer months to develop an online course that can "go live" in the following fall semester.

K–12 education

Similar to online instruction and online music instruction in higher education, K–12 online learning is becoming more widespread. According to the most recent data, all 50 states provide some form of K–12 online learning. Approximately 275,000 students attended fully online schools and over 600,000 were enrolled in one-semester online courses during the 2011–2012 school year, about 5 percent of K–12 students nationally. Blended schools and programs appear to be growing, but accurate numbers are not available because blended learning is not specifically reported as such. However, blended learning is expected to continue as an area of growth and innovation, in part because of the limited number of students who might wish to attend a fully online school. The data include a few references to high school courses in the visual and performing arts, but there is no specific mention of online music courses (Watson, Murin, Vashaw, Gemin, & Rapp, 2012). There is also a small but growing body of research on online learning at this level. Most of the research compares standardized test achievement of students enrolled in asynchronous online courses with that of students in traditional synchronous face-to-face courses.

The National Education Association (NEA) published a guide for teaching online courses at the high school level (NEA, 2002) to address the specific characteristics and needs of high school students engaged in online learning. The opportunity to offer a broader range of courses is among the benefits particularly relevant to online music instruction. For example, in the case of music education, a specialized nonperformance course like music theory might be offered online when it cannot be accommodated within the existing schedule. The guide emphasizes that the criteria it sets forth refer only to individual courses, as there are concerns about online completion of significant portions of a high school education. The appropriateness of online learning for younger students is questioned, and caution is urged regarding use of online instruction with students younger than middle school age. The criteria for online high school courses, particularly those that address curriculum, instructional design, teacher quality, student roles, and assessment, would be useful in pre-service teacher/music teacher education. A later NEA publication (2006) focuses on K–12 online educators, addressing the skills needed for effective online teaching and the kind of professional development that will help teachers acquire those skills. Among the principles supporting this professional development are a basis in research on online pedagogy and delivery, and demonstration of mastery of all features of online teaching. Training and practice with communication, feedback, facilitation of discussions and group projects, and adaptation of curriculum, materials, and online tools are specified as areas for professional development along with complementary assistance from mentors who are master online teachers.

Pre-service teacher preparation

Pre-service music teacher education typically does not include instruction in how to teach online, but with the growth of online learning opportunities at the K–12 level, this situation must change. The lack of this kind of instruction is part of a larger issue that involves learning how to teach with technology. Although music teacher education programs may include a music technology course, this kind of course typically deals with using the technology and does not address technology-supported teaching. This lack of practical pedagogical applications compounds the problem. There is a small body of published research and a number of articles on online music teaching at this level, but if this research is not within the music education professor's primary area of interest, it may well be overlooked. Integration of technology and modeling of technology-supported teaching throughout the music education curriculum are also uncommon. It is not surprising, then, that instruction in how to teach online is not represented in music teacher education, as it extends the use of technology in the face-to-face music classroom to use of digital technologies in an online environment and requires adjustment of familiar techniques and strategies. Music education students ordinarily learn about and experience a standard body of traditional pedagogical approaches. However, there are also pedagogical frameworks for teaching with technology and for online instruction. The TPACK framework, for example, provides a way to think about teaching with technology at any level, and it can be useful in the design and development of online experiences and courses as well (see chapter 4). Recent research highlights the importance of the TPACK framework in pre-service training for online teaching. A survey of K–12 online teachers (Archambault, 2011) revealed that they felt most prepared in pedagogy, content, and pedagogical content, but least prepared in all areas involving technology—technological pedagogical knowledge, technological content knowledge, and technological pedagogical content knowledge. Recommendations included integrating technology into pre-service courses and creating specific courses or course modules that address issues of online instruction. Online collaborative learning (OCL) theory was previously described as most effective for adult learners in higher education; however, its collaboration and creative problem-solving characteristics may be well suited to middle school through secondary-level online music courses that involve creative collaborations (see chapter 5).

Standards for K–12 online education have been developed by the NEA (2006), by the International Association for K–12 Online Learning (iNACOL, 2011), and by the Quality Matters™ Program, which developed a rubric for grades 6–12 online and blended courses. These standards can also be used for professional development and for design of online teaching field experiences for pre-service teachers (Kennedy & Archambault, 2012). The NEA's *Guide to teaching online courses* (2006) makes recommendations for preparing pre-service teachers for online teaching. Minimum recommended instruction includes content evaluation of Internet resources, compliance with copyright provisions, identification of outstanding educational websites, awareness of accessibility issues, use of appropriate web etiquette, and design of lesson plans that promote students' Internet research skills. The report also recommends a required online course on online pedagogy and practice. Experiences in this course would include instruction and practice with synchronous and asynchronous discussions, discussion facilitation, collaborative experiences designed to build community, content delivery, and lesson creation incorporating peer feedback. Online student teaching experiences are also recommended, one of which could be teaching in an online course under the mentorship and supervision of a master online teacher.

If implemented, the NEA's recommendations would undoubtedly provide a solid foundation for online music teaching at the K–12 level. However, given the current demands on music education curricula, addition of another course may not always be reasonable or possible. Experiencing online music learning in context, as modules within their existing music education courses, and taking small steps that lead to a more comprehensive form of online learning such as a blended course or a flipped classroom model might provide a better introduction to online learning for pre-service music teachers. In this way, music education students would learn principles and practical applications of online learning in a musical context and with direct application to their future professional lives. For example, students in instrumental methods courses might create electronic portfolios that include practice journals, digital or audio recordings of their performances, and reflections on their own progress. This kind of electronic portfolio can be readily used with beginning instrumental students. Instrumental methods courses are also an ideal venue for reviewing current research on online applied lessons at the middle school level and using web-based VoIP (voice over Internet Protocol) software applications to replicate the research. Exposure to this research and introductory experiences with the techniques reported in the studies can pave the way for future online music teaching in which beginning or intermediate students might receive an occasional online lesson and submit their recorded performances to the teacher for evaluation. Use of this kind of technology with instrumental music students can increase their motivation to practice and it can encourage collaborative activities. In a general music methods course, music education majors might create class wikis or WebQuests (inquiry-oriented lessons with most required information derived from web-based resources) on selected composers or musical styles. WebQuests have been used successfully at the K–12 level and can easily be created around music topics. Wikis and WebQuests provide relevant and engaging experiences, particularly for students from elementary through middle school levels. They also ease the prospective music educator into the practice of online instruction. Use of a blended model in selected music education methods courses or other music courses would provide firsthand experience with a form of online learning that is common in K–12 settings. Advancing from a blended model, students may explore development of fully online high school courses in music theory or popular music to provide relevant, engaging, and important learning opportunities for this audience that would not be possible otherwise. Finally, the need to educate pre-service music teachers in techniques of online teaching provides another reason for music education professors to pursue professional development opportunities in this area.

REFERENCES

Archambault, L. (2011). The practitioner's perspective on teacher education: Preparing for the K–12 online classroom. *Journal of Technology and Teacher Education, 19*(1), 73–91.

Bawane, J., & Spector, J. M. (2009). Prioritization of online instructor roles: Implications for competency-based teacher education programs. *Distance Education, 30*(3), 383–397.

Beglau, M., Hare, J. C., Foltos, L., Gann, K., James, J., Jobe, H., Knight, J., & Smith, B. (2011). *Technology, coaching, and community: Partners for improved professional development in primary and secondary education.* International Society for Technology in Education. Retrieved from https://www.iste.org/

Boettcher, J., & Conrad, R. (2010). *The online teaching survival guide: Simple and practical pedagogical tips.* San Francisco: Jossey-Bass.

Harris, J. B. (2008). TPCK in in-service education: Assisting experienced teachers' "planned improvisations." In AACTE Committee on Innovation and Technology (Ed.), *Handbook of technological pedagogical content knowledge (TPCK) for educators* (pp. 251–271). New York: Routledge.

Hebert, D. G. (2008b). Reflections on teaching the aesthetics and sociology of music online. *International Review of the Aesthetics and Sociology of Music, 39*(1), 93–103. Retrieved from JSTOR database.

Heuer, B. P., & King, K. P. (2004). Leading the band: The role of the instructor in online learning for educators. *Journal of Interactive Online Learning, 3*(1), 1–11. Retrieved from http://www.ncolr.org/

International Association for K–12 Online Learning. (2011). National standards for quality online teaching. Version 2. Retrieved from http://www.inacol.org/

International Society for Technology in Education. (2011). ISTE NETS for technology coaches (NETS•C). Retrieved from https://www.iste.org/

Kennedy, K., & Archambault, L. (2012). Design and development of field experiences in K–12 online learning environments. *Journal of Applied Instructional Design, 2*(1), 35–49. Retrieved from http://www.jaidpub.org

King, A. (1993). From sage on the stage to guide on the side. *College Teaching, 41*(1), 20–35.

NEA. (2002). *Guide to online high school courses.* Retrieved from http://www.nea.org/assets/docs/onlinecourses.pdf

NEA. (2006). *Guide to teaching online courses.* Retrieved from http://www.nea.org/assets/docs/onlineteachguide.pdf

Watson, J., Murin, A., Vashaw, L., Gemin, B., & Rapp, C. (2012). *Keeping pace with K–12 online learning: An annual review of policy and practice.* Evergreen, CO: Evergreen Education Group. Retrieved from http://kpk12.com/

CHAPTER 9
Best Practices

Whatever seems to be working should be seen as something that might be improved.
—Frank Mayadas in Gary E. Miller, *Asynchronous learning networks
and distance education: An interview with Frank Mayadas of
the Alfred P. Sloan Foundation*

EFFECTIVE PRACTICES FOR ONLINE LEARNING

Much literature on effective online instruction deals with best practices or effective practices, and the terms may be more or less interchangeable based on their use in the literature. Among the many resources for such practices in higher education are Chickering & Gamson's classic seven principles for good practice in undergraduate education (1987). These practices, which were researched and developed for undergraduate education, can apply as well to graduate education, and as suggested by their title, they have broad application across disciplines. Other scholars and researchers have aligned the seven principles with various technologies and have used them as the basis for design and delivery of online instruction. Various organizations and institutions have also developed sets of best practices for online course design and online pedagogy, including the Quality Matters™ (QM™) program; California State University, Chico; the Illinois Online Network (ION); the Sloan Consortium; and the Multimedia Educational Resource for Learning and Online Teaching (MERLOT). However, at the time of this writing, no best practices specific to online learning in music have been put forth, nor are there any practices relevant to particular music disciplines that would provide more targeted guidance for current and prospective online music instructors.

Following is a brief review of published practices that provides a sampling of best or effective practices in online learning.

SEVEN PRINCIPLES FOR GOOD PRACTICE IN UNDERGRADUATE EDUCATION

The seven principles for good practice in undergraduate education (Chickering & Gamson, 1987) are research-based principles intended as guidelines for improving undergraduate teaching and learning. The work that led to formulation of the principles was co-sponsored by the American Association for Higher Education and the Education Commission of the States with support from the Johnson Foundation. The principles, developed by a panel of higher education scholars and authored by Arthur Chickering & Zelda Gamson, were originally intended to guide the design and delivery of traditional courses and programs, but have since been extended to learning with technology and online learning. According to these principles, good practice in undergraduate education

1. Encourages contacts between students and faculty.
2. Develops reciprocity and cooperation among students.
3. Uses active learning techniques.
4. Gives prompt feedback.
5. Emphasizes time on task.
6. Communicates high expectations.
7. Respects diverse talents and ways of learning. (Chickering & Gamson, 1987, p. 3)

The authors emphasize that the seven principles are not rules but guidelines, that they are research-based, and that many instructors and students have already experienced them. They note that while the individual practices are important, their use in combination increases their effects by tapping the larger educational forces of activity, cooperation, diversity, expectations, interaction, and responsibility (1987, p. 4). They also point out that the principles work as well within professional programs as within the liberal arts and for different types of students. Additionally, the principles address larger pedagogical factors that may be applied as appropriate to specific subject matter in various disciplines. By extension then, they can be applied to education in the music disciplines and also to graduate education. Clearly, most of these principles are centered on constructivist-based teaching practices, notably the use of active learning strategies and authentic instructional tasks, collaborative learning, and the use of multiple and diverse learning formats.

Chickering & Ehrmann (1996) collaborated in describing suitable ways to align then-current technologies with the seven principles. Motivated by an interest in realizing the potential of new technologies and using the appropriate technological tool for any given instructional strategy, they emphasized the use of interactive, relevant, and motivational materials that would be consistent with the aims of the seven principles, and they noted the need for faculty professional development in this area. E-mail, computer conferencing, and web-based tools were cited in support of student/faculty contact, as well as student study groups, collaborative learning, and discussions. They noted the large number of technologies available to support active learning techniques, particularly apprentice-style learning, including use of technology as a tool to create computer-based music.

Principles of effective teaching: Lessons learned for online instruction

Graham, Cagiltay, Craner, Lim, & Duffy (2001) used the seven principles for good practice in undergraduate education to evaluate four online courses and subsequently developed a set of lessons learned to parallel the seven principles: (1) Instructors should provide clear guidelines for interaction with students; (2) well-designed discussion assignments facilitate meaningful cooperation among students; (3) students should present course projects; (4) instructors need to provide two types of feedback: information feedback and acknowledgment feedback; (5) online courses need deadlines; (6) challenging tasks, sample cases, and praise for quality work communicate high expectations; and (7) allowing students to choose project topics incorporates diverse views into online courses. They did not intend these lessons to be definitive, as they emerged from a single evaluation of a small number of courses, but rather to spur additional thought and research. Palloff & Pratt (2003) expanded Graham, et al.'s lessons with additional suggestions for best practice, many of which are commonly found in the literature of online teaching and learning. Some are quite general and apply as stated to online music learning, while others, particularly the use of active learning techniques, suggest the use of specific music learning activities. Taken together, the principles, lessons learned, and practical suggestions provide some guidelines for online learning generally, and they may be further elaborated to provide more specific direction for online learning in music.

Principle 1: Good practice encourages student/faculty contact

Chickering & Gamson emphasized the importance of student/faculty contact in developing motivation and student involvement. *Lesson for online instruction: Instructors should provide clear guidelines for interaction with students.*

Instructors should inform students of their response times for e-mail (e.g., 24 hours) and for returning assignments, and then be sure to observe those times. This is critical in terms of learning, support, and student satisfaction.

Principle 2: Good practice develops reciprocity and cooperation among students

Chickering & Gamson noted the social and collaborative nature of good learning, as this kind of interaction can increase students' involvement and deepen their understanding. *Lesson for online instruction: Well-designed discussion assignments facilitate meaningful cooperation among students.*

Because collaboration and participation in discussions are critical to the formation of a learning community, instructors should provide focused discussion questions that engage students with content, open-ended questions, or tasks designed to produce high-quality responses in which students demonstrate understanding and application of knowledge. Additional discussion forums can support small group work on targeted problem-solving tasks and collaborative projects that have potential to broaden and deepen understanding through social interactions. Instructors should post their expectations for discussions; students are more likely to contribute if participation is required and graded, with the grade based on the quality, not the length, of posts.

Principle 3: Good practice uses active learning techniques

Students learn best when they discuss, write about, and apply what they are learning in practical ways. *Lesson for online instruction: Students should present course projects.*

In-service music teachers taking a graduate-level music psychology course might engage in some action research by implementing strategies they are studying in the course in their own classrooms, such as application of effective practice techniques or strategies for managing performance anxiety, followed by reporting the results to the group and leading an online discussion based on their findings. Music educators in a philosophy of music education course might engage the issue of diversity by simulating a debate on the relationship of religion and music education policy and practice.

Individual students can present projects synchronously or asynchronously, and others in the course can comment on the topic, ask questions, or raise issues related to the topic. Engagement with authentic, real-life issues, case studies, or simulations that not only promote interactive learning but also convey high expectations (principle 6) would precede the presentations. Because not all learning in an online course takes place online, students might also conduct research on an issue of interest and report the findings to the group (see box 9.1).

Principle 4: Good practice gives prompt feedback

Instructor feedback gives students important information about what they know and do not know, helps them assess their own learning, and provides recommendations for improvement. *Lesson for online instruction: Instructors need to provide two types of feedback: information feedback and acknowledgment feedback.*

Instructors need to respond to student questions and provide feedback on assignments in a timely fashion. Information feedback could consist of answers to questions or comments and grades on assignments. Acknowledgment feedback could be an e-mail confirming receipt of a student assignment with an indication of when to expect a more detailed response. Instructors can also provide feedback through contributions to discussion forums that might consist of pointing out connections among related issues or concepts, offering clarifications when students seem uncertain, and summarizing major points or threads. In this case, instructors need to maintain a balance, making their presence known but not dominating the discussion, as too much instructor input can stifle student participation and create a question/answer exchange rather than a true discussion. Instructor feedback plays a particularly important role because it promotes student self-efficacy, which in turn supports more time on task.

Principle 5: Good practice emphasizes time on task

Chickering & Gamson point out the critical importance of time on task, and the need for students to develop good time-management skills. *Lesson for online instruction: Online courses need deadlines.*

Online students need an optimum amount of structure; online courses demand more self-discipline, organization, and time management than do face-to-face courses. Due dates for discussions and assignments provide structure, as well as opportunities to evaluate progress and make recommendations that will help students complete the course successfully. Regularly scheduled synchronous meetings can provide consistent contact with the instructor and other students comparable to the structure built into on-campus face-to-face courses. All of these factors tend to convey high expectations for student achievement.

Principle 6: Good practice communicates high expectations

Chickering & Gamson emphasize that projecting high expectations for all students is critical to their academic success: They reiterate the well-known axiom that expectations become self-fulfilling prophecies as students become aware of them and make increased efforts to meet those expectations. *Lesson for online instruction: Challenging tasks, sample cases, and praise for quality work communicate high expectations.*

Instructors can communicate high standards by designing rigorous and challenging online courses, creating challenging assignments that require analysis and synthesis of reading materials, modeling the quality of discussion posts they expect of students, and requiring and fostering active participation. Positive feedback within a discussion forum on particularly thoughtful or insightful posts communicates high expectations as do individual communications with students who fall behind or fail to participate.

Principle 7: Good practice respects diverse talents and ways of learning

Students need to learn in both ways that tap their strengths and ways that are less familiar to them. *Lesson for online instruction: Allowing students to choose project topics incorporates diverse views into online courses.*

Choice in the selection of projects highlights individual student interests and enriches the course with multiple points of view. It is motivating because it allows students to pursue personally meaningful topics and tasks in ways that build upon their individual strengths. Instructors can also incorporate assignments and learning activities that tap into the various learning modalities (visual, auditory, kinesthetic) and learning styles (e.g., collaborative, reflective). By using multiple media and both collaborative and individual strategies, instructors can provide significant experiences for all students while simultaneously challenging them to use less familiar modalities or styles. These kinds of choices also support student self-efficacy.

BEST PRACTICES: EXAMPLES, PROGRAMS, AND RESOURCES

While earlier literature focused on effective use of technologies, recently, there has been more attention to best practice in online instruction, as exemplified by Graham, et al.'s (2001) application of the seven principles for good practice in undergraduate education to online learning. In addition, some organizations and institutions have developed systems or rubrics to evaluate online learning. The Quality Matters™ organization evaluates online course design and trains faculty as Quality Matters™ evaluators, who then assess the quality of courses at their own institutions and offer recommendations for improvement. California State University, Chico, and the Illinois Online Network have developed and made online course design rubrics publicly available. The Sloan Consortium has compiled an extensive list of effective practices related to several aspects of online learning, and MERLOT maintains a collection of exemplary materials that includes online courses.

Quality Matters™ Program (QM™)

The QM™ program was developed beginning in 2003 by the University of Maryland with a primary focus on online course design and evaluation. A program of quality assurance, it consists of three major components: a rubric, a peer review process, and QM™ professional development. It operates on a subscription basis whereby institutions or individuals can purchase various subscription levels to gain access to resources and materials such as training documents, as well as to the course review process, which may culminate in QM™ certification. QM™ uses the peer evaluation process and the course design rubric to determine the effectiveness of online courses and to make recommendations for improvement of their design. A fully annotated copy of the course design rubric is available only by subscription, but a brief version in PDF format is available on the QM™ website and can be useful even in its abbreviated form to anyone designing an online course.

Design issues: Rubrics, peer review, professional development

The QM™ rubric is research-based, developed from existing best practices with a focus on course design and student learning, and updated regularly. The categories are (1) course overview and introduction; (2) learning objectives; (3) assessment and measurement; (4) resources and materials; (5) learner engagement; (6) course technology; (7) learner support; and (8) accessibility. Standards listed within those categories are assigned a number of points from one to three, with three-point standards considered to be essential standards. To meet the QM™ standards and qualify for QM™ certification, courses must meet all 21 three-point essential standards and earn a number of additional points. Examples of essential standards include a clear introduction to the course; course learning objectives that have measurable outcomes and unit objectives that are congruent with course objectives, with all objectives appropriate to the level of the course; assessments congruent with course objectives and learning activities; course materials that support course and unit objectives together with clear explanations of their use in learning activities; learning activities that lead to achievement of the learning objectives and that support interaction; and technologies that support both the learning objectives and student engagement in active learning experiences. The rubric presents a holistic view of the course, so learning objectives align with assessments, instructional materials, learning activities, and course technology, and all online course components are congruent or, in a musical sense, they are in harmony.

Peer reviews can be either unofficial or official. Unofficial reviews are not required to follow the QM™ process, while official reviews do follow those protocols and are conducted by a paid three-member review team consisting of an experienced reviewer, a subject matter expert, and an external reviewer. Reviews are rigorous and result in specific and detailed feedback. If the course passes the review (i.e., meets all the essential standards and receives the required number of points), it is recognized by QM™ and is registered on the QM™ website.

QM™ training workshops and courses provide professional development and certification. Professional development workshops deal with topics including application of the QM™ rubric, building or improving an online course, and building a blended course. Other workshops focus on meeting and aligning QM™ standards. Certifications include a peer reviewer certification, master reviewer training, and independent trainer certification.

California State University, Chico

California State University (CSU), Chico, actively supports and encourages use of academic technologies, particularly online and web-enhanced courses, to create high-quality learning environments. The rubric for online instruction was created to provide a structure for designing and evaluating online courses. The rubric may be used to evaluate and revise existing courses for online offering or to guide the design of new courses specifically for the online environment. Internally, it may be used as a basis for recognizing instructors for exemplary online courses. The complete rubric is available on the CSU, Chico website.

Rubric for online instruction

The CSU rubric is organized into six categories: (1) learner and support resources; (2) online organization and design; (3) instructional design and delivery; (4) assessment and evaluation of student learning; (5) innovative teaching with technology; and (6) faculty use of student feedback. Baseline, effective, and exemplary performance quality levels are provided for each component. Although the primary emphasis is on design, some useful references to process are given in some categories. According to the rubric, exemplary course designs emphasize congruence among course goals, learning objectives, learning activities, and assessments. Various interactions are optimized: student/student, student/instructor, and student/content. Different learning modalities and styles are addressed through the use of multiple kinds of learning activities and supported by a variety of multimedia elements. Learning activities address multiple learning modalities and promote critical thinking and problem-solving. Regular, prompt instructor feedback is provided throughout the course. Finally, a variety of technological tools support communication, and new instructional methods promote interactive student engagement.

Illinois Online Network (ION)

With the goal of helping colleges and universities improve accountability in their online courses, the ION and the Illinois Virtual Campus in partnership with various Illinois higher education institutions, introduced the quality online course initiative (QOCI). Objectives of the initiative include creation of a rubric to help faculty develop and evaluate quality online courses and identification of best practices in online courses. Although it was designed for use in colleges and universities in the state of Illinois, the QOCI rubric is publicly available on the ION website and would be a useful and informative resource for anyone wishing to develop a quality online course.

Quality online course initiative (QOCI) rubric

The QOCI rubric consists of six categories: (1) instructional design; (2) communication, interaction, and collaboration; (3) student evaluation and assessment; (4) learner support and resources; (5) web design; and (6) course evaluation. Five categories are provided to indicate the level to which a course provides evidence of meeting a particular criterion: nonexistent, developing, meets, exceeds, and not applicable. The instructional design category accounts for use of varied instructional approaches that relate to multiple learning styles, learning strategies, and learning preferences. Items in this category include structure, such as sequencing and grouping of material to facilitate student achievement of course goals; clear statement of course goals; alignment of learning objectives with course goals; instructional strategies that use multiple delivery approaches and address multiple learning styles; and multiple ways for students to demonstrate their knowledge. The second category—communication, interaction and collaboration—considers the impact of course design, assignments, and technology on collaboration among students, as well as on student/instructor/content interaction. Subcategories include provision of opportunities for all three kinds of interaction; discussion forums organized to support these various interactions; and clearly stated expectations and due dates for group work. The student evaluation and assessment and learner support categories are related to institutional processes in those areas. Subcategories reflect the alignment of goals and objectives and use of multiple approaches listed under other categories of the rubric. They include alignment of assessment and evaluation with learning objectives; use of multiple methods of assessment; and timing and type of feedback to students. Web design issues refer to technical issues related to course management systems, such as standards for use of multimedia. Course evaluation provides opportunities for student feedback on various issues, which is used for course improvement.

Sloan-C effective practices

The Alfred P. Sloan Foundation's Sloan Consortium (Sloan-C) compiled a list of effective practices (Moore, 2012) for online learning based on the five pillars of quality online education (Moore, 2005), which serve as a framework for the design, delivery, and evaluation of quality online instruction. Included are effective practices for student satisfaction, learning effectiveness, scale (formerly cost-effectiveness), access, and faculty satisfaction. And just as the five pillars are "related and interdependent" (Moore, 2012, p. 93), quality in each category of practices also influences quality in other categories.

The specific practices are submitted by Sloan-C members and member institutions. They have been deemed excellent by reason of five criteria: innovation (inventiveness or originality); replicability (capability of being replicated in multiple learning environments); potential impact (capability of advancing the field if widely adopted); supporting documentation (evidence of effectiveness); and scope (relationship with other categories of quality elements). Practices are framed by questions that arise frequently, although as the field continues to develop, new and different issues and questions will continue to appear. The collection is seen as a work in progress that should evolve to incorporate new possibilities enabled by new technologies: "...the questions are by no means comprehensive, and the practices suggest a multitude of innovations still to be developed and shared" (Moore, 2012, p. 112). The following sampling of broadly applicable questions and effective practices may serve as a starting point for development of practices more directly related to online learning in music.

Student satisfaction, learning effectiveness, scale, access, and faculty satisfaction

The report *A Synthesis of Sloan-C Effective Practices, December 2011* presents a brief narrative about Sloan-C's goals in each of the five categories, followed by a set of practices relevant to that category. A short description of each practice is given, with links to a detailed description of the practice, the authors, and their institutions. Practices most relevant to this discussion are those concerning student satisfaction, learning effectiveness, and faculty satisfaction. Scale and access, while important, are less directly related to instructional issues, and are therefore not detailed to the same extent as the other three categories.

Student satisfaction implies that students are successful in online learning and are pleased with their online learning experiences. Analysis of student attitudes includes these contributing factors: a satisfactory orientation to online learning; student services rated at least as good as those on campus; satisfactory interaction with instructor and other students; learning experiences that meet student expectations; and outcomes relevant to students' academic and professional goals. Student services comparable to on-campus services are thought to support equivalent quality between online and on-campus courses. Effective practices in these categories are framed within questions of how schools can introduce students to online learning (a comprehensive online resource center for online students; an online student guide), help them make good choices regarding time management and course selection (videos in which the professor welcomes students to the course), build an online learning community (emphasis within a course on the importance of student/faculty interaction; a course community website where students can share pictures and work; use of cohorts), assess student satisfaction (student use of a teacher-created template for organizing the online week), increase student satisfaction with learning (use of convenient, flexible, relevant, and engaging activities such as case studies and e-portfolios), and use technology to enhance online learning (use of audio feedback to students; student use of online collaborative document editors).

The goal for learning effectiveness is that online learning quality is comparable to that of traditional programs. Evaluation of learning effectiveness includes these factors: the critical role of interaction with the instructor, other students, the content, and the interface; comparable learning outcomes between online and on-campus courses; optimum use of the digital medium to improve learning in online courses; and emphasis on communication and building of an online learning community. Three questions frame the learning effectiveness practices: how learning design can enhance interaction (emphasis on social presence achieved through introductions that include student profiles with photos; posting definitions of effective communication; using student-led discussions; use of the QM™ rubric as a guide for course development), how learning design can enhance collaboration (online peer evaluation of written assignments), how learning design can teach academic honesty (practices that emphasize understanding of academic integrity policies; use of a proctoring service for secure testing), and how institutions can assess learning effectiveness (use of e-portfolios available to the public; use of the community of inquiry model to build online relationships that increase motivation and produce superior learning outcomes).

Scale involves issues of cost-effectiveness associated with offering a high-quality education to a maximum number of students at an affordable cost, including resource sharing and partnering with other institutions as cost-reducing strategies. Practices include larger projects such as statewide library consortia for sharing of instructional resources across multiple institutions.

Access involves facilitating learning opportunities in multiple ways. It includes providing opportunities for diverse learners including at-risk learners, learners with disabilities, and expert learners; using learner-centered courseware; using student feedback to improve offerings and procedures; and monitoring delivery systems for functionality and reliability. Practices include using links to services within course sites and using a flexible design process that provides students with a choice of attendance options.

Faculty satisfaction is related to institutional commitment and policies regarding online instruction, as well as to their own success in online teaching. Contributing factors in this category include improvement in online teaching over time; a reward structure for online teaching and research on online teaching; an equivalent workload between on-campus and online teaching; and institutionally provided training and technical support. Among questions framing the faculty satisfaction practices are the following: how institutions can enhance community among faculty (CSU, Chico's rubric for online instruction, created to guide and encourage exemplary online courses and teaching; a best practices online showcase where online instructors can meet and share their best practices), how institutions can prepare faculty for effective online teaching (self-paced faculty development programs and teaching aids; online asynchronous faculty training and support sites; short-term summer faculty development programs), how they can reward online faculty (online teaching showcases; recognition for innovative uses of technology to improve learning; modifications of promotion and tenure processes; addition of technology scholarship to the reward structure), and how technology can enable faculty activities (provision of an online faculty instructional design toolkit requiring little instructional design expertise; faculty development blog; MERLOT collection of online instructional materials).

Effective practices for blended learning

In a study of literature on effective practices for blended course design, McGee & Reis (2012) found characteristics unique to blended courses that distinguish them from fully online courses. A qualitative meta-analysis revealed some common principles concerning instructional design, pedagogical strategies, online and classroom technology use, assessment strategies, and course implementation and student readiness (p. 7). The findings highlighted consistent recommendations, particularly for redesign of traditional courses for blended instruction. However, attempts to compile best practices for blended learning are complicated by the existence of multiple conceptualizations of what blended learning is. For example, practices relevant to an on-campus course that includes asynchronous discussions may not be applicable to a flexible learning model in which students can choose to attend particular classes online or in person, nor to an online course that blends asynchronous discussions with synchronous online meetings. These practices are more thoroughly discussed in chapter 7.

Multimedia educational resource for learning and online teaching (MERLOT)

The Multimedia Educational Resource for Learning and Online Teaching (MERLOT), a program of California State University, is an open, online collection of peer-reviewed higher education online learning materials and a group of faculty development support services. Developed in 1997, its strategic goal is improvement of online teaching and learning effectiveness by making exemplary peer-reviewed materials available that can be incorporated into other online courses. Membership in MERLOT is free and entitles members to contribute materials, as well as to submit learning materials for evaluation. MERLOT also holds an annual conference and publishes the *Journal of Online Learning and Teaching* (JOLT), a peer-reviewed online publication featuring scholarly uses of multimedia instructional resources.

Content for online teaching and learning

Learning materials on the MERLOT site are categorized within 19 material types and 20 technical formats, and organized into 19 academic discipline communities, including music. The material types include animations, case studies, e-portfolios, online courses, simulations, and tutorials. Technical formats include Flash, image, PDF, podcast, QuickTime, video, and wiki. For each discipline, there is a portal with links to teaching (suggested uses for materials that include self-study, small-group, and whole-class assignments), people (peer reviewers), learning materials (subject matter categories with links), and more.

The MERLOT music portal provides ready access to music-related materials and resources. Learning materials listed here are considered learning objects that can be reused in multiple ways and in multiple courses. The portal is organized in subject matter categories of aural skill and ear training; composition; music appreciation; music education; music history; music technology; performance; theory and analysis; and world music. Search options allow selection by subject matter category and material type, with more than 50 examples of online courses available for viewing. Detailed information on these materials includes a brief description, keywords, primary audience, and mobile compatibility. Some course listings display peer review information including a rating, while others have not been peer-reviewed. In addition, registered members may log in to post comments on any material. If comments are available, the user is identified, and a rating is displayed along with an indication of whether the material was used in the classroom. These materials and courses may be useful in generating ideas for online courses, as well as providing some ready-made supplementary materials.

WHAT WORKS: THE GOOD, THE BAD, AND THE BEST YOU CAN DO

Lists and descriptions of best practices for online teaching and learning can serve instructors well as general guidelines, but to be truly useful, they must be contextual, addressing issues specific to the discipline in which they are to be used. As Christensen, Horn, & Johnson pointed out, "No longer will research on best practices or what works best on average across education suffice" (2008, p. 162). Many of the best and effective practices for online learning are intentionally general and apply to music learning in a broad, nonspecific sense; however, online music instructors will develop relevant applications of some of the practices at increasingly fine-grained levels. In music, the particular application will vary depending upon the music subdiscipline, and even within the music subdisciplines, there will be variations. For example, in building upon the principle "Good practice uses active learning techniques" (Chickering & Gamson, 1987), online music instructors will first consider characteristics of active learning and typical active learning assignments, and then look to the various music subdisciplines—music history, music theory, music education, music technology— for specific active learning techniques in those content areas. And they will look to the technologies that can support those or comparable activities in the online environment or that will enable activities that are possible only with the use of Internet resources.

The collections of practices demonstrate the many varied ways that individuals and institutions approach important issues of online teaching and learning. Although they were developed by and for particular institutions, programs, or courses, their appearance in a peer-reviewed collection suggests professional endorsement of their quality. However, that implied endorsement should not be taken to imply broad applicability in every situation. These practices should be considered examples of well-thought-out responses to issues and needs of online learning in specific environments. As such, we do not want to simply transplant a practice from one institution, program, or course to another, but rather to rethink the practice as it might be incorporated into a new or different context and what adaptations might be warranted in view of the mission, characteristics, and goals in our own setting. Therefore, the preferred approach would be replicating the process that resulted in that practice in one's own environment to create a solution uniquely applicable to one's own setting. Ultimately, in music as in other disciplines, excellent online teaching consists of more than simply integrating best practices, many of which focus on the use of specific tools and techniques, into one's teaching.

Having journeyed through the *Seven Principles for Good Practice in Undergraduate Education* (Chickering & Gamson, 1987), through the same seven principles linked to technology (Chickering & Ehrmann, 1996) and then applied to online learning (Graham, et al., 2001; Palloff & Pratt, 2003); having proceeded to implications for best practice suggested by the five pillars of quality online education (Moore, 2005); having analyzed rubrics for online teaching (QM™; CSU, Chico); and having examined multiple successful practices employed by individual instructors and institutions, it would be beneficial to return once more to a broader view, to reflect upon the many possible practices, and to consider a few more timeless teaching principles. Perhaps a more productive approach to the development of best or excellent practice (not practices) in online music instruction would be to shift the focus from discrete practices to the larger picture—the art of teaching music online. This view can provide a framework in which the science of online music teaching and learning can take shape, one in which the more global features of the art of online teaching complement the specific best practices that emerge from systematic research on various techniques and strategies within our own music subdisciplines. It can provide focus and overall direction for the development of excellent online teaching, in which prospective and current online music instructors may develop their own best approaches.

Successful college teaching

We might take a cue from Ken Bain's well-known volume *What the Best College Teachers Do* (2004), and begin to examine the more elusive characteristics of excellent online music instructors. Bain notes that his conclusions transcend common comparisons of rival approaches and styles, such as "guide on the side" versus "sage on the stage," and states that

> ...the key to understanding the best teaching can be found not in particular practices or rules but in the *attitudes* of the teachers, in their *faith* in their students' ability to achieve, in their *willingness* to take their students seriously and to let them assume control of their own education, and in their *commitment* to let all policies and practices flow from central learning objectives and from a mutual respect and agreement between students and teachers. (pp. 78–79)

He defines the best teachers as those who have "achieved remarkable success in helping their students learn in ways that made a sustained, substantial, and positive influence on how those students think, act, and feel" (2004, p. 5). Evidence for this achievement varies by individual and discipline. It was obtained through observations, videotapes, conversations, examination of course materials, and more. Conclusions were based on broad questions in six areas: what the best teachers know and understand; how they prepare to teach; what they expect of their students; what they do when they teach; how they treat their students; and how they check their progress and evaluate their efforts. In using the findings to improve teaching, he offers the following advice:

> We cannot take single pieces of the patterns noted here and simply combine them with other, less effective or even destructive habits and expect them to transform someone's teaching any more than adopting Rembrandt's brush strokes would, by itself, replicate his genius. We must understand the thinking, attitudes, values, and concepts that lie behind pedagogical masterpieces, observe practices carefully but then begin to digest, transform, and individualize what we see....So too must teachers adjust every idea to who they are and what they teach. (pp. 20–21)

In describing successful teaching, Bain explains, "First, some underlying principles cut across practice and shape the learning environment....Second, a few key techniques propel the application of those principles" (2004, p. 99). The underlying principles are these: Create a natural critical learning environment;

get their attention and keep it; start with the students rather than the discipline; seek commitments; help students learn outside of class; engage students in disciplinary thinking; and create diverse learning experiences. He emphasizes that if these principles are to be successful, professors must implement them in a "performance in front of students" (p. 117). We might consider this performance to constitute the art of teaching. The teaching performance is driven by the techniques or the craft of teaching, which Bain organizes into two major categories: "the ability to talk and the ability to get students to talk" (p. 117). Included in the ability to talk are "good talk, warm language, and making explanations." Getting students to talk is treated separately.

Creation of a "natural critical learning environment," the first of the underlying principles, is the central point around which most of the other principles seem to cluster. "Natural" refers to the use of authentic tasks and questions that students consider important and interesting; "critical" refers to the need for students to engage in critical thinking. Bain identifies five elements that constitute that environment. First is the use of intriguing and authentic questions or problems that seem important to students and that are similar to issues dealt with by professionals in the field. We might paraphrase Jerome Bruner in this context: "The student learning music *is* a musician, and it is easier for him or her to learn music behaving like a musician than doing something else" (Bruner, 1977, p. 14). The "something else" might be readings about conclusions in a discipline rather than direct involvement in inquiry within that discipline. This is a key issue for online learning: A natural critical learning environment can be created in a face-to-face setting, as described by Bain, or in an online one. The difference would be in the specifics of how to create it, given the physical and technological differences between the two settings. The second element is helping students understand the importance of the questions or problems; the third, engaging them in higher-order thinking about the questions—comparing, applying, and making judgments about them; the fourth, encouraging students to develop their own answers or explanations; and the fifth, leaving students with the next questions about the original problem.

First among the techniques of the craft of teaching—the ability to talk and the ability to get students to talk—is what Bain refers to as "good talk" (p. 117), a conversational tone that includes instructor interaction with students, encouragement for students to interact with each other, a change of pace at ten-minute intervals, and the use of humor. Warm language, commonly understood as telling a story or bringing a topic to life by providing details and explanations, is designed to draw the listener into the topic; cool language involves talking about a topic without the more engaging details that capture the listener's imagination. In making explanations, an instructor offers a generalization or analogy that helps students understand subject matter in familiar terms, and then moves on to more specific and complex aspects. An important factor in getting students to talk reflects back directly to the natural critical learning environment: discussion of a topic that seems important to students and that engages them in solving a problem (i.e., discussion of ideas rather than discussion of readings).

Successful online college teaching

Bain's ideas have been applied to online learning in a university-wide faculty development program (Brinthaupt, Fisher, Gardner, Raffo, & Woodard, 2011). Participants explored ways to foster student engagement, stimulate intellectual development, and build rapport with online students. The ideas they put forth are similar to those found in other models, notably in Moore's (1989) three types of interaction—interaction of students with other students, with the instructor, and with content; in the community of inquiry theory (Garrison, 2011) with its focus on social, cognitive, and teaching presences; and in the seven principles of good practice for undergraduate education (Chickering & Gamson, 1987). The similarities highlight the many connections that can be made among these theories and models. Fostering student engagement, for example, includes developing a community of learners, furthering interaction among students and faculty, using humor in purposeful ways, and using discussion forums and wikis to support collaborative learning. Stimulating intellectual development brings into play Bain's "natural critical learning environment," which is built upon generative questioning and engagement with authentic tasks together with use of technology like video to create authentic content, and use of wikis, blogs, and discussion forums to explore questions. Building rapport with online students may involve use of video introductions and individual feedback on assignments and other learning activities. Bain states, "The best teaching creates a sense that everyone is working together and the questions, issues, and problems are authentic: they seem important to students and are similar to those that professionals in the field might undertake" (Bain, 204, p. 100). His statement aligns with the three components selected by Brinthaupt, et al. (2011) and their implications: A sense that everyone is working together suggests student engagement supported by rapport among students and instructors, while promotion of intellectual development implies engagement

Box 9.2

A question or problem for students in a music history or music research course might be presented through a brief scenario such as the following:

Your parents are selling great-great-grandma's house, and you are helping sort through some of her effects. You are given the task of examining the contents of a trunk that was shipped from Germany in the late 1800s. Inside the trunk, you find a musical score that appears to be handwritten. You notice that the name "Schumann" appears on the score where you would expect to find the composer's name, and you wonder whether this could be an original score. How can you determine the nature and value of this score? What would you look for? Who could you consult to help you figure this out?

In the process of investigating this problem, students would acquire a vocabulary for discussing authentication of historical documents, learn the technical procedures—internal and external criteria—for determining authenticity, sift through historical information relevant to the problem, frame important questions about it, and engage in processes of musicological inquiry used by professionals in the field. In an online course, the scenario could be presented as a problem that students will attempt to solve together. A first step might be posting potential investigative strategies to an asynchronous discussion forum and developing a consensus on how to proceed in collaboration with each other and the instructor. Small groups might be assigned or choose to work on the various tasks involved in the investigation, reporting their findings and drawing conclusions based on their collective findings.

with authentic tasks. The authors argue that while these components should not depend on delivery mode, technology does exert an influence on how they are demonstrated. Specific application to online music instruction would take this kind of work to the next level and provide contextual guidance, as well as inspiration for online music instructors (see box 9.2).

Anecdotal examples from the field

Understanding how someone approached a teaching issue and observing how that approach did or didn't resolve it is more helpful than simply adopting a best practice that may not suit one's own situation. Discovering what works, what does not work, and why it does or does not work is more useful, as successes often emerge from multiple failed or less successful attempts and depend upon the particular students and the particular context. Therefore, these anecdotes are presented as examples of how some online music instructors have thought about and approached various issues and challenges of online learning in music, along with their results and sometimes their next steps, which were purposefully devised and sometimes improvised to address their particular situations. "To an experienced educator, teaching is much like a jazz performance: a well-practiced fusion of careful, creative planning and spontaneous improvisation" (Harris, 2008, p. 251).

What's it all about?

Professor A reported that during a synchronous chat about five weeks into her course, a graduate student interrupted the discussion, saying "What is this course all about? I just don't get it." The (stunned) professor wondered whether the student had read the syllabus, as a detailed course description and major topics were provided there. Additionally, in the first synchronous meeting, which this student attended, the professor explained how all the major topics connected to each other and displayed a simple concept map of the course. To dispel the student's confusion, she again explained the flow of topics in the course and how they related to each other. The professor realized that although she always kept the big picture in mind, she could not assume that the students would do so, and that more direction would be needed in addition to the introductions included in weekly class folders on the course site. The student's question prompted the professor to rethink the way she initially presents an overall picture of the course and to begin subsequent synchronous meetings with a review of where they were in the course, how that would lead to where they were going next, and to point out connections along the way.

Technical difficulties

Professor B scheduled student presentations for the last two synchronous sessions of his course. Students were instructed to give brief summaries of their individual projects and to be prepared to respond to questions and comments from other participants. One student was unable to log in to the live classroom on the evening of her assigned presentation and was not available on the alternate evening because of her school's concert schedule. The student was understandably frustrated by the situation and concerned about her grade. The professor quickly resolved the situation and eased the student's mind. He informed her that grades are not affected by technical difficulties, and he made the presenter tools for the learning management system's synchronous meeting available. The student was able to record her presentation and archive it. The other students were then able to view her presentation, comment on it, and ask questions in a discussion forum he created for that purpose.

Getting together

Professor C wanted to foster collaborative learning in her graduate-level course. The plan was for students to identify major issues of a general topic in a full-group synchronous meeting, to form small groups based on issues of interest, and for those small groups to meet in synchronous discussions to explore the topics and reach consensus on a solution. Final results were to be presented in another full-group synchronous meeting. Students soon reported that it was very difficult to arrange common meeting times, and that they would prefer to do individual projects. However, the idea behind the project was to explore a single issue from different perspectives in order to arrive at a solution that could work in various situations. Therefore, the professor, still wanting to use a collaborative approach, revised the assignment as a wiki, with pages for each of the major issues. Using the wiki, students were able to contribute and collaborate without the added stress of arranging additional meetings within their busy schedules. This professor will continue to use wikis for selected collaborative assignments.

There must be a better way

Professor D had been assigning a research paper in her online graduate music psychology courses, but she wanted a better indication of what her students were actually learning, what they took away from the course, and how they were able to apply what they learned in class in their teaching. It seemed that there had to be an alternative that would be academically challenging and provide the practical information she sought. She changed the research paper requirement to a learning portfolio (e-portfolio) assignment. The learning portfolio was to include a narrative describing key concepts the students learned during the course, what connections they perceived among the concepts, what they learned about how to use or apply the concepts in their teaching, and how their thinking changed as a result of their study. The portfolio also included samples of work such as short essays on selected topics (e.g., how current neuroscientific research suggests changes they might make in their teaching practice). The e-portfolios were more satisfactory as a final project because they contained traditional academic work (papers) and, more important, they provided documented evidence of student learning. The professor intends to retain and possibly refine this assignment.

Inversions

In a face-to-face music technology course, Professor E is experimenting with the flipped classroom, a type of blended model. (A flipped or inverted classroom reverses the traditional sequence: in-class lecture followed by homework. Instead, students do homework that typically consists of listening to recorded lectures, completing digital readings, and participating in a discussion forum in preparation for an active class in which they work on projects.) He created video and screencast tutorials that students watch outside of class and used class time for practical applications and projects. He feels that this model makes more time available for creativity in class, and he designs creative activities that make use of procedures demonstrated in the recorded presentations.

Music and math

Professor F adapted the Khan Academy model for use in her online music theory course. She creates videos for her music theory course in which she solves analytical and part-writing "puzzles," engaging her students in musical problem-solving by using techniques that work for math and science problem-solving. In addition, her students use a free online notation program to complete short theory exercises.

Momentum toward the finish line

Professors G and H try to link all the courses in their graduate music education programs and create transitions between them. Their introductory research and bibliography courses incorporate various types of writing assignments including a blog, an annotated bibliography, a review of the literature, and a final paper in which students describe a research problem. The research problem is elaborated and discussed in a music psychology course. It is developed into a research proposal in a music research design course and finally carried out as a practical final project. The blog is maintained throughout the process.

In conclusion, as we move forward with online learning in music, promising and effective practices may be more appropriate descriptors than best practices. Given the various approaches and pedagogical strategies available to us, the fundamental question is what practices are best for whom in what context. For music in higher education, those contexts include undergraduate and graduate students, music majors and music in general studies, and the various music subdisciplines that comprise degree programs in music and music in general studies. Practices that seem promising in graduate-level music studies may be less effective at the undergraduate level, though upon repeated trials, promising practices may prove effective. Best practices are not generic; they are contextual. Identification of promising and effective practices should lead to development of principles for good practice in online music learning. And these practices and principles carry implications for professional development as well. It will be important to continue to experiment with techniques and strategies for online learning in music and to share the results for the benefit of all who are engaged in online music instruction in higher education.

REFERENCES

Bain, K. (2004). *What the best college teachers do*. Cambridge, MA: Harvard University Press.

Brinthaupt, T. M., Fisher, L. S., Gardner, J. G., Raffo, D. M., & Woodard, J. B. (2011). What the best online teachers should do. *MERLOT Journal of Online Learning and Teaching, 7*(4), 515–524.

Bruner, J. (1977). *The process of education*. Cambridge, MA: Harvard University Press.

Chickering, A. W., & Erhmann, S. C. (1996). Implementing the seven principles: Technology as lever. *AAHE Bulletin, 49*(2), 3–6.

Chickering, A. W., & Gamson, Z. F. (1987). Seven principles for good practice in undergraduate education. *AAHE Bulletin, 39*(7), 3–7.

Christensen, C. M., Horn, M. B., & Johnson, C. W. (2008). *Disrupting class. How disruptive innovation will change the way the world learns*. New York: McGraw-Hill.

Graham, C., Cagiltay, K., Lim, B., Craner, J., & Duffy, T. M. (2001). Seven principles of effective teaching: A practical lens for evaluating online courses. *The Technology Source* (March/April). Retrieved from http://technologysource.org/article/seven_principles_of_effective_teaching/

Harris, J. B. (2008). TPCK in in-service education: Assisting experienced teachers' "planned improvisations." In AACTE Committee on Innovation and Technology (Ed.), *Handbook of technological pedagogical content knowledge (TPCK) for educators* (pp. 251–271). New York: Routledge.

Illinois Online Network. Illinois quality online course initiative rubric. Retrieved from http://www.ion.uillinois.edu/initiatives/qoci/index.asp

McGee, P., & Reis, A. (2012). Blended course design: A synthesis of best practices. *Journal of Asynchronous Learning Networks, 16*(4), 7–22. Retrieved from http://sloanconsortium.org/jaln/v16n4/blended-course-design-synthesis-b est-practices

Miller, G. (1997). Asynchronous learning networks and distance education: An interview with Frank Mayadas of the Alfred P. Sloan Foundation. Reprinted from *American Journal of Distance Education, 11*(3), 71–75. Retrieved from http://sloanconsortium.org/mayadas_interview_97

Moore, J. C. (2005). *The Sloan Consortium quality framework and the five pillars.* Retrieved from http://sloanconsortium.org/publications/freedownloads

Moore, J. C. (2012). A synthesis of Sloan-C effective practices, December 2011. *Journal of Asynchronous Learning Networks, 16*(1), 91–115. Retrieved from http://sloanconsortium.org/jaln/v16n1/synthesis-sloan-c-effective-practi ces-december-2011

Palloff, R. M., & Pratt, K. (2003). *The virtual student: A profile and guide to working with online learners.* San Francisco: Jossey-Bass.

Quality Matters™ rubric standards 2011–2013 edition with assigned point values. Retrieved from https://www.qualitymatters.org/

Rubric for online instruction. (2009). California State University, Chico. Retrieved from http://www.csuchico.edu/roi/

CHAPTER 10

Trends, Tools, Techniques, and Transformation

The information technology lens on the future has always been a cloudy one. We see through the glass darkly, discovering later that we have understated the enormity of change wrought by existing or unimagined technologies while we have overstated the pace of change.

—Richard N. Katz, *Scholars, scholarship, and the scholarly enterprise in the digital age*

ON THE HORIZON

Any attempt to predict the future of online learning, and by association, online learning in music, is almost certain to miss the mark: Predictions can be notoriously inaccurate. However, well-researched extrapolation from current trends to the near future can provide valuable insights and reasonable direction for planning. We can look to historical cycles in the development of computer-based technologies for insight into what technologies might become available for education in the near future. We can examine the evolution of distance education for insights into current practice and what might be the next logical steps. We can look to broad theories of innovation, such as the theory of disruptive innovation, for insight into developments likely to impact our current models of education. We can observe current technologies and how people use them in everyday life to develop innovative, new teaching approaches that are more relevant to life in the 21st century.

The New Media Consortium's Horizon Project has been engaged in this kind of effort since 2002, and the first *Horizon Report* was published in 2004. The Horizon Project is a research venture undertaken by an international group of experts in education, technology, and other areas. This group identifies significant trends and challenges that will be important within higher education for the coming five years. The group also identifies emerging technologies that are likely to have significant impact on teaching, learning, and creative inquiry over the next five years. The purpose of the report is not to predict—the examples cited in the report are drawn from various institutions that are already working with all the featured technologies—but to point out emerging technologies that show potential for broader impact among other institutions. The findings have implications for both the traditional classroom and online learning.

Similarly, since 2004, the EDUCAUSE Center for Applied Research (ECAR) has conducted an annual survey of undergraduate students and information technology to identify ownership and usage patterns, skills with and preferences for various technologies, and the effect of digital technologies on their college experiences. The annual ECAR report on undergraduate students and information technology considers trends in the changing behaviors and opinions of undergraduate students as indicators of the technology needs of future students. Unlike many other reports, this one represents the student perspective on digital technologies for everyday and instructional use. It analyzes current undergraduate student behaviors as indicators of mainstream technology use that can inform future faculty technology adoption in both traditional classrooms and online settings. Like the *Horizon Report*, the ECAR report does not predict, but rather studies short-term and long-term trends and extrapolates to near future needs.

Near-, mid-, and long-term technologies: *Horizon Reports*

The *NMC Horizon Report* is published annually in three editions—higher education, K–12 education, and museum education. Each report features key trends and significant challenges that will be important in the next five years, along with six emerging technologies likely to be widely implemented within three adoption horizons over the coming five years: a near-term horizon of the next 12 months, a mid-term horizon of two to three years, and a far-term horizon of four to five years. The *Horizon Reports* for higher education identify and describe trends, challenges, and emerging technologies that are likely to have significant impacts on teaching, learning, and creative inquiry in higher education. Key trends identified in the 2013 higher education edition (Johnson, et al., 2013) include openness, massively open online courses, informal learning, learning analytics, the changing role of educators, and hybrid learning models. Significant challenges that directly affect online learning include faculty training in digital media literacy, comfort with the status quo, demand for personalized learning, challenges presented by new models of education, and lack of use by academics of new technologies for teaching, learning, and research. However, the report points out that circumstances within particular institutions are likely to be the most important influence on decisions regarding technology adoption.

Technologies identified for entry into higher education mainstream use within a one-year timeframe include massively open online courses (MOOCs) and tablet computing. While MOOCs were not included in any adoption category of the previous year's report, they appear as the first technology in the near-term category of the 2013 report. Based on their rapid growth and the intense interest generated by the free offerings of major providers, the report projects continued growth and increased influence of MOOCs within the next year. In line with current thinking about personalized learning, MOOCs provide opportunities for individuals to pursue specific interests without needing to enroll in a particular institution or program. Features common to most MOOCs include centrally located course materials that include recorded lectures, automated assessment software, cloud-based collaboration services, and online discussion forums. While the quality of materials is high and the MOOC model is seen as promising, the pedagogy is rooted in a traditional lecture format. "Open" refers primarily to there being no charge; however, there is some movement toward charging for certifications. Although there are questions about challenges involved with these large-scale models, including quality, interaction, sustainability, and assessment strategies, they are stimulating discussions about online learning. Among examples of MOOCs offered across various disciplines is a course focused on music listening that can be taken for credit (Indiana University-Purdue University, Indianapolis, and the Purdue University Department of Music and Arts Technology: "Music for the Listener"). The popularity of tablets in higher education is partly a result of the bring-your-own-device movement. By loading their choice of apps, textbooks, and other content, students can create their own personalized learning environments. Tablets equipped with WiFi or cellular network capabilities provide anytime/anyplace access to course materials via learning management system mobile apps.

Technologies expected to be widely adopted within the mid-term horizon of two to three years include games and gamification and learning analytics. Game-based learning appeared in the two previous *Horizon Reports* (Johnson, Adams, & Cummins, 2012; Johnson, Smith, Willis, Levine, & Haywood, 2011); these reports highlighted the usefulness of games in simulating real-world experiences and their ability to promote student collaboration, problem-solving, procedural thinking, and engagement in learning. The 2013 report expands this category to games and gamification, moving beyond integration of games into the curriculum and broadening the perspective to gamer culture and game design. In gamified curricula, game elements are integrated into learning activities other than games. In these environments, students have the opportunity to earn points or other kinds of rewards by meeting certain challenges, and they may have some choice in the types of assignments they complete in order to earn the points or rewards. Among examples of games and gamification is an orchestra simulation game that uses high-definition panoramic video and surround sound to replicate the experience of playing in an orchestra (McGill University: "Open Orchestra"). Learning analytics, included in the report for the third year, deals with use of large amounts of student data, particularly data available through learning management systems (LMS), to customize learning platforms and personalize the learning experience by suggesting additional resources to students.

Projected for adoption within the far-term horizon of four to five years are 3-D printing and wearable technology. Although there are some musical applications of both technologies, including experiments with 3-D records and musical instruments and a playable T-shirt-based drum machine, they are less directly applicable to online learning and therefore will not be explored further.

Massively open online courses (MOOCs)

The term massively open online courses or MOOCs was coined by Bryan Alexander and Dave Cormier to describe a course taught in 2008 by Stephen Downes and George Siemens, titled "Connectivism and Connective Knowledge" (Hill, 2012, p. 92). It referred to web-based courses that could be taken by anyone anywhere in the world, with potential for thousands of students. The original concept was that the course and materials would be open source and free, with an option to pay a fee for university credit. Pedagogically, the vision was for collective continued knowledge production through connections and discussions among course participants. As implemented currently, MOOCs focus more on content mastery in topic areas conducive to independent study, and therefore the components of the term MOOC bear some clarification. There is no firm definition of massive, as these courses may attract as few as 100 to over 100,000 participants. Open refers primarily to no charge or tuition for courses. Content is rarely open or available for reuse, and a password is usually required for participation. MOOCs are delivered in an online format; however, some may include opportunities for face-to-face interaction.

Three major MOOC platforms were founded in 2012, with courses typically hosted on readily accessible sites such as wikis, blogs, Google sites, or a proprietary LMS. Course offerings at the time of this writing tend toward computer science, math, and the sciences, although one provider offers a greater variety that includes a number of music courses (e.g., Western Music History through Performance, History of Rock, Introduction to Guitar, and others). The music history MOOCs may provide recorded performances together with interactive discussions in which historical context, musical significance, and musical structure of the repertoire are explored. The applied music MOOC offers video demonstrations and integrated quizzes along with assignments that require submission of self-recorded examples for peer review. These courses are primarily at an introductory level, as might be expected of early offerings in a novel format. They reflect the earlier online music courses documented in the research literature, many of which could be categorized as music appreciation courses or introductory skills courses. Course formats, which are similar among the major providers, include short lecture videos, quizzes with automated electronic feedback integrated into the videos, and final exams. One provider incorporates peer assessments in which several students grade each homework assignment using a grading rubric, and another uses a live course manager comparable to a teaching assistant. Interactivity in these courses includes question/answer forums, discussion forums, meetups, wikis, and Facebook study groups. In some cases, students form their own study groups independent of the course structure.

Materials and content of MOOCs may be of high quality; however, the pedagogy is lecture-based, consisting of short videos featuring well-known professors at elite universities. Although the professors may be notable, the pedagogy adheres to an outdated model of talking heads and multiple-choice quizzes, in effect an outmoded pedagogy delivered by means of a current medium. The major providers emphasize the interactivity that is included in their courses; however, one author points out that this model "doesn't create a learning community; it creates a crowd" (Guthrie, 2012). The large number of participants precludes faculty availability to individual students, so MOOCs depend more on student/student interaction and self-directed learning. Grading is problematic, especially for nontechnical subject matter or content that is not readily accommodated by multiple-choice quizzes. Cheating is a concern, and there have been instances of multiple students submitting identical homework; however, the providers do offer proctored exams. Because anyone can enroll in these courses, some students may be underprepared for the level of work required, and the resulting uneven knowledge base may render discussions unproductive. Scale is an issue as well: Scaling lectures to this magnitude may be achieved with some success, but scaling learning is more challenging. If interaction and customization of learning are basic to online learning, then a key question is how to achieve them in these massive courses—how to move beyond mass production to mass personalization.

There has been considerable hype around the appearance and rapid rise of MOOCs, and arguments are advanced both for and against this model. It is evident, however, that MOOCs at a minimum have changed the landscape of online learning and are undoubtedly impacting face-to-face learning as well. Indeed, the discussion about MOOCs highlights the many challenges of online learning and should stimulate further examination of what is most important in online learning, as well as strategies that might improve it. Previous technological innovations have followed a characteristic pattern, first mirroring or replicating what is already being done, then doing it better than it is currently being done, and finally doing what could not be done before. If MOOCs develop along this path, they will eventually transform online education. Currently, they replicate one way of learning, and they level the playing field by offering free courses to anyone who wants to learn. And though they are not a silver bullet that provides the answer to all the pedagogical challenges facing higher education, they contain multiple elements that can be used to inform and transform other kinds of learning in multiple disciplines, including music.

MOOCs serve primarily as informal learning: Students select those topics that are most interesting to them. Among those who may find MOOCs useful are professionals who want to update their skills or gain new ones, or anyone who simply wants to explore a topic of interest. High school students preparing for college might find certain MOOCs appropriate to their needs, and it is possible that these kinds of courses could become the advanced placement courses of the future, although music theory is the only advanced placement music course currently available. Current college students might enroll in courses not available at their own institutions; however, it is not clear how MOOCs may fit into the current structure of higher education. At the time of this writing, the American Council on Education's College Credit Recommendation Service (ACE CREDIT) has evaluated and recommended college credit for several courses offered by one of the major providers. To gain this credit, students would register for the course and take a proctored exam, for which there is a fee, at the conclusion of the course. At the college level, certain MOOCs might serve as prerequisites for upper-level courses or as supplementary work for those who need more help in introductory-level courses. Along these lines, Christensen has projected a future for higher education in which universities evolve into hybrid institutions, licensing some courses from large online providers while offering more specialized courses on campus (Howe, 2013). Alternatively, one of the major providers describes how institutions might move traditional lectures from face-to-face classes to a MOOC and use face-to-face class meetings for discussion and other learning activities, an option that aligns with the concept of the flipped or inverted classroom. One professor, based upon his experience teaching a History of Rock MOOC, reported thinking of a MOOC as "a very organized series of public lectures based on the structure of a college course" (Covach, 2013). He felt that a MOOC is most valuable as a way to offer academic knowledge to a broad audience and stated that, in the future, MOOCs might be used as part of traditional for-credit college courses. At the time of this writing, there is some movement of the MOOC providers toward offering conventional online courses for credit, and one of the providers has developed a model for credit-bearing courses that would be taken by tuition-paying students enrolled at a university that has contracted to offer such courses.

Tablet computing

The increasing popularity of tablets in higher education is partly a result of the bring-your-own-device movement. By loading their choice of apps, textbooks, and other content, students can create personalized learning environments and seamlessly access their course materials as needed. However, the more important consideration may be the value that tablets may add to online learning due to connectivity capabilities and integration with social networks. WiFi or cellular network capabilities allow students to access course content and activities via LMS mobile apps. Some sources suggest that mobile devices do not lend themselves to sustained discourse and reflection; however, LMS apps may provide students with opportunities to post ideas to discussion forums they thought out previously but did not have time to type and post. Tablet access enables timely contributions to collaborative projects so that momentum is not lost and projects are not delayed simply because participants are not at their desktop computers. In addition, various music apps support composition projects, study of music theory concepts, and music listening. Apps for note-taking and annotation enable students to create and share digital notebooks that include text, images, and audio. Students can listen to audio lectures or podcasts on their tablets, and instructors and students alike can create micro-lectures—short, focused, audio or video presentations—for upload to the LMS and subsequent listening or viewing on tablets. Students who already own tablets will undoubtedly use them to access their online courses when possible. In certain online music courses, tablets with appropriate apps may become tools of choice (e.g., bibliography aids and note-taking/annotation apps in music education research courses). Finally, experimental music programs that include a tablet in the tuition or course fee are being designed and may be expected to gain momentum.

Games and gamification

The *Horizon Report* cites McGill University's "Open Orchestra" as an example of a simulation game. Like any game, it provides feedback and results in motivation to improve. Games can be considered flow activities (Csikszentmihalyi, 1990), creative activities in which people become so completely engaged that they lose track of time and place.

> …game play is about working harder and harder, receiving constant feedback
> on your progress, and progressing to the next level when you've mastered the

---

Box 10.1

A sample problem scenario in music might begin with the observation that audiences for classical music are dwindling. Students would assume various roles that include an amateur music lover who has stopped attending concerts, a symphony musician, a music professor, and a college music student. The challenge is to examine the problem, study the perspectives of the persons involved, identify and discuss the underlying issues with the other concerned parties, and propose a strategy to attract new audiences. All of these tasks require higher-level thinking and use of skills relevant to the music profession, including taking on leadership roles when important issues are concerned.

This discussion could easily be accommodated in an asynchronous discussion or in a wiki where various facets of the problem and potential solutions could be clearly displayed. As a practical, real-world application of the activity, a viable solution might be applied in the community as an outreach project to reinvigorate the audience for classical music. The simulation engages students in an authentic learning experience that replicates a real-life situation and requires them to employ the same strategies they would use in the actual situation.

---

last one. It is about striving for perfection. There is no bell curve in game play. (Davidson, 2011, p. 158)

Clearly, games are useful for training and motivation, but perhaps gamification, the integration of game elements or gamer culture into nongame activities, is more relevant and readily applicable to online learning at this juncture. Game-like simulations can stimulate critical thinking and problem-solving, whereby students take on roles of stakeholders in a problem area and debate the most feasible solution (see box 10.1).

A DISRUPTIVE INNOVATION

The theory of disruptive innovation was proposed in order to describe changes in industry. It has been applied to K–12 education with some success, and it can be useful in addressing current challenges in higher education with regard to online learning generally and online learning in music in particular (Christensen, Horn, Caldera, & Soares, 2011). This theory, which applies across multiple sectors from industry to consumer products to professional services, posits two types of innovation: sustaining innovation and disruptive innovation. A sustaining innovation makes an existing product or service bigger or better: An example would be schools or departments of music with more majors and better practice rooms. A disruptive innovation interrupts that process by introducing a product or service that may not be of the same high quality as existing options but is more affordable and easier to use. It usually begins in an area where there is no competition, targeting people who are not served by the existing product or service, and subsequently improves to the point where it may replace a previous choice. For example, earlier online courses often consisted primarily of digital versions of traditional lectures and tests and were subject to slow Internet speeds, so their quality did not match that of face-to-face courses. These courses probably would not have attracted students already enrolled in traditional programs; however, working adults, such as in-service music teachers, might have found them appealing, as they could enroll in an online program while remaining in their current teaching positions, read or listen to a lecture in the evening at their own home, and avoid a late afternoon commute and a rigid course schedule. As the disruptive innovation improves, it begins to compete with the existing or traditional offerings; the addition of videoconferencing to an online course increases its similarity to a classroom experience, while discussion forums, tutorials, and other enhancements provide options that a conventional face-to-face course does not. Ultimately, the innovation improves to such an extent that it becomes attractive even to students in traditional programs or institutions.

Staker (2011) observed: "Online learning appears to be a classic disruptive innovation with the potential not just to improve the current model of educational delivery, but to transform it" (p. 1). An example of this process might be development of an online master's program in music education targeted toward music teachers who do not have convenient access to a college or university that offers such a program, and who would need to leave their teaching positions in order to earn a master's degree. This kind of innovation offers a financially viable and convenient solution: Students can remain in their current positions while pursuing the degree, and they can study at times that best fit their teaching schedules. Technological changes such as improved LMSs and synchronous communication technologies eventually support expansion of the system to serve both distant and local or on-campus students, while the flexibility and convenience are attractive to both audiences. Among the first online music offerings were courses and programs designed for in-service music teachers who found it difficult to accommodate their teaching responsibilities to the schedule requirements of on-campus courses. However, the flexibility offered by online courses was also appealing to on-campus students, and the clientele for online learning expanded to include local and on-campus students. In addition, online activities began to be included in face-to-face courses, and blended courses began to appear.

Many recommendations for action regarding the disruptive innovation of online learning are targeted toward university administrators, and they highlight the need to adapt in order to avoid what is perceived as almost certain decline. However, one recommendation that is accessible at the level of individual schools, departments, or disciplines is this: "...use this new technology to disrupt the existing classroom model to extend convenience to many more students as well as provide a better learning experience" (Christensen, et al., 2011, p. 6).

Improving and transforming education

Technology use in education has followed a pattern, first helping us to do better or more effectively what we're already doing—to replicate—and then to do things we could not do before—to innovate. A glance through the literature on technology in education reveals a number of statements on the unfulfilled promises of technology in education and questioning whether we are there yet. The truth is that we will never be there: If we think we've arrived, we're already backsliding. We expect that the Internet and digital technologies will improve education and ideally transform it. Transformation, however, is a phenomenon of considerably greater magnitude than individual improvements. We might consider it a kind of metamorphosis that results from collective smaller changes that ultimately alter the entire landscape. The question is: What does transformed musical education in the 21st century look like? Is it teaching hundreds to thousands of students in one massive course? Is it developing compelling learning experiences that actively engage students? The existing body of research on online learning in music provides evidence of innovative thinking, ongoing efforts, and some success in achieving specific improvements. Transformation is not achieved by using new tools to do what we've always done, using new technologies in the service of old pedagogies—what has been referred to as the sound of yesterday. For example, posting lengthy video lectures to an online course site does not maximize the potential of the online environment. It simply mirrors what we may always have done, but uses a new technological means to achieve it. The potential of the online environment for education in the age of web 2.0 is in connections, in supporting participatory activities and collaboration. Rethinking our subject matter and pedagogy in light of these current technologies can reinvigorate existing good practice and ultimately lead to transformation.

MOOCs are already prompting change in higher education. Although there are reasonable concerns about some of their pedagogical features, a more balanced perspective suggests that they will provide new opportunities for learners. Among these opportunities are just-in-time mini-courses that answer the need for more customized education or training. This kind of training might become an attractive choice for in-service music educators seeking targeted professional development opportunities or coursework required for continuation of certification. In addition to the music MOOCs offered through major providers, a few schools of music have developed and offered music MOOCs using other platforms, and pending review and evaluation of these courses, more may follow. Just as the lines continue to blur between online and face-to-face learning, a similar phenomenon may occur with current and new forms of online teaching. More institutions will offer online music courses or programs, and offerings are likely to include the best MOOC-like features, while MOOCs may continue to move toward the mainstream of credit-bearing courses.

Online learning as just "learning"

Online learning is a disruptive innovation that is influencing how we think about and approach our subject matter and pedagogy. Online strategies are filtering down to the traditional classroom, transforming face-to-face courses, and various models of blended courses are being developed. Students enroll in the courses they need or want without regard to delivery mode; courses are becoming just courses. Students in traditional programs supplement their face-to-face coursework with online courses, sometimes including MOOCs, and in some cases, students in online programs supplement their coursework with traditional options. In this postmodality era (Cavanagh, 2012), the boundaries between course delivery modes continue to blur, and students select the courses they want irrespective of delivery mode. Propelled by flexibility, convenience, access, and choice, online learning is becoming simply learning.

NEUROSCIENCE AND ONLINE LEARNING

Neuroscience is a relatively young field, and despite the thousands of articles published on the topic, neuroscientists are among the first to point out that there is still much we do not know about the brain. Peer-reviewed neuromusical studies run into the hundreds: Nearly 500 such articles have been compiled in an online database (Edwards, 2008). However, few articles apply the findings to music teaching and learning. Findings of neuromusical research are such that they may be most useful in applied and online applied music situations, but the more general findings will be most useful in informing online music learning.

The psychology of e-learning is an emerging field of study that can contribute to the understanding and further development of online learning in music. In this context, e-learning is defined as a learning system that "uses various electronic techniques as its primary medium for learning" and may take the form of "virtual learning, online learning, distance learning, and Web-based learning" (Yan, Hao, Hobbs, & Wen, 2003, p. 286). Psychological studies of e-learning include research on cognitive aspects and social processes of learning: These are the categories most pertinent to online learning in music. A recommended research agenda for the psychology of e-learning includes empirical research on psychological factors and processes that support e-learning, efforts to develop theories of e-learning to inform research and practice, as well as interdisciplinary research on e-learning (from a variety of psychology disciplines) and development of research-based applications that can benefit e-learners in all disciplines. In this chapter, a similar agenda for online learning in music is outlined.

Mayer (2003) proposed a science of e-learning, the investigation of how people learn in e-learning environments. Elements include evidence from research studies, a research-based theory of how people learn in e-learning environments, and applications consisting of research-based principles for design of e-learning environments (p. 297). In framing a research agenda, Mayer cautions against media comparisons, pointing out that differences are due to the pedagogical approaches that e-learning enables. The primary focus is on the question "Which aspects of e-learning environments help which kinds of learners to learn which kinds of knowledge?" (p. 299). Mayer's work was concerned with the effects of multimedia learning; however, this question is also of interest to those involved in design and development of online courses and programs in music.

What current brain science can tell us about how people learn online

Findings from neuroscientific research have enlightened us with regard to how the brain works, and we have been particularly interested in findings about how the brain processes music. This new knowledge entices us to apply and use it in our everyday teaching. However, we need to be cautious in interpreting and applying research results to avoid such oversimplifications and premature applications as have resulted, for example, in the "Mozart Effect" and "music makes you smarter" myths. In this regard, Zull (2011) advises: "We should not be looking for instant remedies, clever pedagogical tricks, or isolated facts. Rather, we should seek a deeper understanding of the 'learning organ' and how the journey toward mind can be facilitated" (p. 14). In light of changes in education brought about by technology, he states, "The challenge that faces us now is to blend the growing insights about human learning with the power of technology. This is a goal of education in our time" (p. 231). It is also good to keep in mind Hodges's assertion: "We are just at the beginning stages of applying neuroscientific findings to music teaching" (2010, p. 3). With Zull's (2002) learning cycle as a starting point, Hodges proposes some tentative applications of the research to music teaching and learning. The applications are targeted toward K–12 music educators, but they may be adapted to higher education in an online environment. Key concepts include active learning, the effect of emotion on learning, personally meaningful learning, learning as multisensory, and learning through social interactions. Of central importance is the combination of active involvement, positive emotion, flow, and meaningful learning: "Students are most likely to have powerful learning experiences when they intensely focus on meaningful tasks that match their skill levels" (p. 6). This combination is also important in adult learning and can be achieved in an online environment as well.

Additionally, the more ways people encounter a concept—through text, image, sound—the more secure it becomes in memory. And people learn through social interactions—from expert models and from each other in group discussions and collaborative projects. Finally, due to the structure of neural pathways, sensory input is rapid but integration of that input with previous knowledge and experience requires more time and reflection, which can be achieved in the online environment with the use of blogs and asynchronous discussions.

Hodges's applications align well with other efforts to use neuroscience to inform learning (Zull, 2011) and online learning in particular (Clemons, 2005; Meyer, 2004). Zull recommends designing an environment that encourages discovery, using expert modeling, incorporating challenges that require creative action, using multisensory approaches, individualizing learning, and promoting metacognition. An inquiry model that uses collaborative discourse contributes to a discovery-oriented environment: Students brainstorm, organize their ideas, explore options, and reach a solution or consensus. Expert modeling can be achieved online with the use of audio or video presentations by experts in the field (e.g., TED [technology, entertainment, and design] talks or musical instrument demonstrations by members of military bands). Simulations, role-playing, and case studies provide material for creative problem-solving. Instructors and students can use multisensory approaches, presenting content and contributing to discussions with multiple media—text, images, audio, or video. Individualized learning is a crucial ingredient in meaningful learning experiences: Delving into topics pertinent to students' individual situations is motivating. Online journals or blogs offer excellent support for metacognitive work.

Current brain science is revealing how people learn and how people learn music. Other research efforts are increasing our understanding of how to use that knowledge to help people learn music online, and sometimes the results serve to confirm existing good practice. The hope is that this knowledge and its application will produce improvements in online pedagogy and online learning that will lead to a genuine transformation of education and online learning in music.

THE FUTURE OF ONLINE LEARNING IN MUSIC

Sir Ken Robinson probably said it best: "We may not be able to predict the future but we can help to shape it" (2011, p. 17). Again, we may not be able to predict, but based upon current trends, we can extrapolate and take action to shape our own future. The future is now.

New developments, new possibilities

The pattern of implementation of new technologies has been fairly consistent over time: First they are used to do better what we're already doing, and then they are used to do something we could not do before. Each new technological development opens the door to new possibilities for educational applications and new opportunities to explore those possibilities on a small or large scale, through formal or informal research. It is not possible to predict exactly how current innovations—MOOCS, tablet computing, games and gamification—will change online music learning in higher education. However, on the basis of their current status, it is fairly certain that they will be more widely adopted and will cause institutions to adapt with changes in formats and pedagogy. The 2013 *Horizon Report* outlined some key trends, some of which are currently occurring in music institutions: music MOOCs, informal learning experiences within traditional courses, the changing role of the instructor, and development of multiple models of online learning from fully online to various configurations of blended learning.

Advancing the research

To date, there has been relatively little research on online learning in music at the higher education level. As noted previously, the challenges with this kind of research include appropriate representation of concepts and use of pedagogies suitable to the various music subdisciplines. National studies that reported online learning outcomes at least as effective as those of traditional face-to-face learning (or no significant difference) attributed learning advantages to differences in curriculum materials, pedagogical aspects, and learning time, rather than to the delivery medium (Means, et al., 2010). Others have pointed out the misconceptions associated with the "no significant difference" phenomenon. The evidence for online learning's effectiveness together with the design flaws associated with media comparisons suggest that we need better research questions. Rather than continue to conduct comparison studies focused on delivery medium, it would be more productive to examine instructional practices in systematic ways in order to identify those that lead to high-quality student learning and result in student satisfaction. This kind of research can lead to development of appropriate instructional models and practical teaching strategies that will help us advance online learning in music. Following are some directions for future research that can prove useful for assessing and improving online learning in music.

Theory-based approaches focused on how people learn what aspects of music in an online environment would be particularly beneficial (e.g., studies of online music course design using the TPACK framework, or studies of the appropriateness of pedagogical strategies based on the online collaborative learning [OCL] theory for various types of online music courses). This kind of research would complement the existing studies of constructivist approaches in online settings (Keast, 2010; Keast, 2009; Brewster, 2005; Bauer & Daugherty, 2001). It could be a step toward developing models specific to online learning in the music subdisciplines and possibly a theory of online learning in music.

Differences among music subdisciplines require different pedagogical approaches, and multiple models of online learning are becoming available. Studies should be conducted to determine which kinds of music courses are best for online delivery and which models of online learning—fully online, synchronous, asynchronous, blended—are most suitable for the various types of music courses, including the technologies and pedagogies appropriate to each model. This kind of research might include exploration of effective practices in specific content areas (e.g., music education, music history or musicology, music theory, and applied studies).

Online music courses and entire online music degree programs continue to be developed. Research on their effectiveness would be useful for both evaluation purposes and direction in the development of new online music programs. A small number of such studies exist (Kos & Goodrich, 2012; Groulx & Hernly, 2010; Walls, et al., 2005; Walls, et al., 2004); however, additional work in this vein is desirable.

Given data on course and program effectiveness, qualitative research to determine what specific features of online learning contribute to individual student learning, student satisfaction, and professional success would be valuable, as it would contribute to a more comprehensive picture of the effectiveness of online music programs and courses, indicate what approaches will lead to high-quality learning outcomes, and provide an accessible source of practical teaching strategies. The course designs, instructional strategies, technologies, and online resources that best support student learning in specific content areas would be of interest.

Some of the existing program effectiveness studies include brief descriptions of courses offered within those programs. Similar studies of practice would be a useful next step in determining what pedagogical techniques work best for what type of music instruction in an online environment. These studies might focus on the techniques and strategies used by successful online instructors, how they changed their approaches to suit the online environment, and how they determined what constitutes high-quality music learning experiences in various types of music courses.

In a similar vein, a taxonomy of music learning activity types comparable to those developed for the K–12 level (Bauer, Harris, & Hofer, 2012b) should be explored and developed for use in higher education.

Blended learning is underrepresented in the literature. Studies of blended programs and courses would be valuable, particularly to instructors who may be unable or unwilling to teach online but who want to integrate online experiences into their current face-to-face courses in a systematic way. A body of research on blended learning in music would reveal the variety of models already being used, provide usable strategies for redesigning courses for blended delivery, offer examples of effective practices for blended learning, stimulate additional innovative approaches, and lend further support to the idea of online learning as just learning.

Online synchronous applied music study is an area of increasing interest. Comparison studies involving personal computers and readily available desktop videoconferencing technology have been useful. Future research may focus on effective pedagogical practices developed specifically for online applied lessons. Improvements in desktop videoconferencing technology will provide improved audio and video quality and further enhance the pedagogy of online synchronous applied music lessons. Internet2 technology has made performing and teaching music over the Internet a reality. Musical events transmitted over Internet2—performances, master classes, and workshops—are typically offered on an ad hoc basis. However, recent efforts are being directed toward making these events more widely accessible, identifying and developing approaches that go beyond one-time performances, and strategically integrating more frequent events into the curriculum. Challenges include determining the purposes for which these events will be used and their potential impact on existing curricula, developing pedagogical applications, integrating them into courses and programs, integrating them into faculty pedagogy and research, and assessing the value and significance of the sessions. Research involving these pioneering efforts has potential to significantly enrich music curriculum and elevate the level of online music performance and pedagogy whether or not it is supported by Internet2 technology.

While "early adopters" who chose to teach online may have been technologically inclined and may have sought additional information or training as needed, other faculty who are asked to teach online often do not have a similar background or inclinations. If we want to advance quality online music instruction, we need knowledgeable and committed online instructors. Comprehensive faculty development/coaching programs for prospective online music instructors should be developed to help faculty gain experience with the various models of online learning and identify and address their concerns. Preliminary research in this area might focus on skills needed for successful online teaching (e.g., classroom management techniques that promote formation of a learning community), which in turn would set the stage for development of benchmarks and standards for professional development in online music pedagogy.

In summary, online learning in music is a young field with a small but growing body of research. It has much in common with online learning in general; however, there are also many issues unique to online music learning because of the multifaceted nature of music study. In moving forward, we in the various music subdisciplines have much to learn from each other, as well as from individuals in other disciplines. The short list of suggestions for advancing the scholarship of online music learning represents a beginning agenda based on existing research, current issues and concerns, and near future trends. A more comprehensive agenda can be developed with the combined efforts of those involved with online learning in all its aspects, and there is much to be gained from this effort: "We may not be able to predict the future but by acting on the ideas produced in our imagination, we can help to create it" (Robinson, 2011, p. 142).

REFERENCES

Bauer, W. I., & Daugherty, J. F. (2001). Using the Internet to enhance music teacher education. *Journal of Music Teacher Education*, 11(1), 27–32.

Bauer, W. I., Harris, J., & Hofer, M. (2012b). *Music learning activity types*. Retrieved from College of William and Mary, School of Education, Learning Activity Types Wiki: http://activitytypes.wmwikis.net/file/view/MusicLearningATs-June2012.pdf

Cavanagh, T. B. (2012). The postmodality era: How "online learning" is becoming "learning." In D. G. Oblinger (Ed.), *Game changers: Education and information technologies* [PDF e-book version] (pp. 215–227). Retrieved from http://net.educause.edu/ir/library/pdf/pub7203.pdf

Christensen, C. M., Horn, M. B., Caldera, L., & Soares, L. (2011). *Disrupting college: How disruptive innovation can deliver quality and affordability to postsecondary education*. Center for American Progress and Innosight Institute. Retrieved from http://www.innosightinstitute.org/innosight/wp-content/uploads/2011/02/future_of_higher_ed-2.3.pdf

Clemons, S. A. (2005). Brain-based learning: Possible implications for online learning. *International Journal of Instructional Technology and Distance Learning*, 2(9). Retrieved from http://itdl.org/journal/sep_05/article03.htm

Covach, J. (2013). To MOOC or not to MOOC? *Music Theory Online*, 19(3). Retrieved from http://mtosmt.org/issues/mto.13.19.3/mto.13.19.3.covach.php

Csikszentmihalyi, M. (1990). *Flow: The psychology of optimal experience*. New York: Harper & Row.

Dahlstrom, E. (2012). *ECAR study of undergraduate students and information technology, 2012*. Louisville, CO: EDUCAUSE Center for Applied Research. Retrieved from http://www.educause.edu/ecar

Davidson, C. N. (2011). *Now you see it: How technology and brain science will transform schools and business for the 21st century*. New York: Penguin Books.

Edwards, R. D. (2008). The neurosciences and music education: An online database of brain imaging neuromusical research (doctoral dissertation). Retrieved from ProQuest Dissertations and Theses database (UMI No. 3307191).

Guthrie, D. (2012). Jump off the Coursera bandwagon. *Chronicle of Higher Education* (December 17). Retrieved from http://chronicle.com

Hill, P. (2012). Online educational delivery models: A descriptive view. *EDUCAUSE Review*, 47(6), 84–86, 88, 90, 92, 94–97.

Hodges, D. A. (2010). Can neuroscience help us do a better job of teaching music? *General Music Today*, 23(2), 3–12.

Howe, J. (2013). Clayton Christensen wants to transform capitalism. *Wired online: Business* (February 12). Retrieved from http://www.wired.com/business/2013/02/mf-clayton-christensen-wants-to-transform-capitalism/all/

Johnson, L., Adams, S., & Cummins, M. (2012). *The NMC Horizon Report: 2012 higher education edition*. Austin, TX: The New Media Consortium. Retrieved from http://www.nmc.org/publications/

Johnson, L., Adams Becker, S., Cummins, M., Estrada, V., Freeman, A., & Ludgate, H. (2013). *The NMC Horizon Report: 2013 higher education edition*. Austin, TX: The New Media Consortium. Retrieved from http://www.nmc.org/publications/

Johnson, L., Smith, R., Willis, H., Levine, A., & Haywood, K., (2011). *The 2011 Horizon Report*. Austin, TX: The New Media Consortium. Retrieved from http://www.nmc.org/publications/

Katz, R. N. (2010). Scholars, scholarship, and the scholarly enterprise in the digital age. *EDUCAUSE Review*, 45(2), 44–56.

Mayer, R. E. (2003). Elements of a science of e-learning. *Journal of Educational Computing Research*, 29(3), 297–313.

Meyer, K. (2004). How recent brain research can inform the design of online learning. *Journal of Educators Online*, 1(1), 1–17.

Robinson, K. (2011). *Out of our minds: Learning to be creative* (rev. ed.). Chichester, UK: Capstone Publishing.

Staker, H. (2011). *The rise of K–12 blended learning: Profiles of emerging models*. Innosight Institute. Retrieved from http://www.christenseninstitute.org/

Yan, Z., Hao, H., Hobbs, L. J., & Wen, N. (2003). The psychology of e-learning: A field of study. *Journal of Educational Computing Research*, 29(3), 285–296.

Zull, J. E. (2002). *The art of changing the brain: Enriching the practice of teaching by exploring the biology of learning*. Sterling, VA: Stylus Publishing.

Zull, J. E. (2011). *From brain to mind: Using neuroscience to guide change in education*. Sterling, VA: Stylus Publishing.

APPENDIX A

Electronic Code of Federal Regulations, §600.2

Correspondence course:

(1) A course provided by an institution under which the institution provides instructional materials, by mail or electronic transmission, including examinations on the materials, to students who are separated from the instructor. Interaction between the instructor and student is limited, is not regular and substantive, and is primarily initiated by the student. Correspondence courses are typically self-paced.
(2) If a course is part correspondence and part residential training, the Secretary considers the course to be a correspondence course.
(3) A correspondence course is not distance education.

Distance education means education that uses one or more of the technologies listed in paragraphs (1) through (4) of this definition to deliver instruction to students who are separated from the instructor and to support regular and substantive interaction between the students and the instructor, either synchronously or asynchronously. The technologies may include—

(1) The internet;
(2) One-way and two-way transmissions through open broadcast, closed circuit, cable, microwave, broadband lines, fiber optics, satellite, or wireless communications devices;
(3) Audio conferencing; or
(4) Video cassettes, DVDs, and CD–ROMs, if the cassettes, DVDs, or CD–ROMs are used in a course in conjunction with any of the technologies listed in paragraphs (1) through (3) of this definition.

Program Profiles: Online Music Programs/NASM-Accredited Institutions

GRADUATE DEGREES IN MUSIC EDUCATION

Auburn University: Master of Music Education
Boston University: Master of Music in Music Education
Boston University: Doctor of Musical Arts in Music Education
East Carolina University: Master of Music in Music Education
Kent State University: Master of Music in Music Education
Ohio University: Master of Music Education
Stephen F. Austin University: Master of Music, Music Education Track
University of Florida (Gainesville): Master of Music in Music Education
University of Hawaii at Manoa: Master of Arts in Music Education
University of Montana: Master of Music Education
University of South Florida: Master of Arts in Music Education
University of Southern Mississippi: Master of Music Education

GRADUATE DEGREES IN MUSIC THERAPY

Indiana University-Purdue University at Indianapolis (IUPUI): Master of Science in Music Therapy

GRADUATE DEGREES IN MUSIC TECHNOLOGY

Indiana University-Purdue University at Indianapolis (IUPUI): Master of Science in Music Technology

UNDERGRADUATE DEGREES IN MUSIC

Valley City State University, N. Dakota: Composite Bachelor of Science/Arts in Music

AUBURN UNIVERSITY, AUBURN, AL

Degree-granting, regional accreditation, education accreditation, not-for-profit, public. A department of music in the college of liberal arts in a state-supported university.

Website: http://auburn.edu/academic/college_of_education/musiceducation/distance.html

Degree title: Master of Music Education

Kimberly C. Walls, Ph.D., Department Head of Curriculum & Teaching
  E-mail: wallski@auburn.edu
  Phone: 334-844-4434

Jane M. Kuehne, Ph.D., Program Coordinator
  E-mail: kuehnjm@auburn.edu
  Phone: 334-844-6852

Program features

The Master of Music Education is a 30–33 credit program. All coursework can be completed at a distance. Courses are primarily offered synchronously through computer audio and videoconferencing software, and are delivered both on-campus and at a distance. Programs include certification tracks for N–12 Instrumental or N–12 Vocal. General music specialists choose either track and tailor the coursework toward General Music. A residency consisting of attendance at a two-day seminar each summer of enrollment is required. Initial certification-related coursework is offered only on-campus, and some electives require summer meetings. Individuals who complete this program will be eligible to apply for an Alabama Class A professional educator certificate or Master's level certification in other states. Note: The Ed.S. program is under review to add an official distance education program option, but all of the coursework is available through distance learning. The Ph.D. degree requires more on-campus coursework, but some courses can be taken through distance education.

Application requirements include a Bachelor's or higher degree from a regionally accredited college or university; a minimum overall GPA of 2.75 that must be documented on the official transcript from the degree-granting institution and must be the GPA that was used as the basis for granting the degree; a professional educator certificate at the Bachelor's level in Music Education (valid and renewable); a clear background check; all official transcripts; competitive GRE scores for the Verbal and Quantitative tests; three letters of recommendation that address professional and academic qualifications; a current résumé; and a portfolio and/or interview if requested.

BOSTON UNIVERSITY, BOSTON, MA

Degree-granting, regional accreditation, not-for-profit, private. A school of music in the college of fine arts in a university.
Website: http://musiceducation.bu.edu/
Degree title: Master of Music in Music Education
Susan Wharton Conkling, Ph.D., Chair of Music Education
    E-mail: drc@bu.edu
    Phone: 617-353-5093

Program features

The MM in Music Education is a 32-credit program consisting of eight 4-credit required courses, each seven weeks in duration. Students may begin the program at any of five start times per year. Required coursework includes Music Education (16 cr.), Musicology and Music Theory (8 cr.), and approved electives (8 cr.). Students typically take two courses per semester, and they may attend summer (elective) courses on-campus in addition to the required online courses. The NASM-required MM Comprehensive exam is a curriculum project, embedded in the final course. The degree can be completed in 17 to 20 months of study.

Application requirements include completion of a Bachelor's degree in Music or Music Education from a regionally accredited college or university; a cumulative GPA of 3.0 or higher; current or recent classroom teaching experience; a professional portfolio; an analytic paper such as one written for a Music Theory, Music History, or Music Education course; a teaching video; and an interview. A Music Theory proficiency exam is given.

BOSTON UNIVERSITY, BOSTON, MA

Degree-granting, regional accreditation, not-for-profit, private. A school of music in the college of fine arts in a university.
Website: http://musiceducation.bu.edu/
Degree title: Doctor of Musical Arts in Music Education

Susan Wharton Conkling, Ph.D., Chair of Music Education
  E-mail: drc@bu.edu
  Phone: 617-353-5093

Program features

The DMA in Music Education is a 48-credit program consisting of eleven 4-credit required courses, each seven weeks in duration. Required coursework includes Music Education and Professional Education (20 cr.), Theory and Musicology (12 cr.), approved electives (12 cr.), research and directed study (1 credit/residency), and dissertation (3 cr.). Attendance at the one-week on-campus residency is required in order to begin the final DMA course, the dissertation. Students typically take two courses per semester, and they may attend summer (elective) courses on-campus in addition to the required online courses. Courses can be completed continuously in 5.5 semesters. There are qualifying examinations in Theory, Musicology, and Music Education. Degree completion takes a minimum of three years. Completion of the dissertation may take one to two years.

Application requirements include completion of Bachelor's and Master's degrees in Music from regionally accredited institutions; at least three years of music teaching experience at primary, secondary, or university level; leadership through activities such as designing curriculum, mentoring new teachers, serving on executive boards of professional organizations, and publishing articles; a cumulative GPA of 3.0 or higher; a portfolio; a statement of research interest; a 500-word response to one of three "provocative" statements; a teaching video and 500-word reflection; GRE or MAT testing results; and an interview. A music theory proficiency exam is given.

EAST CAROLINA UNIVERSITY, GREENVILLE, NC

Degree-granting, regional accreditation, education accreditation, not-for-profit, public. A school of music in a college of fine arts and communication in a state-supported university.
Website: http://www.ecu.edu/music/
Degree title: Master of Music in Music Education
Michelle Hairston, Ed.D., Chair, Music Education Department
  E-mail: hairstonm@ecu.edu
  Phone: 252-328-4871

Program features

The MM in Music Education is a 33–35 semester hour program. The program is predominantly online; the Pedagogical Studies option is entirely online.

Courses are delivered using a course management system with synchronous and asynchronous technologies (discussion forums, some "real-time" chat, small-group work). There are two options: one in teacher education (approved for North Carolina teacher licensure), the other without licensure preparation. Students choose an emphasis from Pedagogical Studies (entirely online), Choral Conducting (residency required), Instrumental Conducting (residency required), Performance (residency required), Music Theory/Composition (residency required), Suzuki Pedagogy (residency required), and Music Therapy (residency required; within the no licensure option). Required coursework includes Music Education Core (16 s.h.), Teacher Education (3 s.h.), Advanced Analysis (3 s.h.), and courses in the chosen area of emphasis.

Application requirements include the equivalent of a Bachelor of Music degree from an accredited institution, a minimum 3.0 GPA, and a successful portfolio review.

KENT STATE UNIVERSITY, KENT, OH

Degree-granting, regional accreditation, education accreditation, not-for-profit, public. A school of music in a college of the arts in a state-supported university.

Website: http://musicedmasters.kent.edu/
Degree title: Master of Music in Music Education
Patricia Grutzmacher, Ph.D., Coordinator of Music Education and Online Curriculum

E-mail: music@kentstateonline.com
Phone: 877-223-1114 ext. 3311

Program features

The MM in Music Education is a 31-credit program consisting of 3-credit required courses, each seven weeks in duration. Students may begin the program at any of six start dates per year, two each in spring, summer, and fall. Two courses are offered each semester, with a one-week break between courses. Required coursework includes Foundations of Music Education, Music Education/Research, a choice of two electives in Music Education Methods, and a Capstone Project (4 cr.). Students may choose a choral, instrumental, or general music emphasis. The degree can be completed entirely online in approximately 20 months.

Application requirements include a Bachelor's degree in Music Education from an accredited institution; a teaching certificate or licensure from one of the 50 states in the U.S.; a minimum music GPA of 3.0; and a minimum B average overall (2.77). Formal music teaching experience in public or private school systems is desirable. Neither the GRE nor an audition is required.

OHIO UNIVERSITY, ATHENS, OH

Degree-granting, regional accreditation, education accreditation, not-for-profit, public. A school of music in the college of fine arts in a state-supported university.
Website: http://www.ohio.edu/finearts/music/
Degree title: Master of Music Education
Dorothy Bryant, Ph.D, Chair, Professional Studies Area, Chair of Music Education
  E-mail: bryantd@ohio.edu
  Phone: 740-593-4243

Program features

Coursework for the Master of Music Education is accessed online and is designed to be relevant and flexible to the needs of individual teachers. It emphasizes research and writing skills along with classroom implementation of new methods and materials. Required coursework includes Music Education, History, and Theory of Music. The degree can be completed at a distance with the exception of on-campus entrance and exit (oral) exams, and two summers of intensive two-week courses.

  Application requirements include a writing sample on assessment in music (diagnostic); a 15-minute rehearsal or teaching video; and a résumé or portfolio.

STEPHEN F. AUSTIN STATE UNIVERSITY, NACOGDOCHES, TX

Degree-granting, regional accreditation, education accreditation, not-for-profit, public. A school of music in the college of fine arts in a state-supported university.
Website: http://www.music.sfasu.edu/academics.php?link=grad
Degree title: Master of Music, Music Education Track
Manny Brand, Director, School of Music, Professor, Music Education
  E-mail: mbrand@sfasu.edu
  Phone: 936-468-1170
Stephen Lias, DMA, Associate Director for Graduate Studies and International Initiatives
  E-mail: slias@sfasu.edu
  Phone: 936-468-4056

Program features

The Master of Music, Music Education Track is a 31- or 36-credit program, depending on the track (thesis or no thesis). Courses carry 2 or 3 credits. The Elementary/General Music concentration in the Music Education Track can be completed entirely online. Required coursework for the Elementary/General Concentration (thesis) includes Music Core (11 cr.) and Music Education Specialization (20 cr.), for a total of 31 credits. Required coursework for the Elementary/General Concentration (no thesis) includes Music Core (11 cr.), Music Education Specialization (14 cr.), and music electives (11 cr.), for a total of 36 credits.

Application requirements include a baccalaureate degree from an NASM-accredited institution; 18 semester hours of undergraduate work in the major field; Graduate Music Entrance Exam; an admission interview; and a written statement outlining objectives for graduate study and career plans.

UNIVERSITY OF FLORIDA, GAINESVILLE, FL

Degree-granting, regional accreditation, education accreditation, not-for-profit, public. A school of music in the college of fine arts in a state-supported institution.
Website: http://musiceducation.arts.ufl.edu/
Degree title: Master of Music in Music Education
William I. Bauer, Ph.D., Director, Online Master of Music in Music Education Program
E-mail: wbauer@ufl.edu
Phone: 352-273-3182

Program features

The MM in Music Education is a 33-credit program consisting of 3-credit, eight-week required courses and a 16-week culminating Capstone course. Two courses are offered during each 16-week semester. Students may begin the program at any of three start times per year: fall, spring, and summer. Required coursework includes Music Education Foundation Courses (12 cr.), Music Foundation Courses (9 cr.), Supplemental Courses (9 cr.), and Graduate Music Education Capstone Course (3 cr.). The minimum time for degree completion is two years.

Application requirements include a Bachelor in Music Education or Bachelor in Music with professional teaching experience (K–12 classroom or alternative setting, e.g., private music teacher) and a 3.0 undergraduate GPA.

UNIVERSITY OF HAWAII AT MANOA, HONOLULU, HI

Degree-granting, regional accreditation, education accreditation, not-for-profit, public. A department of music in the college of arts and humanities in a state-supported university.

Website: http://www.hawaii.edu/uhmmusic/degrees/MA_MusEd_Online.htm

Degree title: Master of Arts in Music Education

Barbara McLain, Ph.D., Online Program Administrator

    E-mail: payne@hawaii.edu

    Phone: 808-956-2172

Program features

The MA in Music Education is a 30-credit program consisting of 3-credit courses. One to three online courses are offered each semester, and course length varies: fall (16 weeks), spring (16 weeks), and summer (6–8 weeks). Required coursework includes Required Courses (6 cr.), General Musicianship (6 cr.), Music Education (9 cr.), Plan B Project for Music Education (3 cr.), and music electives (6 cr.). All courses in this program are asynchronous, but some may require a class chat room interaction session at a specific time during the week. Many instructors use the University of Hawaii's learning management system to organize and present digital content and communicate with students. In addition, instructors are required to provide online office hours in the course chat room periodically during the semester to assist students with questions. Courses are taught and monitored by faculty who are currently employed by the fully accredited University of Hawaii Music Department: No graduate assistants or "facilitators" are utilized in this program. A minimum of five semesters or two years and two summers is required for degree completion.

Application requirements for degree admission include an undergraduate degree in music education or post-baccalaureate licensure; a minimum undergraduate GPA of 3.0; one year of fulltime music teaching experience; a video/DVD teaching demonstration. Casual enrollment is encouraged for anyone needing re-licensure credits or prior to admission, to insure that students have sufficient skills and equipment to complete the degree. Casual enrollment for many online graduate courses is available to any student with an undergraduate degree (music preferred) via the UH Outreach College and involves a simple two-page online application form and instructor consent.

UNIVERSITY OF MONTANA, MISSOULA, MT

Degree-granting, regional accreditation, education accreditation, not-for-profit, public. A department of music in the school of fine arts in a state university.

Website: http://umt.edu/music/degrees/MM-education-online
Degree title: Master of Music Education
Lori Gray, DMA, Music Education Program Coordinator
  E-mail: lori.gray@umontana.edu
  Phone: 406-243-6889

Program features

The Master of Music Education is a 30-credit (thesis option) or 36-credit (non-thesis option) online/summer program consisting of 2- or 3-credit courses. Required coursework includes Music Education/Research, Performance/Ensemble, Conducting, Music History, Music Theory, and electives.

Application requirements include a completed undergraduate degree in Music Education or approved equivalent, a teaching philosophy statement, a letter stating objectives in pursuing graduate study, and three letters of recommendation.

UNIVERSITY OF SOUTH FLORIDA, TAMPA, FL

Degree-granting, regional accreditation, education accreditation, not-for-profit, public. A school of music in a college of visual and performing arts in a state research university.
Website: http://music.arts.usf.edu/content/go/music-education/
Degree title: Master of Arts in Music Education
David A. Williams, Ph.D., Associate Director, Academic Advisor for the program
  E-mail: davidw@usf.edu
  Phone: 813-974-9166

Program features

The MA in Music Education is a 30-credit program consisting of 3- or 6-credit courses offered in a completely online format. Classes are accessible via an asynchronous online design. Courses are offered during the fall and spring semesters each year and during summers. Required coursework includes Music Education courses (9 cr.); Music Literature, Theory, or History Courses (6 cr.); electives including at least one Music Education Course (9 cr.); Directed Research/Music Education Research Project (6 cr.); and a comprehensive exam.

Application requirements include a Bachelor's degree in Music or Music Education; a minimum 3.0 GPA; and a minimum of two years' K–12 music teaching experience or the equivalent.

UNIVERSITY OF SOUTHERN MISSISSIPPI, HATTIESBURG, MS

Degree-granting, regional accreditation, education accreditation, not-for-profit, public. A school of music in the college of arts and letters in a state-supported university.
Website: http://www.usm.edu/music/graduate-0
Degree title: Master of Music Education
Amanda Schlegel, Ph.D.
   E-mail: amanda.schlegel@usm.edu
   Phone: 601-266-5754

Program features

The Master of Music Education is a 30-credit online/hybrid program consisting of 3-credit courses. Options include Music Education and Music Education seeking licensure. Required coursework includes five required courses (Music Education/Research, Music History, Curriculum Development, Music Theory); five electives in Music Education chosen from online, summer intensive workshops, or traditional face-to-face courses; and a comprehensive exam. All classes are streamed or uploaded to YouTube. Students take two to three courses in the fall and spring and three to four courses during the summer to finish in 18–24 months. The minimum time for degree completion is 18 to 24 months.

Application requirements include a Bachelor's degree in Music Education including student teaching and licensure; B or better in music courses; a minimum 2.75 GPA in the last two years of undergraduate study; the GRE General Test; a writing sample, research, or report written in the last year or a three- to five-page literature review on a music education topic; and three letters of recommendation.

INDIANA UNIVERSITY-PURDUE UNIVERSITY, INDIANAPOLIS, IN

Degree-granting, regional accreditation, not-for-profit, public. A department of music and arts technology in the school of engineering and technology in a state research university.
Website: http://music.iupui.edu/degrees/ms-MusicTherapy.shtml
Degree title: Master of Science in Music Therapy
Fred J. Rees, DMA, Chair
   E-mail: frees@iupui.edu
   Phone: 317-274-4000
G. David Peters, Ed.D., Head of Graduate Study
   E-mail: gpeters@iupui.edu
   Phone: 317-274-4000

Program features

The MS in Music Therapy is a 30-credit, fully online program that uses synchronous and asynchronous technologies to provide instructional time and build a sense of community. Required coursework includes Music Therapy, Music Technology, and elective courses; core courses (18 cr.), cognate courses (6 cr.), and approved electives (6 cr.).

Application requirements include evidence of Music Therapy board certification; a minimum 3.0 GPA for the undergraduate degree; any information that demonstrates personal experience in music technology and musicianship (e.g., authored CDs or websites, original compositions); and an in-person or telephone interview with the Coordinator of Music Therapy. The GRE is recommended but not required.

INDIANA UNIVERSITY-PURDUE UNIVERSITY, INDIANAPOLIS, IN

Degree-granting, regional accreditation, not-for-profit, public. A department of music and arts technology in the school of engineering and technology in a state research university.

Website: http://music.iupui.edu/degrees/ms-MusicTechnology.shtml
Degree title: Master of Science in Music Technology
Fred J. Rees, DMA, Chair
   Email: frees@iupui.edu
   Phone: 317-274-4000
G. David Peters, Ed.D., Head of Graduate Study
   Email: gpeters@iupui.edu
   Phone: 317-274-4000

Program features

The MS in Music Technology is a 30-credit program offered as a traditionally delivered on-campus course, but students have the option to take the entire program over the Internet. Courses are offered during fall, spring, and summer semesters. Required coursework includes core courses (18 cr.); cognate courses (6 cr.); and approved electives (6 cr.). There is a residency requirement for on-campus students of three consecutive summers or one summer and a contiguous academic term.

Application requirements include a Bachelor's degree and evidence of substantial music instruction, performance and literacy; a minimum 3.0 GPA for the undergraduate degree; a performance videotape, audio cassette, CD, DVD or on-campus audition on a musical instrument or conducting of a music ensemble; any additional information that demonstrates personal experience in music technology and musicianship (e.g., authored

CDs or websites, original compositions); and an in-person or telephone interview with the Head of Graduate Studies. The GRE is recommended but not required.

VALLEY CITY STATE UNIVERSITY, VALLEY CITY, ND

Degree-granting, regional accreditation, education accreditation, not-for-profit, public. A department of music in a state university.
Website: http://www.vcsu.edu/academics/divisions/finearts/music-dept/
Degree title: Composite Bachelor of Science/Arts in Music
Beth Klingenstein, Ph.D., Department of Music Chair, Music Advisement Coordinator
  E-mail: beth.klingenstein@vcsu.edu
  Phone: 701-845-7269

Program features

The Composite Bachelor of Science/Arts in Music is a 120-credit program consisting of 1- to 3-credit courses offered during a regular 15-week semester, with a few courses offered during the four- or eight-week summer terms. Courses are offered synchronously through real-time videoconferencing, simultaneously with face-to-face on-campus courses. Interactivity is provided through the whiteboard, application sharing, chat, and online polling. Online office hours are provided. Online courses are recorded and archived to provide access for students unable to attend scheduled class sessions. Full-time students average 12–16 credits per semester. Distant students who are employed full-time are advised to limit themselves to a maximum of 6 credits per semester. With prior approval, students enroll for ensemble and applied credit at a university in their home area, preferably an NASM-accredited institution.

Application requirements include an application to the university; an online theory and aural skills placement examination; a DVD video recording of a performance audition; and a program plan, showing the approved applied instructor and ensemble.

APPENDIX C
Resources for Online Music Instruction

STANDARDS

Distance learning programs: Interregional guidelines for the evaluation of distance education (online learning)
http://web.njcu.edu/programs/vision2015/Uploads/msche_guidelines-for-the-evaluation-of-distance-education.pdf

National Association of Schools of Music, *Handbook 2013–2014*
http://nasm.arts-accredit.org/index.jsp?page=Standards-Handbook

Moore, J. C. (2005). *The Sloan Consortium quality framework and the five pillars.*
http://sloanconsortium.org/publications/freedownloads

THEORIES OF ONLINE LEARNING

Technological, pedagogical, and content knowledge (TPACK)
http://www.tpack.org/
Community of inquiry (CoI)
https://coi.athabascau.ca/
Online collaborative learning theory (OCL)
http://lindaharasim.com/

REPORTS, TRENDS, AND DATA

EDUCAUSE Center for Analysis and Research (ECAR)
http://www.educause.edu/ecar
Horizon Report (annual)
http://www.nmc.org/horizon-project
Sloan Consortium/Babson Research Group Reports on Online Learning in the U.S.
http://sloanconsortium.org/publications/survey/index.asp

RUBRICS
Illinois quality online course initiative rubric
http://www.ion.uillinois.edu/initiatives/qoci/index.asp
Quality Matters™ rubric standards 2014-2016 edition with assigned point values
https://www.qualitymatters.org/
Rubric for online instruction, California State University, Chico
http://www.csuchico.edu/roi/

INSTRUCTIONAL RESOURCES
Connect4Education
http://www.connect4education.com/
EDUCAUSE Learning Initiative's *7 Things You Should Know About...*™ series
http://www.educause.edu/research-and-publications/7-things-you-should-know-about
iTunes U
http://www.apple.com/education/ipad/itunes-u/
https://itunes.apple.com/us/genre/itunes-u/id40000000?mt=10
Library of Congress Podcasts
http://www.loc.gov/podcasts/
Multimedia Educational Resource for Learning and Online Teaching (MERLOT)
http://music.merlot.org/
YouTube EDU
http://www.youtube.com/t/education

JOURNALS: MUSIC
Journal of Music, Technology & Education
http://www.intellectbooks.co.uk/journals/view-issue,id=2431/
Journal of Technology in Music Learning
http://www.atmimusic.com/jtml/

JOURNALS: GENERAL
Campus Technology
http://www.campustechnology.com
International Journal of Instructional Technology & Distance Learning
http://www.itdl.org/index.htm
International Review of Research in Open and Distance Learning
http://www.irrodl.org/index.php/irrodl
Journal of Asynchronous Learning Networks
http://sloanconsortium.org/publications/jaln_main

Journal of Interactive Online Learning
http://www.ncolr.org
Journal of Online Learning and Teaching
http://jolt.merlot.org
Online Journal of Distance Learning Administration
http://www.westga.edu/~distance/ojdla

COURSE MANAGEMENT SYSTEMS
Blackboard
http://www.blackboard.com/
Canvas
http://www.instructure.com/
Desire2Learn
http://www.desire2learn.com/
Moodle
https://moodle.org/
Sakai
http://www.sakaiproject.org/

BIBLIOGRAPHY

AACTE Committee on Innovation and Technology (Ed.). (2008). *Handbook of techno-logical pedagogical content knowledge (TPCK) for educators*. New York: Routledge.

AACTE Committee on Innovation and Technology. (2008). Afterword: TPCK action for teacher education: *It's about time!* In AACTE Committee on Innovation and Technology (Ed.), *Handbook of technological pedagogical content knowledge (TPCK) for educators* (pp. 289–300). New York: Routledge

Adams, J. (2007). Then and now: Lessons from history concerning the merits and problems of distance education. *Studies in Media Information Literacy Education, 7*(1), 1–14.

Allen, I. E., & Seaman, J. (2003). *Sizing the opportunity: The quality and extent of online education in the United States, 2002 and 2003*. Sloan-C™. Retrieved from http://sloanconsortium.org/publications/survey/index.asp

Allen, I. E., & Seaman, J. (2010). *Class differences: Online education in the United States, 2011*. Babson Survey Research Group and Quahog Research Group, LLC. Retrieved from http://sloanconsortium.org/publications/survey/index.asp

Allen, I. E., & Seaman, J. (2011). *Going the distance: Online education in the United States, 2011*. Babson Survey Research Group and Quahog Research Group, LLC. Retrieved from http://sloanconsortium.org/publications/survey/index.asp

Allen, I. E., & Seaman, J. (2013). *Changing course: Ten years of tracking online educa-tion in the United States*. Babson Survey Research Group and Quahog Research Group, LLC. Retrieved from http://sloanconsortium.org/publications/survey/index.asp

Allen, I. E., Seaman, J., & Garrett, R. (2007). *Blending in: The extent and promise of blended education in the United States*. Sloan-C™. Retrieved from http://sloancon-sortium.org/publications/survey/index.asp

Allen, I. E., Seaman, J., Lederman, D., & Jaschik, S. (2012a). *Conflicted: Faculty and online education, 2012*. Inside Higher Ed. Babson Survey Research Group and Quahog Research Group, LLC. Retrieved from http://babson.qualtrics.com/SE/?SID=SV_bJHd6VpmahG2NGB

Allen, I. E., Seaman, J., Lederman, D., & Jaschik, S. (2012b). *Digital faculty: Professors, teaching, and technology, 2012*. Inside Higher Ed. Babson Survey Research Group and Quahog Research Group, LLC. Retrieved from http://babson.qualtrics.com/SE/?SID=SV_bJHd6VpmahG2NGB

Al-Shalchi, O. N. (2009). The effectiveness and development of online discussions. *MERLOT Journal of Online Learning and Teaching, 5*(1), 104–108.

American Federation of Teachers. (n.d.). Technology and distance education. Retrieved from http://www.aft.org/issues/highered/technology.cfm

Anderson, J. Q., Boyles, J. L., & Rainie, L. (2012). *The future of higher education.* Pew Research Center's Internet and American Life Project. Retrieved from http://www.pewinternet.org/

Anderson, L. W., & Krathwohl, D. R. (2001). *A taxonomy for learning, teaching, and assessing: A revision of Bloom's taxonomy of educational objectives.* New York: Addison Wesley Longman.

Anderson, R. S., Bauer, J. F., & Speck, B.W. (2002). *Assessment strategies for the on-line class: From theory to practice.* San Francisco: Jossey-Bass.

Anderson, T. (Ed.). (2008). *The theory and practice of online learning* (second ed.). Edmonton, Alberta, CA: AU Press, Athabasca University. Retrieved from http://www.aupress.ca/index.php/books/120146

Anderson, T., & Dron, J. (2011). Three generations of distance learning pedagogy. *The International Review of Research in Open and Distance Learning, 12*(3), 80–97.

Anderson, T., Rourke, L., Garrison, D. R., & Archer, W. (2001). Assessing teacher presence in a computer conferencing context. *Journal of Asynchronous Learning Networks, 5*(2), 1–17. Retrieved from http://sloanconsortium.org/jaln/v5n2/assessing-teacher-presence-computer-conferencing-context

Archambault, L. (2011). The practitioner's perspective on teacher education: Preparing for the K–12 online classroom. *Journal of Technology and Teacher Education, 19*(1), 73–91.

Archambault, L., & Crippen, K. (2009). Examining TPACK among K–12 online distance educators in the United States. *Contemporary Issues in Technology and Teacher Education, 9*(1), 71–88.

Ash, K. (2011). Group outlines K–12 online course standards. *Education Week, 30*(15), 5–6.

Austin, J. (2007). *Navigating a flat world: The promise and peril of online graduate music education programs.* Paper presented at the September 2007 Symposium on Music Teacher Education, Greensboro, NC.

Bain, K. (2004). *What the best college teachers do.* Cambridge, MA: Harvard University Press.

Baker, D. L. (2011). Designing and orchestrating online discussions. *MERLOT Journal of Online Teaching and Learning, 7*(3), 401–411.

Bangert, A. W. (2004). The seven principles of good practice: A framework for evaluating on-line teaching. *The Internet and Higher Education, 7,* 217–232.

Baran, E., Chuang, H., & Thompson, A. (2011). TPACK: An emerging research and development tool for teacher educators. *TOJET: The Turkish Online Journal of Educational Technology, 10*(4), 370–377. Retrieved from http://www.tojet.net/articles/v10i4/10437.pdf

Barry, N. (2003). Integrating web based learning and instruction into a graduate music education research course. *Journal of Technology in Music Learning, 2*(1), 2–8.

Bates, A. W. (1995). *Technology, open learning and distance education.* London and New York: Routledge.

Batson, T. (2011). The classroom is 'distance learning;' The web is connected learning. *Campus Technology* (May 18). Retrieved from http://campustechnology.com/articles/2011/05/18/the-classroom-is-distance-learning-while-the-web-is-connected-learning.aspx

Bauer, W. I. (2001). Student attitudes toward web-enhanced learning in a music education methods class: A case study. *Journal of Technology in Music Learning, 1*(1), 20–30.

Bauer, W. I. (2009). Using technology to support research-based principles of learning. *The TI:MES, 1*(1), 9–10. Retrieved from http://www.ti-me.org/

Bauer, W. I. (2010a). Technological pedagogical and content knowledge for music teachers. In D. Gibson & B. Dodge (Eds.), *Proceedings of Society for Information Technology & Teacher Education International Conference 2010* (pp. 3977–3980). Chesapeake, VA: AACE.

Bauer, W. I. (2010b). Technological pedagogical and content knowledge, music, and assessment. In T. S. Brophy (Ed.), *The practice of assessment in music education: Frameworks, models, and designs* (pp. 425–434). Chicago: GIA Publications.

Bauer, W. I. (2012). The acquisition of musical technological pedagogical and content knowledge. *Journal of Music Teacher Education, 22*(2), 51–64.

Bauer, W. I., & Daugherty, J. F. (2001). Using the Internet to enhance music teacher education. *Journal of Music Teacher Education, 11*(1), 27–32.

Bauer, W. I., Harris, J., & Hofer, M. (2012a). Grounded tech integration using K–12 music learning activity types. *Learning & Leading, 40*(3), 30–32.

Bauer, W. I., Harris, J., & Hofer, M. (2012b). *Music learning activity types.* Retrieved from College of William and Mary, School of Education, Learning Activity Types Wiki: http://activitytypes.wmwikis.net/file/view/MusicLearningATs-June2012.pdf

Bawane, J., & Spector, J. M. (2009). Prioritization of online instructor roles: Implications for competency-based teacher education programs. *Distance Education, 30*(3), 383–397.

Beglau, M., Hare, J. C., Foltos, L., Gann, K., James, J., Jobe, H., Knight, J., & Smith, B. (2011). *Technology, coaching, and community: Partners for improved professional development in primary and secondary education.* International Society for Technology in Education. Retrieved from https://www.iste.org/

Bennett, K. (2010). A case study of perceptions of students, teachers, and administrators on distance learning and music education in Newfoundland and Labrador: A constructivist perspective (doctoral dissertation). Retrieved from ProQuest Dissertations and Theses database (UMI No. MR64792).

Bernard, R. M., Abrami, P. C., Borokhovski, E., Wade, C. A., Tamim, R. M., Surkes, M. A., & Bethel, E. C. (2009). A meta-analysis of three types of interaction treatments in distance education. *Review of Educational Research, 79,* 1243–1288.

Bernard, R., Abrami, P., Lou, Y., Borokhovski, E., Wade, A., & Wozney, L. (2004). How does distance education compare with classroom instruction? A meta-analysis of the empirical literature. *Review of Educational Research, 74*(3), 379–439.

Bernstein, L. (1976). *The unanswered question: Six talks at Harvard.* Cambridge, MA: Harvard University Press.

Berz, W. L., & Bowman, J. (1994). *Applications of research in music technology.* Reston, VA: Music Educators National Conference.

Berz, W. L., & Bowman, J. (1995). An historical perspective on research cycles in music computer-based technology. *Bulletin of the Council for Research in Music Education, 126,* 15–28.

Bloom, B. S. (Ed.) (1956). *Taxonomy of educational objectives. The classification of educational goals. Handbook I: Cognitive domain.* New York: McKay.

Boettcher, J. V. (2007). Ten core principles for designing effective learning environments: Insights from brain research and pedagogical theory. *Innovate, 3*(3). Retrieved from http://citeseerx.ist.psu.edu/viewdoc/summary?doi=10.1.1.186.6518

Boettcher, J., & Conrad, R. (2010). *The online teaching survival guide: Simple and practical pedagogical tips*. San Francisco: Jossey-Bass.

Bonk, C. J. (2002). *Online teaching in an online world*. Retrieved from http://www.publicationshare.com/docs/faculty_survey_report.pdf

Bransford, J. D., Brown, A. L., & Cocking, R. R. (Eds.) (2000). *How people learn: Brain, mind, experience, and school*. Washington, DC: National Academy Press. Retrieved from http://www.nap.edu

Brewster, M. S. (2005). The effects of a constructivist-inspired web-based summary portal on examination performance in music for an online course (doctoral dissertation). Retrieved from ProQuest Dissertations and Theses database (UMI No. 3180074).

Briggs, L. I. (2013). Marrying into MOOCs. *Campus Technology, 26*(7), 9–11.

Brinthaupt, T. M., Fisher, L. S., Gardner, J. G., Raffo, D. M., & Woodard, J. B. (2011). What the best online teachers should do. *MERLOT Journal of Online Learning and Teaching, 7*(4), 515–524.

Brown, G. (2011). *LMS, tear down this wall!* Retrieved from http://campustechnology.com/0711_brown

Brown, J. S. (2006). New learning environments for the 21st century: Exploring the edge. *Change* (Sept./Oct.), 18–24.

Bruner, J. (1977). *The process of education*. Cambridge, MA: Harvard University Press.

Burke, L. A. (2005). Transitioning to online course offerings: Tactical and strategic considerations. *Journal of Interactive Online Learning, 4*(2), 94–107. Retrieved from www.ncolr.org/

Bush, J. (2001). Introducing the practitioner's voice through electronic mentoring. *Journal of Technology in Music Education, 1*(1), 4–9.

Carney, R. D. (2010). Using web-based instruction to teach music theory in the piano studio: Defining, designing, and implementing an integrative approach (doctoral dissertation). Retrieved from ProQuest Dissertations and Theses database (UMI No. 3417740).

Cavanagh, T. B. (2012). The postmodality era: How "online learning" is becoming "learning." In D. G. Oblinger (Ed.), *Game changers: Education and information technologies* [PDF e-book version] (pp. 215–227). Retrieved from http://net.educause.edu/ir/library/pdf/pub7203.pdf

CDW-G. (2012). *Learn now, lecture later*. Retrieved from http://www.cdwnewsroom.com/2012-learn-now-lecture-later-report/

Chaney, D., Chaney, E., & Eddy, J. (2010). The context of distance learning programs in higher education: Five enabling assumptions. *Online Journal of Distance Learning Administration 13*(4). Retrieved from http://www.uncg.edu/oao/PDF/5%20Assumptons%20OJDLA.pdf

Chen, Y-J. (2001). Dimensions of transactional distance in the World Wide Web learning environment: A factor analysis. *British Journal of Educational Technology, 32*(4), 459–470.

Chickering, A. W., & Erhmann, S. C. (1996). Implementing the seven principles: Technology as lever. *AAHE Bulletin, 49*(2), 3–6.

Chickering, A. W., & Gamson, Z. F. (1987). Seven principles for good practice in undergraduate education. *AAHE Bulletin, 39*(7), 3–7.

Christensen, C. M., & Eyring, H. J. (2011). *The innovative university: Changing the DNA of higher education from the inside out.* San Francisco: Jossey-Bass.

Christensen, C. M., Horn, M. B., Caldera, L., & Soares, L. (2011). *Disrupting college: How disruptive innovation can deliver quality and affordability to postsecondary education.* Center for American Progress and Innosight Institute. Retrieved from http://www.innosightinstitute.org/innosight/wp-content/uploads/2011/02/future_of_higher_ed-2.3.pdf

Christensen, C. M., Horn, M. B., & Johnson, C. W. (2008). *Disrupting class. How disruptive innovation will change the way the world learns.* New York: McGraw-Hill.

Chuang, W. (2000). Formative research on the refinement of web-based instructional design and development guidance systems for teaching music fundamentals at the pre-college level (doctoral dissertation). Retrieved from ProQuest Dissertations and Theses database (UMI No. 9993557).

Clemons, S. A. (2005). Brain-based learning: Possible implications for online learning. *International Journal of Instructional Technology and Distance Learning, 2*(9). Retrieved from http://itdl.org/journal/sep_05/article03.htm

Coming to terms: ALN. (2003). *Sloan-C View 2*(4), pp. 1, 3. Retrieved from http://sloanconsortium.org/publications/view/v2n4/coverv2n4.htm

Conrad, D. (2005). Building and maintaining community in cohort-based online learning. *Journal of Distance Education, 20*(1), 1–21. Retrieved from http://www.jofde.ca/index.php/jde/article/view/78/59

Covach, J. (2013). To MOOC or not to MOOC? *Music Theory Online, 19*(3). Retrieved from http://mtosmt.org/issues/mto.13.19.3/mto.13.19.3.covach.php

Cox, S. (2008). A conceptual analysis of technological pedagogical content knowledge (doctoral dissertation). Retrieved from ProQuest Dissertations and Theses database (UMI No. 3318618).

Csikszentmihalyi, M. (1990). *Flow: The psychology of optimal experience.* New York: Harper & Row.

Dabbagh, N. (2007). The online learner: Characteristics and pedagogical implications. *Contemporary Issues in Technology and Teacher Education, 7*(3), 217–226.

Dabbagh, N., & Bannan-Ritland, B. (2005). *Online learning: Concepts, strategies, and applications.* Upper Saddle River, NJ: Pearson Education.

Dahlstrom, E. (2012). *ECAR study of undergraduate students and information technology, 2012.* Louisville, CO: EDUCAUSE Center for Applied Research. Retrieved from http://www.educause.edu/ecar

Damasio, A. (1999). *The feeling of what happens: Body and emotion in the making of consciousness.* New York: Harcourt.

Dammers, R. J. (2009). Utilizing internet-based videoconferencing for instrumental music lessons. *Update: Applications of Research in Music Education, 28*(1) 17–24.

Davidson, C. N. (2011). *Now you see it: How technology and brain science will transform schools and business for the 21st century.* New York: Penguin Books.

Davidson, C. N. (2012). Size isn't everything. *Chronicle of Higher Education* (December 10). Retrieved from http://chronicle.com

DePlatchett, N. (2008). Placing the magic in the classroom: TPCK in arts education. In AACTE Committee on Innovation and Technology (Ed.), *Handbook of technological pedagogical content knowledge (TPCK) for educators* (pp. 167–192). New York: Routledge.

Deubel, P. (2007). What's online education all about? *THE Journal* (April 19). Retrieved from http://thejournal.com/articles/2007/04/19/whats-online-education-all-about.aspx

Diaz, D. P. (2000). Carving a new path for distance education research. *The Technology Source* (March/April). Retrieved from http://technologysource.org/article/carving_a_new_path_for_distance_education_research/

Diaz, V., & Brown, M. (2010). *Blended learning: A report on the ELI focus session* (White paper). EDUCAUSE. Retrieved from http://net.educause.edu/ir/library/pdf/ELI3023.pdf

DiPietro, M., Ferdig, R., Black, E. W., & Preston, M. (2008). Best practices in teaching K–12 online: Lessons learned from Michigan Virtual School teachers. *Journal of Interactive Online Learning*, 7(1), 10–35. Retrieved from http://www.ncolr.org/

Dirr, P. J. (1999). Distance and virtual learning in the United States. In G. M. Farrell (Ed.), *The development of virtual education: A global perspective* (pp. 23–48). Vancouver, CA: Commonwealth of Learning. Retrieved from http://www.col.org/resources/publications/Pages/detail.aspx?PID=277

Don, G., Garvey, C., & Sadeghpour, M. (2009). Theory and practice: Signature pedagogies in music theory and performance. In R. A. R. Gurung, N. L. Chick, & A. Haenie (Eds.), *Exploring signature pedagogies: Approaches to teaching disciplinary habits of mind* (pp. 81–98). Sterling, VA: Stylus Publishing.

Downs, A. (2006). Online professional development for teachers: An interview with Chris Dede. *Harvard Education Letter*, 22(4), 1–2. Retrieved from http://www.hepg.org/hel/article/308

Dye, K. G. (2007). Applied music in an online environment using desktop videoconferencing (doctoral dissertation). Retrieved from ProQuest Dissertations and Theses database (UMI No. 3259242).

Dziuban, C., & Moskal, P. (2011). A course is a course is a course: Factor invariance in student evaluation of online, blended, and face-to-face learning environments. *The Internet and Higher Education*, 14(4), 236–241.

Dziuban, C. D., Hartman, J. L., & Moskal, P. D. (2004). *Blended learning*. Boulder, CO: EDUCAUSE Center for Applied Research. Retrieved from http://www.educause.edu/ecar

Eakes, K. (2009). A comparison of a sociocultural and a chronological approach to music appreciation in face-to-face and online instructional formats (doctoral dissertation). Retrieved from ProQuest Dissertations and Theses database (UMI No. 3365532).

Edwards, R. D. (2008). The neurosciences and music education: An online database of brain imaging neuromusical research (doctoral dissertation). Retrieved from ProQuest Dissertations and Theses database (UMI No. 3307191).

Electronic code of federal regulations. Retrieved from http://ecfr.gpoaccess.gov/cgi/t/text/text-idx?c=ecfr&sid=0900b7322acc5a5a10c558b8fe15ad7b&rgn=div8&view=text&node=34:3.1.3.1.1.1.23.2&idno=34

Farrell, G. M. (Ed.). (1999). *The development of virtual education: A global perspective*. Vancouver, CA: Commonwealth of Learning. Retrieved from http://www.col.org/resources/publications/Pages/detail.aspx?PID=277

Fasimpaur, K. (2013). Massive and open: MOOCs are the next big thing in online learning. *Learning and Leading*, 40(6), 12–17.

Fink, L. D. (2013). *Creating significant learning experiences: An integrated approach to designing college courses* (rev. ed.). San Francisco: Jossey-Bass.

Flohr, J. W., & Hodges, D. A. (2002). Music and neuroscience. In R. Colwell (Ed.), *MENC Handbook of Cognition and Development* (pp. 7–39). New York: Oxford University Press.

Flores, J. G. (2010). *Enabled by broadband, education enters a new frontier*. Retrieved from http://www.usdla.org/assets/pdf_files/OnlineWhitePaper-V10312.pdf

Flores, J. G. (2011). *Expanding the classroom: Mobile learning across America.* Retrieved from http://www.usdla.org/assets/pdf_files/USDLAWhitePaper. English.FINAL.9.15.pdf

Folio, C., & Kreinberg, S. (2009/2010). Blackboard and wikis and blogs, oh my: Collaborative learning tools for enriching music history and music theory courses. *College Music Symposium, 49/50,* 164–175.

Forum: Has the quality of online learning kept up with its growth? (2010). In Online learning 2010: Taking measure of online education. *Chronicle of Higher Education* (November 3). Retrieved from http://chronicle.com/article/ Online-Learning-The-2010/129636/

Franklin, J. L. (2008). Dimensions of sound in virtual online immersive environments: A theoretical exploration (doctoral dissertation). Retrieved from ProQuest Dissertations and Theses database (UMI No. 3340474).

Fung, V. (2004). Perception of the need for introducing flexible learning in graduate studies in music education: A case study. *College Music Symposium, 44,* 107–120.

Garrison, D. R. (2006). Online collaboration principles. *Journal of Asynchronous Learning Networks, 10*(1), 25–34.

Garrison, D. R. (2011). *E-learning in the 21st century: A framework for research and practice* (second ed.). London: Routledge/Taylor and Francis.

Garrison, D. R., & Anderson, T. (2003). *E-learning in the 21st century: A framework for research and practice.* London and New York: RoutledgeFalmer.

Garrison, D. R., Anderson, T., & Archer, W. (2000). Critical inquiry in a text-based environment: Computer conferencing in higher education. *The Internet and Higher Education, 2*(2/3), 87–105.

Garrison, D. R., Anderson, T., & Archer, W. (2001). Critical thinking, cognitive presence, and computer conferencing in distance education. *American Journal of Distance Education, 15*(1), 7–23.

Garrison, D. R., & Cleveland-Innes, M. (2005). Facilitating cognitive presence in online learning: Interaction is not enough. *American Journal of Distance Education, 19*(3), 133–148.

Garrison, D. R., & Vaughan, N. D. (2008). *Blended learning in higher education: Framework, principles, and guidelines.* San Francisco: Jossey-Bass.

Garton, S., & Richards, K. (2007). Is distance education for teacher education second best? *The Teacher Trainer, 21*(3), 5–8. Retrieved from http://www.tttjournal.co.uk

Gilbert, S. W. (2004). If it ain't broke, improve it: Thoughts on engaging education for us all. *Journal of Asynchronous Learning Networks, 8*(1), 39–53. Retrieved from http://sloanconsortium.org/jaln/v8n1/if-it-ain039t-broke-improve-it-thou ghts-engaging-education-us-all

Graham, C., Cagiltay, K., Craner, J., Lim, B., & Duffy, T. M. (2000). *Teaching in a web-based distance learning environment: An evaluation summary based on four courses* (CLRT Technical Report No. 13-00).

Graham, C., Cagiltay, K., Lim, B., Craner, J., & Duffy, T. M. (2001). Seven principles of effective teaching: A practical lens for evaluating online courses. *The Technology Source* (March/April). Retrieved from http://technologysource.org/article/ seven_principles_of_effective_teaching/

Grasha, A. F. (2002). *Teaching with style: A practical guide to enhancing learning by understanding teaching and learning styles.* Retrieved from http://www.ilte.ius.edu/pdf/ teaching_with_style.pdf

Green, B. (2003). The comparative effects of computer-mediated interactive instruction and traditional instruction on music achievement in guitar performance (doctoral dissertation). Retrieved from ProQuest Dissertations and Theses database (UMI No. NQ86051).

Green, K. R., Pinder-Grover, T., & Millunchick, J. M. (2012). Impact of screencast technology: Connecting the perception of usefulness and the reality of performance. *Journal of Engineering Education, 101*(4), 717–737.

Groulx, T. J., & Hernly, P. (2010). Online master's degrees in music education: The growing pains of a tool to reach a larger community. *Update, 28*(2), 60–70.

Gruhn, W. (2004). *Neurodidactics: A new scientific trend in music education?* Paper presented at the July XXVI ISME International Conference, Tenerife, ES. Retrieved from http://www.wgruhn.de/Forschung/tenerife.pdf

Gruhn, W., & Rauscher, F. (2002). The neurobiology of music cognition and learning. In R. Colwell (Ed.), *MENC Handbook of Cognition and Development* (pp. 40–71). New York: Oxford University Press.

Grush, M. (2006). Changing the gold standard for instruction. *Campus Technology* (May 21). Retrieved from http://campustechnology.com/Articles/2006/05/Changing-the-Gold-Standard-for-Instruction.aspx?Page=1

Guthrie, D. (2012). Jump off the Coursera bandwagon. *Chronicle of Higher Education* (December 17). Retrieved from http://chronicle.com

Harasim, L. (2012). *Learning theory and online technologies.* New York: Routledge.

Harris, J. B. (2008). TPCK in in-service education: Assisting experienced teachers' "planned improvisations." In AACTE Committee on Innovation and Technology (Ed.), *Handbook of technological pedagogical content knowledge (TPCK) for educators* (pp. 251–271). New York: Routledge.

Harris, J., & Hofer, M. (2009). Grounded tech integration: An effective approach based on content, pedagogy, and teacher training. *Learning & Leading with Technology, 37*(2), 22–25.

Harris, J., & Hofer, M. (2009). Instructional planning activity types as vehicles for curriculum-based TPACK development. In C. D. Maddux (Ed.), *Research highlights in technology and teacher education 2009* (pp. 99–108). Chesapeake, VA: Society for Information Technology in Teacher Education (SITE). Retrieved from http://activitytypes.wmwikis.net/file/view/HarrisHofer-TPACKActivityTypes.pdf

Harris, J. B., Mishra, P., & Koehler, M. (2009). Teachers' technological pedagogical content knowledge and learning activity types: Curriculum-based technology integration reframed. *Journal of Research on Technology in Education, 41*(4), 393–416.

Hebert, D. G. (2007). Five challenges and solutions in online music teacher education. *Research and Issues in Music Education, 5*(1). Retrieved from http://www.stthomas.edu/rimeonline/vol5/hebert.htm

Hebert, D. G. (2008a). Forms of graduate music education: A response to Kenneth Phillips. *Research and Issues in Music Education, 6*(1). Retrieved from http://www.stthomas.edu/rimeonline/vol6/hebert.htm

Hebert, D. G. (2008b). Reflections on teaching the aesthetics and sociology of music online. *International Review of the Aesthetics and Sociology of Music, 39*(1), 93–103. Retrieved from JSTOR database.

Heuer, B. P., & King, K. P. (2004). Leading the band: The role of the instructor in online learning for educators. *Journal of Interactive Online Learning, 3*(1), 1–11. Retrieved from http://www.ncolr.org/

Hill, P. (2012). Online educational delivery models: A descriptive view. *EDUCAUSE Review, 47*(6), 84–86, 88, 90, 92, 94–97.

Hillman, D. C. A., Willis, D. J., & Gunawardena, C. N. (1994). Learner-interface interaction in distance education: An extension of contemporary models and strategies for practitioners. *American Journal of Distance Education, 8*(2), 30–42.

Hiltz, S. R., & Goldman, R. (Eds.) (2005). *Learning together online: Research on asynchronous learning networks.* New York: Lawrence Erlbaum Associates.

Hinson, A. W. (2004). The effects of web-based music appreciation instruction on students' attitudes toward western art music (doctoral dissertation). Retrieved from ProQuest Dissertations and Theses database (UMI No. 3142432).

Hodges, D. A. (2010). Can neuroscience help us do a better job of teaching music? *General Music Today, 23*(2), 3–12.

Horn, M., & Christensen, C. (2013). Beyond the buzz, where are MOOCs *really* going? *Wired online: Opinion.* Retrieved from http://www.wired.com/opinion/2013/02/beyond-the-mooc-buzz-where-are-they-going-really/

Howe, J. (2013). Clayton Christensen wants to transform capitalism. *Wired online: Business (February 12).* Retrieved from http://www.wired.com/business/2013/02/mf-clayton-christensen-wants-to-transform-capitalism/all/

H.R. 4137—110th Congress. (2007). *Higher Education Opportunity Act.* Retrieved from http://www.govtrack.us/congress/bills/110/hr4137

Hunter, R. W. (2011). Learning in an online jazz history class (doctoral dissertation). Retrieved from ProQuest Dissertations and Theses database (UMI No. 3482765).

Illinois Online Network. Illinois quality online course initiative rubric. Retrieved from http://www.ion.uillinois.edu/initiatives/qoci/index.asp

Imel, S. (1998). *Myths and realities: Distance learning.* ERIC Clearinghouse on Adult, Career, and Vocational Education. Retrieved from http://calpro-online.org/eric/docs/mr00012.pdf

International Association for K–12 Online Learning. (2011). National standards for quality online teaching. Version 2. Retrieved from http://www.inacol.org/

International Society for Technology in Education. (2011). ISTE NETS for technology coaches (NETS•C). Retrieved from https://www.iste.org/

Johnson, L., Adams, S., & Cummins, M. (2012). *The NMC Horizon Report: 2012 higher education edition.* Austin, TX: The New Media Consortium. Retrieved from http://www.nmc.org/publications/

Johnson, L., Adams Becker, S., Cummins, M., Estrada, V., Freeman, A., & Ludgate, H. (2013). *The NMC Horizon Report: 2013 higher education edition.* Austin, TX: The New Media Consortium. Retrieved from http://www.nmc.org/publications/

Johnson, L., Smith, R., Willis, H., Levine, A., & Haywood, K., (2011). *The 2011 Horizon Report.* Austin, TX: The New Media Consortium. Retrieved from http://www.nmc.org/publications/

Kadel, R. (2011). Educator's voice: Unpacking TPACK for successful online faculty development. Retrieved from http://www.pearsonlearningsolutions.com/blog/secondary-channels/teacher-education/educators-voice-unpacking-tpack-for-successful-online-faculty-development-2/

Katz, R. N. (2010). Scholars, scholarship, and the scholarly enterprise in the digital age. *EDUCAUSE Review, 45*(2), 44–56.

Keast, D. A. (2009). A constructivist application for online learning in music. *Research and Issues in Music Education, 7*(1). Retrieved from http://www.stthomas.edu/rimeonline/vol7/keast.htm

Keast, D. A. (2010). Implementation of constructivist techniques into an online activity for graduate students. *Journal of Technology in Music Learning, 4*(2), 41–55.

Keengwe, J., & Kidd, T. T. (2010). Towards best practices in online learning and teaching in higher education. *MERLOT Journal of Online Learning and Teaching*, 6(2), 533–541.

Kelley, B. C. (2006). Design for change: Creating significant learning experiences in the music classroom. *College Music Symposium*, 46, 64–76.

Kelley, B. C. (2009). Inspiration and intellect: Significant learning in musical forms and analysis. *New Directions for Teaching and Learning*, 2009(119), 35–41.

Kennedy, K., & Archambault, L. (2012). Design and development of field experiences in K–12 online learning environments. *Journal of Applied Instructional Design*, 2(1), 35–49. Retrieved from http://www.jaidpub.org

Kennedy, K., & Archambault, L. (Eds.). (2013). *Partnering for success: A 21st century model for teacher preparation.* International Association for K–12 Online Learning. Retrieved from http://www.inacol.org/cms/wp-content/uploads/2013/10/iNACOL-Partnering-for-Success-October-2013.pdf

Kim, K-J, & Bonk, C. J. (2006). The future of online teaching and learning in higher education: The survey says.... *EDUCAUSE Quarterly*, No. 4, 22–30.

King, A. (1993). From sage on the stage to guide on the side. *College Teaching*, 41(1), 20–35.

Koehler, M., & Mishra, P. (2008). Introducing TPCK. In AACTE Committee on Innovation and Technology (Ed.), *Handbook of technological pedagogical content knowledge (TPCK) for educators* (pp. 3–29). New York: Routledge.

Koehler, M., Mishra, P., Bouck, E. C., DeSchreyver, M., Kereluik, K., Shin, T. S., & Wolf, L. G. (2011). Deep play: Developing TPACK for 21st century teachers. *International Journal of Technology*, 6(2), 146–163.

Koehler, M., Mishra, P., Hershey, K., & Peruski, L. (2004). With a little help from your students: A new model for faculty development and online course design. *Journal of Technology and Teacher Education*, 12(1), 25–55.

Koehler, M. J., & Mishra, P. (2009). What is technological pedagogical content knowledge? *Contemporary Issues in Technology and Teacher Education*, 9(1), 60–70.

Koole, M., McQuilkin, J. L., & Ally, M. (2010). Mobile learning in distance education: Utility or futility? *Journal of Distance Education*, 24(2), 59–82.

Kos, R. P., Jr., & Goodrich, A. (2012). Music teachers' professional growth: Experiences of graduates from an online graduate degree program. *Visions of Research in Music Education*, 22. Retrieved from http://www.rider.edu/~vrme

Kruse, N. B., Harlos, S. C., Callahan, R. M., & Herring, M. (2013). Skype music lessons in the academy: Intersections of music education, applied music and technology. *Journal of Music, Technology & Education*, 6(1), 43–60.

Lage, M. J., Platt, G. J., & Treglia, M. (2000). Inverting the classroom: A gateway to creating an inclusive learning environment. *Journal of Economic Education*, 31(1), 30–43. Retrieved from JSTOR database.

Lee, C. S. (2003). Introduction to music therapy: An interactive web course via Blackboard 5.5 (doctoral dissertation). Retrieved from ProQuest Dissertations and Theses database (UMI No. 3098610).

Lehman, R. M., & Conceição, S. C. O. (2010). *Creating a sense of presence in online teaching.* San Francisco: Jossey-Bass.

Lockee, B., Moore, M., & Burton, J. (2001). Old concerns with new distance education research. *EDUCAUSE Quarterly*, 24(2), 60–62. Retrieved from http://net.educause.edu/ir/library/pdf/eqm0126.pdf

Lockett, W. (2010). Student perceptions about the effectiveness and quality of online musical instrument instruction (doctoral dissertation). Retrieved from ProQuest Dissertations and Theses database (UMI No. 3419163).

Löfström, E., & Nevgi, A. (2007). From strategic planning to meaningful learning: Diverse perspectives on the development of web-based teaching and learning in higher education. *British Journal of Educational Technology, 18*(2), 312–324.

Lombard, M., & Ditton, T. (1997). At the heart of it all: The concept of presence. *Journal of Computer-Mediated Communication, 3*(0). Retrieved from http://onlinelibrary.wiley.com/enhanced/doi/10.1111/j.1083-6101.1997.tb00072.x/

Lorenzo, G., & Moore, J. C. (2002). *The Sloan Consortium report to the nation: Five pillars of quality online education.* Retrieved from http://sloanconsortium.org/publications/freedownloads

MacKenzie, J. G. (1998). Toodlee-doo: Effective interactive musical instruction across the Internet. Retrieved from http://www.usask.ca/education/coursework/802papers/mckenzie/toodlee_doo.htm

Mayadas, A. F., & Picciano, A. G. (2007). Blended learning and localness: The means and the end. *Journal of Asynchronous Learning Networks, 11*(1), 3–7. Retrieved from http://files.eric.ed.gov/fulltext/EJ842682.pdf

Mayer, R. E. (2003). Elements of a science of e-learning. *Journal of Educational Computing Research, 29*(3), 297–313.

Mazoué, J. G. (2013). The MOOC model: Challenging traditional education. *EDUCAUSE review online* (January). Retrieved from http://www.educause.edu

McCabe, M. (2007). Learning together online: An investigation of the effect of collaborative instruction on students' demonstrated levels of cognition and self-reported course satisfaction in an online music appreciation course (doctoral dissertation). Retrieved from ProQuest Dissertations and Theses database (UMI No. 3257313).

McGee, P., & Reis, A. (2012). Blended course design: A synthesis of best practices. *Journal of Asynchronous Learning Networks, 16*(4), 7–22. Retrieved from http://sloanconsortium.org/jaln/v16n4/blended-course-design-synthesis-best-practices

McLain, B. P. (2005). Estimating faculty and student workload for interaction in online graduate music courses. *Journal of Asynchronous Learning Networks 9*(3), 47–56. Retrieved from http://sloanconsortium.org/jaln/v9n3/estimating-faculty-and-student-workload-interaction-online-graduate-music-courses

Means, B., Toyama, Y., Murphy, R., Bakia, M., & Jones, K. (2010). *Evaluation of evidence-based practices in online learning: A meta-analysis and review of online learning studies.* Center for Technology in Learning, U.S. Department of Education. Retrieved from http://www2.ed.gov/rschstat/eval/tech/evidence-based-practices/finalreport.pdf

Mendenhall, R. W. (2011). How technology can improve online learning—and learning in general. *Chronicle of Higher Education* (November 6). Retrieved from http://chronicle.com/article/How-Technology-Can-Improve/129616/

Merisotis, J. P., & Phipps, R. A. (1999). *What's the difference? A review of contemporary research on the effectiveness of distance learning in higher education.* Report for the Institute for Higher Education Policy. Retrieved from http://www.ihep.org/Publications/publications-detail.cfm?id=88

Meyer, K. (2003). The implications of brain research for distance education. *Online Journal of Distance Learning Administration 6*(3). Retrieved from http://www.westga.edu/~distance/ojdla/fall63/meyer63.html

Meyer, K. (2004). How recent brain research can inform the design of online learning. *Journal of Educators Online, 1*(1), 1–17.

Meyer, K. A. (2007). Student perceptions of face-to-face and online discussions: The advantage goes to.. .. *Journal of Asynchronous Learning Networks, 11*(4), 53–69.

Retrieved from http://sloanconsortium.org/jaln/v11n4/student-perceptions-f
ace-face-and-online-discussions-advantage-goes

Meyer, K. A. (2010). The role of disruptive technology in the future of higher education. *EDUCAUSE Quarterly 33*(1). Retrieved from http://www.educause.edu/ero/
article/role-disruptive-technology-future-higher-education

Middle States Commission on Higher Education. (2006). *Characteristics of excellence
in higher education: Requirements of affiliation and standards for accreditation.*
Retrieved from http://www.msche.org/publications_view.asp?idPublicationTy
pe=1&txtPublicationType=Standards+for+Accreditation+and+Requirements+o
f+Affiliation

Middle States Commission on Higher Education. (2011). *Distance learning programs: Interregional guidelines for the evaluation of distance education (online
learning).* Retrieved from http://web.njcu.edu/programs/vision2015/Uploads/
msche_guidelines-for-the-evaluation-of-distance-education.pdf

Mihailidis, P., & Cohen, J. N. (2013). Exploring curation as a core competency in digital
and media literacy education. *Journal of Interactive Media in Education*, Spring
issue. Retrieved from http://www-jime.open.ac.uk/article/2013-02/pdf

Miller, G. (1997). Asynchronous learning networks and distance education: An interview with Frank Mayadas of the Alfred P. Sloan Foundation. Reprinted from
American Journal of Distance Education, *11*(3), 71–75. Retrieved from http://
sloanconsortium.org/mayadas_interview_97

Mishra, P., & Koehler, M. J. (2006). Technological pedagogical content knowledge: A framework for teacher knowledge. *Teachers College Record*, *108*(6), 1017–1054.

Mishra, P., Koehler, M. J., & Henriksen, D. (2011). The seven trans-disciplinary habits of mind: Extending the TPACK framework towards 21st century learning.
Educational Technology, March/April, 22–28. Retrieved from http://punya.educ.
msu.edu/publications/mishra-koehler-henriksen2011.pdf

Mooney, C. (Ed.) (2011). Online learning: Virtual education goes mainstream. The
2011 special edition. *Chronicle of Higher Education* (November 6). Retrieved from
http://chronicle.com/section/Online-Learning/491/?inl

Moore, J. C. (2003). *Elements of quality: Synthesis of the August 2002 seminar.* Retrieved
from http://sloanconsortium.org/publications/freedownloads

Moore, J. C. (2005). *The Sloan Consortium quality framework and the five pillars.* Retrieved
from http://sloanconsortium.org/publications/freedownloads

Moore, J. C. (2012). A synthesis of Sloan-C effective practices, December 2011.
Journal of Asynchronous Learning Networks, *16*(1), 91–115. Retrieved from
http://sloanconsortium.org/jaln/v16n1/synthesis-sloan-c-effective-practi
ces-december-2011

Moore, M. G. (1989). Editorial: Three types of interaction. *American Journal of Distance
Education*, *3*(2), 1–7.

Moore, M. G. (1993). Theory of transactional distance. In D. Keegan (Ed.), *Theoretical
principles of distance education* (pp. 22–38). New York: Routledge.

Morford, J. B. (2007). Constructivism: Implications for postsecondary music education and beyond. *Journal of Music Teacher Education*, *16*, 75–83. doi: 10.1177/10
570837070160020108.

Mossavar-Rahmani, F., & Larson-Daugherty, C. (2007). Supporting the hybrid
model: A new proposition. *MERLOT Journal of Online Learning and Teaching*,
3(1), 1–12.

Music anywhere, anytime. (2011). International Symposium on Synchronous Distance
Learning. Retrieved from http://dl.msmnyc.edu/events/2011/ISSDL

Nakashima, J. (2009). "Experiencing music 2200" online: A critical case study of the curriculum transfer process (doctoral dissertation). Retrieved from ProQuest Dissertations and Theses database (UMI No. MR57449).

Natale, C. F. (2011). *Teaching in the world of virtual K–12 learning: Challenges to ensure educator quality.* Educational Testing Service. Retrieved from http://www.ets.org

National Association of Schools of Music. (2013). *Handbook 2013–2014.* Retrieved from http://nasm.arts-accredit.org/index.jsp?page=Standards-Handbook

NEA. (2002). *Guide to online high school courses.* Retrieved from http://www.nea.org/assets/docs/onlinecourses.pdf

NEA. (2006). *Guide to teaching online courses.* Retrieved from http://www.nea.org/assets/docs/onlineteachguide.pdf

Neal, J. (2011). The online challenge: Why not teach music history unconventionally? *Journal of Music History Pedagogy,* 2(1), 81–98. Retrieved from http://www.ams-net.org/ojs/index.php/jmhp/

Nelson, J., Christopher, A., & Mims, C. (2009). TPACK and Web 2.0: Transformation of teaching and learning. *TechTrends,* 53(5), 80–85.

Oblinger, D. G. (Ed.) (2012). *Game changers: Education and information technologies.* EDUCAUSE. Retrieved from http://www.educause.edu/research-and-publications/books

Online learning 2010: Taking measure of online education. (2010). *Chronicle of Higher Education* (November 3). Retrieved from http://chronicle.com/article/Online-Learning-The-2010/129636/

Orman, E. K., & Whitaker, J. A. (2010). Time usage during face-to-face and synchronous distance music lessons. *American Journal of Distance Education,* 24(2), 92–103.

Palloff, R. M., & Pratt, K. (2003). *The virtual student: A profile and guide to working with online learners.* San Francisco: Jossey-Bass.

Palloff, R. M., & Pratt, K. (2007). *Building online learning communities. Effective strategies for the virtual classroom.* San Francisco: Jossey-Bass.

Palloff, R. M., & Pratt, K. (2011). *The excellent online instructor: Strategies for professional development.* San Francisco: Jossey-Bass.

Pappano, L. (2012). The year of the MOOC. *New York Times* (November 2). Retrieved from http://www.nytimes.com

Parker, K., Lenhart, A., & Moore, K. (2011). *The digital revolution and higher education: College presidents, public differ on value of online learning.* Washington, DC: Pew Research Center.

Patrick, S., & Powell, A. (2009). A summary of research on the effectiveness of K–12 online learning. *International Association for K–12 Online Learning.* Retrieved from http://www.inacol.org

Peterson, A. D. (2011). The impact of neuroscience on music education advocacy and philosophy. *Arts Education Policy Review,* 112(4), 206–213.

Phillips, K. H. (2008). Graduate music education. *Research and Issues in Music Education* 6(1). Retrieved from http://www.stthomas.edu/rimeonline/vol6/phillips1.htm

Phipps, R., & Merisotis, J. (2000). *Quality on the line: Benchmarks for success in internet-based education.* The Institute for Higher Education Policy. Retrieved from http://www.ihep.org/Publications/publications-detail.cfm?id=69

Picciano, A. G. (2002). Beyond student perceptions: Issues of interaction, presence, and performance in an online course. *Journal of Asynchronous Learning Networks,* 6(1), 21–40.

Pike, P. D., & Shoemaker, K. (2013). The effect of distance learning on acquisition of piano sight-reading skills. *Journal of Music, Technology & Education, 6*(2), 147–162.

Power, M. (2008). The emergence of a blended online learning environment. *Journal of Online Teaching and Learning, 4*(4). Retrieved from http://jolt.merlot.org/vol4no4/power_1208.htm

Power, M., & Vaughan, N. (2010). Redesigning online learning for international graduate seminar delivery. *Journal of Distance Education, 24*(2), 19–38. Retrieved from http://www.jofde.ca/index.php/jde/article/view/649/1103

Quality Matters™ rubric standards 2011–2013 *edition with assigned point values.* Retrieved from https://www.qualitymatters.org/

Radford, A. W. (2011). *Learning at a distance: Undergraduate enrollment in distance education courses and degree programs.* U.S. Department of Education National Center for Education Statistics. Retrieved from http://nces.ed.gov/pubsearch/pubsinfo.asp?pubid=2012154

Rees, F. J. (2002). Distance learning and collaboration in music education. In R. Colwell & C. Richardson (Eds.), *The new handbook of research on music teaching and learning* (pp. 257–273). New York: Oxford University Press.

Rees, F. J. (2003). Hitting the right note with video conferencing. *Syllabus* (June). Retrieved from http://campustechnology.com/Articles/2003/05/Hitting-the-Right-Note-with-Video-Conferencing.aspx?p=1

Reese, J. A. (2013). Online status: Virtual field experiences and mentoring during an elementary general music methods course. *Journal of Music Teacher Education.* Advance online publication. doi: 10.1177/1057083713506119

Reese, S., Repp, R., Meltzer, J., & Burrack, F. (2002). The design and evaluation of use of a multimedia web site for online professional development. *Journal of Technology in Music Learning, 1*(2), 24–37.

Rickard, W. (2010). *The efficacy (and inevitability) of online learning in higher education* (White paper). Retrieved from Pearson Learning Solutions website: http://www.pearsonlearningsolutions.com

Riley, P. (2013). Video-conferenced classes: American pre-service music educators teach composition skills to students in Japan. *Journal of Technology in Music Learning, 5*(1), 51–69.

Robinson, K. (2011). *Out of our minds: Learning to be creative* (rev. ed.). Chichester, UK: Capstone Publishing.

Ross, V. (2001). Offline to online curriculum: A case study of one music course. Retrieved from http://www.westga.edu/~distance/ojdla/winter44/ross44.html

Rubric for online instruction. (2009). California State University, Chico. Retrieved from http://www.csuchico.edu/roi/

Russell, T. L. (Ed.) (1999). *The no significant difference phenomenon: A comparative research annotated bibliography on technology for distance education: As reported in 355 research reports, summaries, and papers.* North Carolina State University.

Ryder, C. O. (2004). The use of internet-based teaching strategies in teaching vocal anatomy, function, and health to high school choral music students, and its effect on student attitudes and achievement (doctoral dissertation). Retrieved from ProQuest Dissertations and Theses database (UMI No. 3136262).

Saba, F. (2011). Distance education in the United States: Past, present, future. *Educational Technology, 51*(6), 11–18.

Salavuo, M. (2008). Social media as an opportunity for pedagogical change in music education. *Journal of Music, Technology and Education, 1*(2/3), 121–136.

Saltzberg, S., & Polyson, S. (1995). Distributed learning on the world wide web. *Syllabus, 9*(1), 10.

Savery, J. (2005). BE VOCAL: Characteristics of successful online instructors. *Journal of Interactive Online Learning, 4*(2), 141–152. Retrieved from http://www.ncolr. org/

Scarnati, B., & Garcia, P. (2007). The fusion of learning theory and technology in an online music history course. Retrieved from http://www.editlib.org/p/104338

Schaffhauser, D. (2012a). 4 keys to a better hybrid. *Campus Technology, 26*(4), 18–21.

Schaffhauser, D. (2012b). Tuning the blend. *Campus Technology, 26*(4), 22–24.

Schlager, K. (2008). Distance learning. *Teaching Music, 15*(6), 36–38.

Schmidt, D. A., Baran, E., Thompson, A. D., Mishra, P., Koehler, M. J., & Shin, T. S. (2009). Technological pedagogical content knowledge (TPACK): The development and validation of an assessment instrument for preservice teachers. *Journal of Research on Technology in Education, 42*(2), 123–149.

Schoueman, S. (1999). Instructional design for distance music education (doctoral dissertation). Retrieved from ProQuest Dissertations and Theses database (UMI No. 0801137).

Scott, L. C. (2009). Through the wicked spot: A case study of professors' experiences teaching online (doctoral dissertation). Retrieved from ProQuest Dissertations and Theses database (UMI No. 3379753).

Seaman, J. (2009a). *Online learning as a strategic asset volume I: A resource for campus leaders*: Babson Survey Research Group. Retrieved from http://sloanconsortium. org/publications/survey/APLU_Reports

Seaman, J. (2009b). *Online learning as a strategic asset volume II: The paradox of faculty voices: Views and experiences with online learning*: Babson Survey Research Group. Retrieved from http://sloanconsortium.org/publications/survey/ APLU_Reports

Seddon, F., & Biasutti, M. (2010). Strategies students adopted when learning to play an improvised blues in an e-learning environment. *Journal of Research in Music Education 58*(2), 147–167.

Sela, O. (2010). The power of the model: One step towards developing blended courses in higher education. *MERLOT Journal of Online Learning and Teaching, 6*(4), 820–827.

Sener, J. (2004). Escaping the comparison trap: Evaluating online learning on its own terms. *Innovate, 1*(2). Retrieved from http://citeseerx.ist.psu.edu/viewdoc/dow nload?rep=rep1&type=pdf&doi=10.1.1.186.6321

Shachar, M., & Neumann, Y. (2010). Twenty years of research on the academic performance differences between traditional and distance learning: Summative meta-analysis and trend examination. *MERLOT Journal of Online Learning and Teaching, 6*(2), 318–334.

Shea, P., & Bidjerano, T. (2010). Learning presence: Towards a theory of self-efficacy, self-regulation, and the development of a communities of inquiry in online and blended learning environments. *Computers & Education, 55*, 1721–1731. Retrieved from http://www.sunyresearch.net/hplo/wp-content/uploads/2012/08/ Shea-and-Bidjerano-2010.pdf

Shea, P., Hayes, S., Uzuner-Smith, S., Vickers, J., Bidjerano, T., Gozza-Cohen, M., Jian, S., Pickett, A., Wilde, J., & Tseng, C. (2013). Online learner self regulation: Learning presence, viewed through quantitative content- and social network analysis. *International Review of Research in Open and Distance Learning,*

14(3) 427–461. Retrieved from http://www.sunyresearch.net/hplo/wp-content/uploads/2013/07/Online-Self-Regulation-Shea-2013.pdf

Shelton, K. (2011). A review of paradigms for evaluating the quality of online education programs. *Online Journal of Distance Learning Administration, 4*(1). Retrieved from http://www.westga.edu/~distance/ojdla/

Sherbon, J. W., & Kish, D. L. (2005). Distance learning and the music teacher. *Music Educators Journal, 92*(2), 36–41.

Sherron, G. T., & Boettcher, J. V. (1997). *Distance learning: The shift to interactivity.* Boulder, CO: CAUSE.

Shin, H. (2011). Enabling young composers through the Vermont MIDI project: Composition, verbalization and communication (doctoral dissertation). Retrieved from ProQuest Dissertations and Theses database (UMI No. 3479343).

Shulman, L. S. (1986). Those who understand: Knowledge growth in teaching. *Educational Researcher, 15*(2), 4–14. Retrieved from JSTOR database.

Sinclair, D. R. (2004). The effect of synchronous and asynchronous online communication on student achievement and perception of a music fundamentals course for undergraduate non-music majors (doctoral dissertation). Retrieved from ProQuest Dissertations and Theses database (UMI No. 3132257).

Slotwinski, J. A. (2011). Online communication as a mode of professional development among student teachers in music education (doctoral dissertation). Retrieved from ProQuest Dissertations and Theses database (UMI No. 3448039).

Smith, B. N. (2010). The role of technology in assessment of online music education courses taught at the community college level. In T. S. Brophy (Ed.), *The practice of assessment in music education: Frameworks, models, and designs. Proceedings of the 2009 Florida symposium on assessment in music education* (pp. 435–439). Chicago: GIA Publications.

Smith, E. L. (2013). Using a new taxonomy of significant learning in the theory classroom. *Music Theory Pedagogy Online, 1.* Retrieved from http://jmtp.ou.edu/ejournal/using-new-taxonomy-significant-learning-theory-classroom

Spires, H., Zheng, M., & Pruden, M. (2012). New technologies, new horizons: Graduate student views on creating their technological pedagogical content knowledge (TPACK). In K. Moyle & G. Wijngaards (Eds.), *Student reactions to learning with technologies: Perceptions and outcomes* (pp. 23–41). Hershey, PA: IGI Global.

Staker, H. (2011). *The rise of K–12 blended learning: Profiles of emerging models.* Innosight Institute. Retrieved from http://www.christenseninstitute.org

Staker, H., & Horn, M. B. (2012). *Classifying K–12 blended learning.* Innosight Institute. Retrieved from http://www.christenseninstitute.org/

Stefanov, I. B. (2011). High school music student and teacher perceptions of online learning environments (doctoral dissertation). Retrieved from ProQuest Dissertations and Theses database (UMI No. 3445716).

Swan, K. (2001). Immediacy, social presence, and asynchronous discussion. In J. Bourne & J. C. Moore (Eds.), *Elements of Quality Online Education, Volume 3.* Needham, MA: Sloan-C.

Swan, K. (2004). *Relationships between interactions and learning in online environments.* Needham, MA: Sloan-C Retrieved from http://sloanconsortium.org/publications/books/pdf/interactions.pdf

Swan, K. (2005). A constructivist model for thinking about learning online. In J. Bourne & J. C. Moore (Eds.), *Elements of Quality Online Education: Engaging Communities.* Needham, MA: Sloan-C.

Swan, K., Matthews, D., Bogle, L., Boles, E., & Day, S. (2012). Linking online course design and implementation to learning outcomes: A design experiment. *Internet and Higher Education, 15*, 81–88.

Swan, K., & Shih, L. F. (2005). On the nature and development of social presence in online course discussions. *Journal of Asynchronous Learning Networks, 9*(3), 115–136.

Syed, M. (2001). Diminishing the distance in distance education. *Multimedia, IEEE 8*(3), 18–20.

Tamim, R. M., Bernard, R. M., Borokhovski, E., Abrami, P. C., & Schmid, R. F. (2011). What forty years of research says about the impact of technology on learning: A second-order meta-analysis and validation study. *Review of Educational Research, 81*, 4–28.

Taylor, J. C. (1995). Distance education technologies: The fourth generation. *Australian Journal of Educational Technology, 11*(2), 1–7. Retrieved from http://www.ascilite.org.au/ajet/ajet11/taylor.html

Taylor, J. C. (2001). *The future of learning—learning for the future: Shaping the transition.* 20th International Council on Distance Education World Conference, Dusseldorf, DE [online]. Retrieved from http://www.fernuni-hagen.de/ICDE/D-2001/final/keynote_speeches/wednesday/taylor_keynote.pdf

Twigg, C. A. (2001). *Innovations in online learning: Moving beyond no significant difference.* Troy, NY: Rensselaer Polytechnic Institute, Center for Academic Transformation.

Van Der Werf, M., & Sabatier, G. (2009). *The College of 2020: Students.* Chronicle Research Services. https://www.chronicle-store.com/ProductDetails.aspx?ID=78921&WG=0

Voogt, J., Fisser, P., Pareja Roblin, N., Tondeur, J., & van Braak, J. (2013). Technological pedagogical content knowledge—a review of the literature. *Journal of Computer Assisted Learning, 29*(2), 109–121.

Vrasidas, C. (2000). Constructivism versus objectivism: Implications for interaction, course design, and evaluation in distance education. *International Journal of Educational Telecommunications, 6*(4), 339–362. Retrieved from http://www.cardet.org/vrasidas/pubs/continuum.pdf

Walker, D. (2001). Computer-aided collaboration in a graduate-level music analysis course: An exploration of legitimate peripheral participation (doctoral dissertation). Retrieved from ProQuest Dissertations and Theses database (UMI No. NQ58954).

Walls, K. C. (2008). Distance learning in graduate music teacher education: Promoting professional development and satisfaction of music teachers. *Journal of Music Teacher Education, 18*(1), 55–66.

Walls, K. C., Miranda, M., Schaffer, B., Gilbreath, J., & Good, R. (2005). *Program development and evaluation of a distance learning graduate degree program in music education: Perspectives from students and professors.* Paper presented at the September 2005 Symposium on Music Teacher Education, Greensboro, NC. Retrieved from http://www.auburn.edu/~wallski/Clinics/SMTE05.pdf

Walls, K. C., Wolfe, S., Good, R., Powell, W., & Schaffer, W. (2004). Education at a distance: Perspective from the podium. *Hawaii International Conference on Arts and Humanities Conference Proceedings*, 6334–6349. Retrieved from http://www.hichumanities.org/proceedings_hum.php

Ward, C. L., & Benson, S. N. K. (2010). Developing new schemas for online teaching and learning: TPACK. *MERLOT Journal of Online Learning and Teaching, 6*(2), 482–490.

Watson, J. (2008). *Promising practices in online learning: Blended learning: The convergence of online and face-to-face education*. North American Council for Online Learning. Retrieved from http://www.inacol.org/resources/publications/inacol-reports/4/

Watson, J., Murin, A., Vashaw, L., Gemin, B., & Rapp, C. (2012). *Keeping pace with K–12 online learning: An annual review of policy and practice*. Evergreen, CO: Evergreen Education Group. Retrieved from http://kpk12.com/

WCET. (2008). *WCET survey on academic integrity and student verification*. Retrieved from http://wiche.edu/pub/13442

WCET. (2009). *Best practice strategies to promote academic integrity in online education: Version 2.0*. Retrieved from http://wcet.wiche.edu/wcet/docs/cigs/studentauthentication/BestPractices.pdf

Webster, P. R. (2007). Computer-based technology and music teaching and learning: 2000–2005. In L. Bresler (Ed.), *International Handbook of Research in Arts Education* (pp. 1311–1328). Dordrecht, NL: Springer.

Webster, P. R. (2011a). Construction of music learning. In R. Colwell & P. R. Webster (Eds.), *MENC handbook of research on music learning: Volume 1: Strategies* (pp. 35–83). New York: Oxford University Press.

Webster, P. R. (2011b). Key research in music technology and music teaching and learning. *Journal of Music, Technology and Education* 4(2/3), 115–130.

Wiggins, G., & McTighe, J. (2005). *Understanding by design* (expanded second ed.). Alexandria, VA: Association for Supervision and Curriculum Development.

Wright, M. R. (2007). Texas community college music appreciation courses, online and traditional (doctoral dissertation). Retrieved from ProQuest Dissertations and Theses database (UMI No. 3295380).

Yan, Z., Hao, H., Hobbs, L. J., & Wen, N. (2003). The psychology of e-learning: A field of study. *Journal of Educational Computing Research*, 29(3), 285–296.

Yoshioka, Y. (2003). A web-based tutorial for the beginning piano student (doctoral dissertation). Retrieved from ProQuest Dissertations and Theses database (UMI No. 3115088).

Zull, J. E. (2002). *The art of changing the brain: Enriching the practice of teaching by exploring the biology of learning*. Sterling, VA: Stylus Publishing.

Zull, J. E. (2011). *From brain to mind: Using neuroscience to guide change in education*. Sterling, VA: Stylus Publishing.

INDEX

blended online learning, 99, 124
blog(s), 11, 49, 197
  as alternative writing styles, 68
  in blended learning, 146
  and brain science, 217
  definition of, 139
  as listening journals, 67
  micro-blogs, 143
  in music theory, 103–104
  as reflective tool, 77, 125
  vs. social media, 129, 143
  See also class blogs
Bloom's taxonomy, 72, 73
bring-your-own-device movement, 206,
  210
Brinthaupt, T. M., Fisher, L. S., Gardner,
  J. G., Raffo, D. M., & Woodard, J.
  B., 197
Bruner, J., 196

Cavanagh, T. B., 9–10
chats. *See* discussions, synchronous
Chickering, A. W., & Ehrmann, S. C., 181
Chickering, A. W., & Gamson, Z. F., 179,
  180, 197
choreography, course design as, 122
Christensen, C. M., Horn, M. B., Caldera,
  L., & Soares, L., 212–213
class blogs, 104, 139
class wiki, 65, 67, 124, 159–160, 164
CMS (course management system). *See*
  LMS (learning management system)
coaching, 171–173, 220
cognitive presence, 87, 89, 91–92
  and asynchronous communication, 98
  definition of, 91
  design issues for, 97
  and direct instruction, 97–98
  facilitation of, 92
  indicators of, 91–92
  and practical inquiry, 91–92
CoI (community of inquiry), 87–99
  and asynchronous communication,
    93, 99
  and collaboration, 95
  as collaborative constructivist view,
    82, 99
  compared with OCL (online
    collaborative learning), 114
  convergent thinking in, 92

critical thinking in, 91–92
definition of, 89
divergent thinking in, 92
and online presence, 89
role of instructor in, 91, 92–94, 96
teaching/learning guidelines for,
  95–99
and three-way interaction, 88, 94–95
See also cognitive presence; learning
  presence; social presence; teaching
  presence
collaborative learning, 82, 87, 100
  compared with cooperative learning,
    101
  projects for, 103–104, 200
College Music Society, 173
communication. *See* discussions,
  asynchronous; discussions,
  synchronous
communications media, 83, 85
  and transactional distance, 85
  See also interactive media
communities of practice, 32, 47
community of inquiry, 89, 99, 113
composition, course design as, 115–116
conductor, online teacher as, 149–150,
  164
constructivist approaches, 32, 49, 100,
  219
  limitations of, 100
cooperative learning, 82, 101
correspondence course, 3, 6–7
Council of Regional Accrediting
  Commissions, 21
course-and-a-half, 134
course content
  for blended courses, 138
  coverage of, 120
  digital formats for, 156
  LMS organization of, 126, 152, 155–
    156, 168
  priorities for selection of, 117,
    120–121
  rethinking of, 66, 112
  student contributions to, 159, 164
course design. *See* blended course design;
  online course design
course goals, 22, 120, 138, 152
course objectives, 22, 120, 125, 138, 145
course tools, 118, 142

selection of, 129–130
credit hour policies, 122
CSU, Chico (California State University, Chico), 117, 185
    rubric for online instruction, 187
curator, professor as, 116–117

Dammers, R. J., 31–32
delivery modes
    comparisons of, 12, 16–17, 30, 50, 218
    and learning outcomes, 30, 112, 122
    and pedagogy, 15, 122, 147
design for significant learning. *See* significant learning
dialogue. *See* discourse; discussions, asynchronous; discussions, synchronous
direct instruction, 92, 93–94, 96, 97
    documenting time for, 122
director of learning, 92–93, 148–150, 151, 164
disappearing distinctions, 9–10, 140
    between delivery modes, 9, 215
    between online and face-to-face learning, 144, 214
    and blended learning, 9, 140
    and MOOCs, 214
discourse
    collaborative, 101–102, 124
    See also discussions, asynchronous; discussions, synchronous
discussions, asynchronous
    facilitating, 157–158
    grading rubrics for, 124–125
    instructor participation in, 158
    and reflection, 67, 91, 98, 125
    as written record, 105, 157
discussions, synchronous
    for brainstorming, 67, 157, 163
    and immediacy, 98, 115, 124
    informal chat in, 159
    moderating, 158–159
    recording, 159, 200
    and spontaneity, 98–99
    student presentations in, 159, 164
    technical preparation for, 167
disruptive innovation
    online learning as, 213, 214–215
    online music offerings as, 213
    theory of, 204, 212

distance education
    concept of, 9
    definitions of, 6–7
    effectiveness of, 29
    generations of, 3–4, 10
    guidelines for evaluating, 21
    NASM standards for, 24
    and "transactional distance," 9
distributed learning, 4–5
Dye, K. G., 31

"early adopters," 171, 220
ECAR (EDUCAUSE Center for Applied Research)
    undergraduate information technology report, 205
effective practices, 181–185
    for blended learning, 191–192
    collections of, 134, 189–191, 192–193, 194
    for faculty satisfaction, 191
    for learning effectiveness, 190–191
    for online music learning, 193
    perspectives on, 193–194, 202
    for student satisfaction, 190
e-learning
    definition of, 99
    psychology of, 215
    science of, 215–216
electronic mentoring. *See* online mentoring
e-portfolio(s), 77, 162, 190, 192, 200–201
evaluation, course/program, 21–23, 33, 185
    standards for, 23, 25

FaceBook, 129, 208
facilitation, 92, 93, 96, 97
    by students, 94
faculty development. *See* professional development
federal requirements
    and distance education, 7
    and student verification, 23, 25
feedback, 160–162
    in games, 211
    instructor/student, 105, 160, 161, 183–184
    student/instructor, 160–161

Fink, L. D., 72–73, 77
five pillars of quality online education,
    20–21, 189
flipped classroom, 11, 140–142, 146,
    173, 177
    definition of, 140
    description of, 201

games, 206–207, 211–212
    and critical thinking, 212
    and feedback, 211
    as flow activities, 211
    and "Open Orchestra," 207, 211
    and simulations, 212
gamification, 206–207, 211–212
    definition of, 212
    and game design, 207
    and gamer culture, 207, 212
gamified curricula, 207
Garrison, D. R., 87–88, 197
Garrison, D. R., & Anderson, T., 82,
    87–88
Garrison, D. R., & Vaughan, N. D., 9, 12,
    131
generations of distance education, 3–4,
    10
"gold standard," 16
Graham, C., Cagiltay, K., Lim, B., &
    Duffy, T. M., 181
Groulx, T. J., & Hernly, P., 8, 32, 38, 219
guidelines for online education. See
    standards for online education
"guide on the side," 92, 100, 102,
    147–148, 149, 195

hallmarks for quality distance education,
    21–23
Harasim, L., 82, 99–100
Harris, J., & Hofer, M., 70, 72
Hebert, D. G., 8, 149
HEOA (Higher Education Opportunity
    Act), 18–19
Higher Education Opportunity Act,
    18–19
Hillman, D. C. A., Willis, D. J., &
    Gunawardena, C. N., 87
historical research cycles. See research
    cycles
Hodges, D. A., 216
Horizon Report, 170, 204–207, 218

challenges, 206
far-term technologies, 207
mid-term technologies, 206–207
near-term technologies, 206
trends, 205
See also games; gamification; MOOCs;
    tablet computing
human touch, 90, 114
hybrid course, 131–132
hybrid learning. See blended learning

icebreaker activities, 156
iChat, 40
"illusion of non-mediation," 89, 163
immediacy, 98, 115, 121, 124, 156
immediacy behaviors, 85
implementation patterns
    in online education, 11–12, 66
    research on, 12
    in technology integration, 11–12, 66,
        209, 213, 218
    See also research cycles
instructor, online. See teacher, online
interaction
    and community of inquiry model,
        94–95
    learner/content, 86
    learner/instructor, 86
    learner/interface, 87
    learner/learner, 87
    and learning effectiveness, 20
    three-way, 69, 81, 86, 88, 114
interactive media, 83–84
    effective use of, 84
Internet2, 220
inverted classroom. See flipped classroom
ION (Illinois Online Network), 187–189
    and QOCI (quality online course
        initiative) rubric, 188–189
ISTE (International Society for
    Technology in Education), 172
    and NETS for Coaches, 172–173
iTunesU, 156
ITV (interactive television), 3

jazz courses, 44, 66, 67,
"just learning"
    blended learning as, 9
    online learning as, 10, 214–215
Kahn Academy, 121, 201

NETS (National Education Technology
    Standards), 172
NETS•C (National Education Technology
    Standards for Coaches), 172–173
neuromusical research, 215
    applying results of, 216–217
neuroscience, 215–217
    and online learning, 217
    and psychology of e-learning, 215
    and science of e-learning, 215–216
"no significant difference" phenomenon,
    49, 111
    misconceptions about, 218

OCL (online collaborative learning)
    theory, 99–106
    collaborative discourse in, 101–102
    compared with CoI (community of
        inquiry), 114
    compared with constructivism, 100
    compared with cooperative learning,
        101
    convergent thinking in, 101, 105
    definition of, 100, 106
    discussion forums in, 104–106
    divergent thinking in, 101, 105
    knowledge building in, 101
    online environments for, 103–106
    in online music instruction, 106
    online tools for, 103–104
    pedagogy of, 102–103
    processes of, 101
    role of teacher in, 100, 102–103, 149
    text-based discussion in, 105–106
online course design
    balance in, 129
    as choreography, 122
    communication and collaboration in,
        124–125
    community building in, 113–114
    as composition, 115–116
    congruence in, 120
    content-focused model of, 115
    as creative process, 112
    as curation, 116–117
    curricular priorities in, 120–121
    developing models for, 219
    effective practices for, 179, 186, 187
    goals and objectives in, 120
    learning materials in, 121–122

as orchestration, 115, 125
preliminary questions for, 112–113
and presence, 114–115
process-oriented model of, 115
redesign for, 113, 115–116
reflection in, 125
rubrics for, 117, 120, 186–187
signature pedagogies in, 140
as sonata form, 116
TPACK framework in, 66, 113,
    117–119
work order in, 117
online course organization
    assignment folders, 126
    backup, 128–129
    course menu, 128
    discussion forums, 128
    learning guide, 126, 155
    learning modules, 126, 127
    learning objectives, 126
    in LMS, 125–128
    as orchestration, 125
online learning
    criticisms of, 8, 16
    definitions of, 5–6
    disappearing distinctions in, 9–10, 12,
        140, 144
    effectiveness of, 12, 15, 20, 28–29, 49
    faculty perspectives on, 17–18
    future of, 204, 218
    growth of, 7–8
    as "just learning," 9–10
    student orientation to, 163, 165–166
    surveys of, 5–6, 7
    theories of, 82, 111, 114, 145, 197
    See also K–12 online learning
online learning community, 113–114
    in CoI framework, 114
    definitions of, 113–114
    formation of, 114, 124, 182
    in OCL theory, 114
    and presence, 114, 150
online mentoring, 8, 47, 49
online music learning
    models for, 218, 219
    in music subdisciplines, 219
    research agenda for, 218–221
    theory of, 219
online music teaching
    art of, 147, 148, 149–150, 194, 196

Printed in the USA/Agawam, MA
December 19, 2014